MUSIC IN THE ROLE-PLAYING GAME

Music in the Role-Playing Game: Heroes & Harmonies offers the first scholarly approach focusing on music in the broad class of video games known as role-playing games, or RPGs. Known for their narrative sophistication and long playtimes, RPGs have long been celebrated by players for the quality of their cinematic musical scores, which have taken on a life of their own, drawing large audiences to live orchestral performances.

The chapters in this volume address the role of music in popular RPGs such as *Final Fantasy* and *World of Warcraft*, delving into how music interacts with the gaming environment to shape players' perceptions and engagement. The contributors apply a range of methodologies to the study of music in this genre, exploring topics such as genre conventions surrounding music, differences between music in Japanese and Western role-playing games, cultural representation, nostalgia, and how music can shape deeply personal game experiences.

Music in the Role-Playing Game expands the growing field of studies of music in video games, detailing the considerable role that music plays in this modern storytelling medium, and breaking new ground in considering the role of genre. Combining deep analysis with accessible personal accounts of authors' experiences as players, it will be of interest to students and scholars of music, gaming, and media studies.

William Gibbons is Associate Professor of Musicology and Associate Dean of the College of Fine Arts at Texas Christian University.

Steven Reale is Associate Professor of Music Theory at Youngstown State University.

Routledge Music and Screen Media Series

Series Editor: Neil Lerner

The **Routledge Music and Screen Media Series** offers edited collections of original essays on music in particular genres of cinema, television, video games and new media. These edited essay collections are written for an interdisciplinary audience of students and scholars of music and film and media studies.

Music in the Role-Playing Game
Heroes & Harmonies
Edited by William Gibbons and Steven Reale

Music and Sound in Silent Film
From the Nickelodeon to *The Artist*
Edited by Simon Trezise and Ruth Barton

Music in Comedy Television
Notes on Laughs
Edited by Liz Giuffre and Philip Hayward

Music in Contemporary Indian Film
Memory, Voice, Identity
Edited by Jayson Beaster-Jones and Natalie Sarrazin

Music in Epic Film
Listening to Spectacle
Edited by Stephen C. Meyer

For a full list of titles in this series, please visit www.routledge.com/series/RMSM

MUSIC IN THE ROLE-PLAYING GAME

Heroes & Harmonies

Edited by
William Gibbons
Texas Christian University

and

Steven Reale
Youngstown State University

NEW YORK AND LONDON

First published 2020
by Routledge
52 Vanderbilt Avenue, New York, NY 10017

and by Routledge
2 Park Square, Milton Park, Abingdon, Oxon, OX14 4RN

Routledge is an imprint of the Taylor & Francis Group, an informa business

© 2020 Taylor & Francis

The right of William Gibbons and Steven Reale to be identified as the authors of the editorial material, and of the authors for their individual chapters, has been asserted in accordance with sections 77 and 78 of the Copyright, Designs and Patents Act 1988.

All rights reserved. No part of this book may be reprinted or reproduced or utilized in any form or by any electronic, mechanical, or other means, now known or hereafter invented, including photocopying and recording, or in any information storage or retrieval system, without permission in writing from the publishers.

Trademark notice: Product or corporate names may be trademarks or registered trademarks, and are used only for identification and explanation without intent to infringe.

Library of Congress Cataloging-in-Publication Data
Names: Gibbons, William (William James), 1981– editor. |
    Reale, Steven, editor.
Title: Music in the role-playing game : heroes & harmonies / edited by
    William Gibbons and Steven Reale.
Description: New York ; London : Routledge, 2019. | Series: Routledge
    music and screen media series | Includes bibliographical references
    and index.
Identifiers: LCCN 2019009437 (print) | LCCN 2019012045 (ebook) |
    ISBN 9781351253208 (ebook) | ISBN 9780815369028 (hardback) |
    ISBN 9780815369042 (pbk.)
Subjects: LCSH:Video game music—History and criticism. |
    Fantasy games.
Classification: LCC ML3540.7 (ebook) | LCC ML3540.7 .M876 2019
    (print) | DDC 781.5/4—dc23
LC record available at https://lccn.loc.gov/2019009437

ISBN: 978-0-8153-6902-8 (hbk)
ISBN: 978-0-8153-6904-2 (pbk)
ISBN: 978-1-351-25320-8 (ebk)

Typeset in Bembo
by Apex CoVantage, LLC

CONTENTS

List of Figures, Tables, and Musical Examples	*vii*
Series Foreword	*xi*

Prologue: The Journey Begins *William Gibbons and Steven Reale*	1

PART I
Magical Melodies   7

1	Song and the Transition to "Part-Talkie" Japanese Role-Playing Games *William Gibbons*	9
2	"The Things I Do for Lust …": Humor and Subversion in *The Bard's Tale* *Karen M. Cook*	21
3	*Mother/EarthBound Zero* and the Power of the Naïve Aesthetic: *No Crying Until the Ending* *Tim Summers*	35

vi Contents

PART II
Mystical Metaphors 55

  4 Alien Waves: Sonic Reverberations of the RPG Interface
in *Lagrange Point* 57
Kevin R. Burke

  5 The Penultimate Fantasy: Nobuo Uematsu's Score
for *Cleopatra no Ma Takara* 76
Dana Plank

  6 Music in the Time of Video Games: Spelunking
Final Fantasy IV 97
Julianne Grasso

  7 Operatic Conventions and Expectations in *Final Fantasy VI* 117
Ryan Thompson

PART III
Meaningful Memories 129

  8 Ludomusical Dissonance in *Diablo III* 131
Michiel Kamp

  9 A Hidden Harmony: Music Theory Pedagogy
and Role-Playing Games 146
Meghan Naxer

10 Soundwalking and the Aurality of *Stardew Valley*:
An Ethnography of Listening to and Interacting
with Environmental Game Audio 159
Kate Galloway

11 Musical Landscapes in *Skyrim* 179
Michiel Kamp and Mark Sweeney

12 Barriers to Listening in *World of Warcraft* 197
Steven Reale

Notes on Contributors 216
Index of Video Games 220
General Index 222

FIGURES, TABLES, AND MUSICAL EXAMPLES

Figures

1.1	Luna singing, *Lunar: Silver Star Story Complete*	15
1.2	Luna's song clears the forest	16
3.1	Status screen in *Mother*	37
3.2	Final battle with Giegue	40
3.3	Ninten and his party perform a musical number at a nightclub	42
3.4	Ninten and Ana share a dance before Ana confesses her love for Ninten	43
4.1	The death of NPC Tum in *Lagrange Point*	58
4.2a	Mapping the Isis Colony Cluster in *Lagrange Point*	59
4.2b	Mapping the audio in *Lagrange Point*	59
4.3a	The process of weapon fusion in *Lagrange Point*	60
4.3b	The resulting synthesis of 2-operator FM	61
4.4	The Bio Corps boss Ledesma	66
5.1	Title screen of *Cleopatra no Ma Takara*	77
5.2	Samurai warriors at Giza, photographed by Antonio Beato (1863)	81
6.1	A sequence of events in *Final Fantasy IV*	99
6.2	A 1:1 mapping between a player's action and an event in the game world. Adapted from Jesper Juul, "Introduction to Game Time" (2004)	103
6.3	An approximate mapping of the delay between a player's action and corresponding event in the game world in *Final Fantasy IV*	103
6.4	Mapping the full sequence from Figure 6.1 on Juul's play time and event time	105

viii Figures, Tables, and Musical Examples

6.5	Messing up Juul's model with music, as promised	112
7.1	Front matter from score to Handel's *Rinaldo* (1711)	120
7.2	Impresario appearing on stage	121
7.3	Celes throwing flowers at the close of the opera scene, midway through Act II	126
10.1	Crafting my avatar (all gameplay fieldwork stills and any annotations by the author)	162
10.2	Opening scenes of *Stardew Valley* gameplay	163
10.3	Annotated gameplay soundwalk map	167
10.4	Sample regions of *Stardew Valley*	169
10.5	Fuzzy Acres Farm over the seasons	171
10.6	Alex and Darby	173
10.7	The Stardrop Saloon	175
11.1	Caspar David Friedrich's *Morning Mist in the Mountains* (1808)	180
11.2	*The Elder Scrolls V: Skyrim* (2011)	180
11.3	"Under an Ancient Sun," spectrogram	186
12.1	The Thousand Needles zone: before (above) and after (below) *Cataclysm*	203
12.2	The entire barrier complex. From left to right, top to bottom: the demon Kil'jaeden; the gates of Orgrimmar; the Eye of the Storm battleground; and the wasteland of Silithus	205
12.3	The blade of Sargeras's sword and the wound of Azeroth now occupy the location of the insect mound in Figure 12.2	207

Tables

3.1	The "Eight Melodies" in *Mother*	38
4.1	Weapon fusion chart by type, *Lagrange Point*	60
4.2	Weapon fusion charts by rank and number of targets, Part 1	61
4.3	Weapon fusion charts by rank and number of targets, Part 2	61
4.4a	Fusing weapons in *Lagrange Point*	62
4.4b	Fusing sine waves in 2-operator FM synthesis	62
4.5	The three functional character types in *Lagrange Point*	63
4.6	The three collaborator types in *Lagrange Point's* music and sound creation	64
4.7	Music track list for *Lagrange Point*	65
4.8	Names given for the 15 preset instrument patches	69
4.9	The Famicom APU's drum kit for *Lagrange Point*	69
12.1	A spectrum of hypothetical synchronic barriers from the perspective of a player who owns a game for which a recent paid expansion features a particular encounter	201
12.2	High-level zones in *World of Warcraft* and *The Burning Crusade*	205

Figures, Tables, and Musical Examples   **ix**

Musical Examples

3.1	Underground Theme from *Mother*, showing the "alien" musical style	46
4.1	A typical distribution of *Lagrange Point*'s audio in "Aqueduct," mm. 9–12	68
4.2	Monophonic drum kit in *Yume Penguin Monogatari*, mm. 1–4	70
4.3	Triangle wave tom and the 2A03 drum kit in "Aqueduct," mm. 9–12	70
4.4	Single- and multi-channel echo in "Bubbles of Light," mm. 7–12	71
4.5	Four-channel echo and harmonics in "Theme of Isis," mm. 1–2	71
4.6	Two-channel echo and harmonics in "The Resurrection of Sabbath," mm. 1–4	72
5.1	Nobuo Uematsu, "Title," mm. 1–10 *Cleopatra no Ma Takara*	77
5.2	Koichi Sugiyama, "Jipang," *Dragon Quest III*	80
5.3	Koichi Sugiyama, "Pyramid," *Dragon Quest III*	84
5.4	Nobuo Uematsu, "Town," *Cleopatra no Ma Takara*	85
5.5	Nobuo Uematsu, "Random Encounter," *Cleopatra no Ma Takara*	85
5.6	Nobuo Uematsu, "Victory Fanfare," *Cleopatra no Ma Takara*	85
5.7	Nobuo Uematsu, "Battle 1," mm. 1–4 *Final Fantasy II*	86
5.8	Nobuo Uematsu, "Shop," *Cleopatra no Ma Takara*	87
5.9	Koichi Sugiyama, "Battle Theme," mm. 1–8, *Dragon Quest III*	88
5.10	Nobuo Uematsu, "Town Theme," mm. 1–10, *Final Fantasy II*	89
5.11	Koichi Sugiyama, "Village Theme," mm. 1–10, *Dragon Quest III*	89
5.12	Nobuo Uematsu, "Goddess Temple," *Cleopatra no Ma Takara*	89
5.13	Nobuo Uematsu, "Credits," mm. 15–24, *Cleopatra no Ma Takara*	90
5.14	Nobuo Uematsu, "Game Over," *Cleopatra no Ma Takara*	91
5.15	Nobuo Uematsu, "Dead Theme," *Final Fantasy II*	92
5.16	Nobuo Uematsu, "Goddess Temple: Underground," *Cleopatra no Ma Takara*	92
5.17	Nobuo Uematsu, "Slumber of Ancient Earth," *Final Fantasy V*	93
6.1	The introduction and opening few bars of "Into the Darkness" from *Final Fantasy IV*	107
6.2	The first half of "Fight 1," the primary battle music of *Final Fantasy IV*	109
6.3	The victory fanfare cue at the conclusion of a successful battle in *Final Fantasy IV*. This loop will repeat until the player has read through the text denoting the acquisition of points and spoils	110
7.1	Transcription of "Locke"	123
7.2	Transcription of "Forever Rachel"	123
7.3	Voice and harp parts from second stanza of Celes's opera aria	125

x Figures, Tables, and Musical Examples

7.4	Voice and harp parts from Celes's theme	126
7.5	Transcription of "Ending Theme (part 1)," excerpt	127
8.1	Bridge cue, *Diablo III*	132
11.1	"From Past to Present," mm. 1–7	183
11.2	"Journey's End," excerpt	184
11.3	"Awake," horn melody	185
11.4	"Far Horizons," excerpt 1	185
11.5	"Far Horizons," excerpt 2	185
11.6	"Unbroken Road," excerpt	192
12.1	Excerpt from "Terrokar Forest" scoring. *World of Warcraft: The Burning Crusade* (Blizzard, 2007). All transcriptions by the author with minor simplifications	199
12.2	Entrance to Orgrimmar cue, *World of Warcraft* original release	204
12.3	Entrance to Orgrimmar cue, post-*Cataclysm*	204
12.4	Excerpt from the Brewfest polka, hordeside	206

SERIES FOREWORD

While the scholarly conversations about music in film and visual media have been expanding prodigiously since the last quarter of the twentieth century, a need remains for focused, specialized studies of particular films as they relate more broadly to genres. This series includes scholars from across the disciplines of music and film and media studies, of specialists in both the audible as well as the visual, who share the goal of broadening and deepening these scholarly dialogues about music in particular genres of cinema, television, video games, and new media. Claiming a chronological arc from the birth of cinema in the 1890s to the most recent releases, the Routledge Music and Screen Media series offers collections of original essays written for an interdisciplinary audience of students and scholars of music, film and media studies in general, and interdisciplinary humanists who give strong attention to music. Driving the study of music here are the underlying assumptions that music, together with screen media (understood broadly to accommodate rapidly developing new technologies), participates in important ways in the creation of meaning and that including music in an analysis opens up the possibility for interpretations that remain invisible when only using the eye.

The series was designed with the goal of providing a thematically unified group of supplemental essays in a single volume that can be assigned in a variety of undergraduate and graduate courses (including courses in film studies, in film music, and other interdisciplinary topics). We look forward to adding future volumes addressing emerging technologies and reflecting the growth of the academic study of screen media. Rather than attempting an exhaustive history or unified theory, these studies—persuasive explications supported by textual and contextual evidence—will pose questions of musical style, strategies of rhetoric, and critical cultural analysis as they help us to see, to hear, and ultimately to understand these texts in new ways.

Neil Lerner
Series Editor

PROLOGUE

The Journey Begins

William Gibbons and Steven Reale

The study of game music—sometimes called "ludomusicology"—is no longer the new kid on the academic block. Alongside the larger field of game studies, the discipline has exploded in the past decade, resulting in a wave of groundbreaking books, chapters, and articles that trace the history and interpretation of music in video games. By nature, these foundational works are for the most part either very broad in scope—tracing the entire history of game music, or introducing frameworks for analysis—or very narrow, usually in the form of individual case studies. This volume represents an effort to explore a middle ground by applying a range of methodological approaches to the study of music in a single game genre: role-playing games, or RPGs. Genre-based approaches to music in film (and, to a lesser degree, television) have been common for some time. Indeed, a genre-based approach is the core concept of the Routledge Music and Screen Media series in which this book appears, which features essay collections dedicated to film genres like horror, epic, documentary, and Westerns; television genres such as science fiction and comedy; in addition to a predecessor volume on video game music. Yet, with some notable exceptions mostly centered around music games, ludomusicologists have been hesitant to embrace genre as a guiding principle.[1] Our decision to do so raises a few important questions. Why choose RPGs for this kind of genre-based study? And what counts as an RPG, anyway?

The first question is the easier of the two to answer. Particularly since the 1990s, RPGs have been celebrated for the quality of their musical scores, many of which have also experienced second lives as concert music in recent years.[2] RPGs require longer playtime than most other genres—often into the hundreds, sometimes even thousands, of hours—which means both that players are exposed to music for long periods of time and that composers and sound designers tend to focus on variety and complexity in their scores to avoid listener fatigue. Furthermore, given the byzantine plots of many RPGs, music can prove an important functional element to players, helping them keep dozens of characters and questlines straight. Finally, there's the question of musical style. The high fantasy settings of many RPGs have long lent themselves to the same types of bombastic, quasi-Wagnerian musical techniques and orchestral textures favored by cinema's fantasy and sci-fi epics (e.g., John Williams's *Star Wars* scores, or Howard Shore's music for the *Lord of the Rings* and *Hobbit* films). By virtue of their proximity both to film and Western concert-music traditions, these styles are accessible and intriguing to music academics, film music fans, and classical music aficionados.

The second question is far more complex, and there are some understandable reasons why game music academics have mostly avoided viewing games through the lens of genre. Most obviously, until recently the discipline lacked the groundwork necessary to contextualize any study of genre within a larger framework. Genre is also more difficult to define in video games than in other media, because every game has (at least!) two genres: one for its narrative and another for its gameplay.[3] For example, *Dragon Quest* (1986) is a fantasy role-playing game—with "fantasy" as the narrative genre and "role-playing game" as the gameplay genre. Then, as with other media, each of these genres can break down into various subgenres, or hybridize by incorporating elements of others. With that complexity in mind, we could meaningfully (if ridiculously) describe *Dragon Quest* as a single-player, quasi-linear, high-fantasy, turn-based Japanese role-playing game. Each of those descriptors helps situate the game and its music in dialogue with a range of other titles over several decades—yet it also becomes obvious how difficult and reductive it might be to generalize too much about game genres.

In fact, it's a challenge just to define what constitutes an RPG in the first place. We might meaningfully make the argument that all narrative games involve "role playing" to some extent, in that players assume the persona(s) of their in-game character(s). The name "role-playing game" is really more of a historical identifier than an accurate description of game content—a holdover from the days of pen-and-paper RPGs, especially *Dungeons & Dragons*. The earliest digital RPGs—games like Richard Garriott's *Akalabeth: World of Doom* (1979) and *Ultima* (1981), or Sir-Tech's *Wizardry: Proving Ground of the Mad Overlord* (1981)—were predominantly efforts to replicate tabletop gaming experiences without all the pesky polyhedral dice. These tabletop origins are clearly evident in early computer RPGs, but in subsequent years the genre has branched in a number of directions.[4] A player today might choose between options as varied as the fantasy single-player action-RPG *The Elder Scrolls: Skyrim* (2011), the massively multiplayer online role-playing game *World of Warcraft* (2004–), the turn-based Japanese role-playing game *Dragon Quest XI* (2017), or the philosophical indie retrogame *Undertale* (2015).

This variety is unquestionably a boon to players, but it also presents a challenge for scholars. For any universal element of RPGs that we might offer—either in

Prologue: The Journey Begins **3**

terms of narrative archetypes or gameplay elements—it would be possible to offer a counterexample. For example, role-playing games tend to focus on developing complex narratives, yet the paradigmatic action-RPG *Diablo* (1996) has almost no story to speak of. RPGs tend to feature a wide range of villainous monsters for players to destroy, but *Rakuen* (2017) includes no combat. RPGs tend to be more about developing characters and managing resources than about twitchy reflexes, but the difficulty of *Bloodborne* (2015) led one of this book's editors to throw his copy into a trash compactor. Rather than offering a clear definition, then, it is useful to consider the "family resemblance" of RPGs—a term Ludwig Wittgenstein developed, appropriately enough, in a study of different types of games.[5] Wittgenstein concluded that there was no single characteristic common to all games, but that they constituted, in his words, "a complicated network of similarities overlapping and criss-crossing: sometimes overall similarities, sometimes similarities of detail."[6] Adapting that formulation for our use, we might say that there are no elements common to all RPGs—not even all the RPGs studied in this volume, in fact—but all RPGs are somehow connected to other games in the genre in a kind of intertextual web.

Most of these criss-crossing elements of RPGs were evident in our contributors' chapters, and, even though we did not dictate the topics, the chapters nonetheless coalesced into some handy thematic groups. A Japanese-vs.-Western RPG distinction was palpable from the outset, with about half of the chapters focusing on JRPGs and the other half on Western RPGs. Though this distinction is fairly loose, it is nonetheless meaningful in terms of both player expectations and musical functions. As one of the editors as written elsewhere:

> Broadly speaking, Western RPGs tend to favor individualized character creation, free exploration, and the creation of dark, "realistic" fantasy worlds; JRPGs, on the other hand, typically privilege colorful, often cartoonish environments and situations, and a linear narrative with pre-established characters ... These differences, though increasingly pronounced in recent years, are the product of a decades-long process of stylistic evolution, driven by technological differences, cultural preferences, and eventually, generic expectations.[7]

Given the continued existence of JRPGs to the present day, it struck us as noteworthy that each of the invited contributors who chose to write on a JRPG chose games released for the Nintendo Entertainment System (NES) or Super Nintendo Entertainment System (SNES)—that is, from the 1980s or early 1990s. There seems to be a vein of nostalgia that informs our experiences with such titles, and that nostalgia extends even to Galloway's decision to write about *Stardew Valley*, a game created by an American designer and released in 2016, but featuring a visual and aural aesthetic very much inspired by those same early 1990s JRPG titles. Nostalgia further suggests that each writer's experience with their chosen

4 William Gibbons and Steven Reale

game is deeply personal—as does the fact that several authors' contributions feature significant autobiographical accounts of their experiences as players. (Indeed, autobiography even crept into this introduction, when one of us divulged our frustration with *Bloodborne*. In Chapter 12, we both acknowledge a similar frustration with *Dark Souls*, an equivalently difficult game from the same design studio).

These fortuitous trends ultimately shaped how we decided to organize the book: the first three chapters provide an overview of genre characteristic and explore the relationship between music and magic; the middle part of the book focuses on JRPGs; and the closing section centers on ways that playing an RPG can be a deeply personal experience. The first chapter, William Gibbons's "Song and the Transition to 'Part-Talkie' Japanese Role-Playing Games," establishes the ground that much of the remainder of the book will tread. It not only establishes some JRPG conventions—and specifically their relationship to sound—but also presents an autobiographical account of the author's amazement as a teenager hearing the transition to fully voiced sound in what had been up to that point a "silent" genre, akin to early films before the rise of talkies.

Karen Cook's contribution, "'The Things I Do for Lust …': Humor and Subversion in *The Bard's Tale*," provides something of a mirror image to Gibbons's account. In a game whose protagonist is ostensibly a musician, *The Bard's Tale* subverts RPG conventions of the interrelated nature between music and magic through its deeply parodic style. But, as Cook shows, ironic subversions of style conventions on one level often reinforce them on the next. In "*Mother/Earthbound Zero* and the Power of the Naïve Aesthetic: *No Crying Until the Ending*," Tim Summers explores how the titular game enacts what he terms a "naïve aesthetic" through its nostalgia for mid- to late-twentieth-century Americana (an ironic nostalgia, as it originates in late twentieth-century Japan). Throughout the game, the protagonist Ninten and his companions explore their world finding fragments of a melody, which, when completed, unleashes the magic necessary to save the planet.

Summers's chapter also functions as a pivot to the heart of the volume: a sequence of chapters that present case studies of NES/SNES JRPGs viewed through large-scale conceits. First, in "Alien Waves: Sonic Reverberations of the RPG Interface in *Lagrange Point*," Kevin Burke employs an extended metaphorical connecting the architecture of the game's custom sound chip and its unusual gameplay mechanics. For example, he shows how the sound chip's production of unusual timbres for the NES creates a sonic parallel to the alien incursion on the game world's interplanetary colony, or how an in-game mechanic whereby players can upgrade weapons parallels FM wave synthesis, where the chip combines sine waves of differing frequencies and amplitudes to create composite timbral curves. Then, in "The Penultimate Fantasy: Nobuo Uematsu's Score for *Cleopatra no Ma Takara*," Dana Plank explores the scoring techniques of one of the best-known video game composers in one of his lesser-known titles. The game, which takes place in ancient Egypt, features many standard exoticist musical tropes in the soundtrack. Plank positions these musical gestures within a larger-scale Japanese fascination with ancient Egypt, and uses the game as a window onto problematic modes of cultural representation.

Uematsu's scores are also the subject of the following two chapters, which address his music for the beloved *Final Fantasy* series. In "Music in the Time of Video Games: Spelunking *Final Fantasy IV*," Julianne Grasso examines representations of time in JRPGs. Specifically, she illustrates how the standard game mechanic whereby JRPGs alternate between exploration and combat in fact requires the player to parse the game's narrative along multiple, simultaneous time streams, and she demonstrates how the music assists the player in making that complicated navigation. Lastly, Ryan Thompson's "Operatic Conventions and Expectations in *Final Fantasy VI*," makes the argument that one of the game's signature set pieces—an opera sequence—highlights an operatic structure to the game as a whole, and he offers his chapter as something like a playbill for the work.

The remaining five chapters concern ways in which RPGs—and their music—can create intensely personal experiences for players; most of these chapters feature autobiographical accounts of their authors' engagement with the games under consideration. Michiel Kamp's "Ludomusical Dissonance in *Diablo III*" begins with a moment of gameplay that caught the author's attention: at one particular spot in one particular level, a portentous musical cue sounded for reasons that weren't immediately clear. The confusing presence of that cue as a musical sign becomes the catalyst for Kamp's broader study on musical signs and how they relate to the gameplay they accompany. In "A Hidden Harmony: Music Theory Pedagogy and Role-Playing Games," Meghan Naxer proposes making the RPG experience deeply personal by rethinking and gamifying music theory pedagogies, adapting some of the practices in RPG game design to help focus students intensely while instructing them in how to overcome their puzzles.

In Chapter 10, "Soundwalking and the Aurality of *Stardew Valley*," Kate Galloway employs the practice of soundwalking through the game's digital environment in a way that establishes a bond between herself-as-player and her in-game avatar. In Chapter 11, "Musical Landscapes in *Skyrim*," Michiel Kamp and Mark Sweeney consider the game's soundtrack in light of the nineteenth-century artistic interest in landscapes—with the chapter's centerpiece being an account (including video footage) of one author's experience viewing the land of Skyrim from a vantage point on a hilltop. The authors argue that *Skyrim*'s visual design can combine with the musical scoring to create "happy accidents" that more closely resemble experiences with nature than is possible in many other artistic media. Finally, Steven Reale's contribution, "Barriers to Listening in *World of Warcraft*," draws on autobiographical accounts of the author's time in Azeroth to highlight ways in which the idiomatic and ever-evolving nature of MMORPGs inevitably prevents players from accessing and experiencing some game content.

The essays in this volume were not designed to give a complete overview of music in RPGs, but rather to begin constructing a network of studies devoted to exploring the roles of music in this rich and diverse genre. What we hope is also made clear by the end of this book is the considerable role that RPGs and their music may play in the lives of those who have spent time exploring their worlds, and that the genre represents a significant—and significantly new—storytelling medium.

Notes

1 Such exceptions would include: *Music Video Games: Performance, Politics, and Play*, ed. Michael Austin (New York: Bloomsbury, 2016); and Kiri Miller, *Playable Bodies: Dance Games and Intimate Media* (New York: Oxford University Press, 2017). For an early examination of the role of genre in game audio, see Tim Summers, "Playing the Tune: Video Game Music, Gamers, and Genre," *ACT: Zeitschrift für Musik & Performance* 2(2) (2011): 2–27. urn:nbn:de:bvb:703-opus-9041 (accessed October 14, 2018).
2 For an overview of the qualities of RPG scores, see William Gibbons, "Music, Genre, and Nationality in Postmillennial Fantasy Role-Playing Games," in *The Routledge Companion to Screen Music and Sound*, ed. Miguel Mera, Ron Sadoff, and Ben Winters (New York: Routledge, 2017): 412–427. On the transition of game music (especially RPG music) into concert halls, see William Gibbons, *Unlimited Replays: Video Games and Classical Music* (New York: Oxford University Press, 2018), Chapter 11; and William Cheng, *Sound Play: Video Games and the Musical Imagination* (New York: Oxford University Press, 2014), Chapter 2.
3 Summers refers to these types as "interactive genre" and "environmental genre," but the distinction remains the same. Summers, "Playing the Tune." On the complexities of genre in games—and the need to theorize them anyway—see, for example, Mark J.P. Wolf, *The Medium of the Video Game* (Austin: University of Texas Press, 2001), Chapter 6; and Gerald Voorhees, Josh Call, and Katie Whitlock, "Series Introduction—Genre and Disciplinarity in the Study of Games," in *Dungeons, Dragons, and Digital Denizens: The Digital Role-Playing Game*, ed. Gerald Voorhees, Josh Call, and Katie Whitlock (New York: Continuum, 2012): 1–10.
4 For an overview of the first few decades of digital RPGs, see Matt Barton, *Dungeons & Desktops: The History of Computer Role-Playing Games* (Boca Raton, FL: CRC Press, 2008).
5 Wittgenstein's concept of "family resemblance" (or Familienähnlichkeit) first appears in print (posthumously) in Philosophical Investigations, trans. G.E.M. Anscombe (New York: Macmillan, 1953).
6 Wittgenstein, *Philosophical Investigations*, 36.
7 Gibbons, "Music, Genre, and Nationality," 413.

PART I
Magical Melodies

1

SONG AND THE TRANSITION TO "PART-TALKIE" JAPANESE ROLE-PLAYING GAMES

William Gibbons

In high school in the 1990s, I was part of a close-knit circle of friends who all, in one way or another, fell pretty squarely in the "nerd" category. One of our geekiest—and, to my mind, most beloved—summer rituals was to gather in the basement of my house and play through Japanese role-playing games (JRPGs), consuming large amounts of iced tea and snacks in the process. To make the games as engrossing (and hilarious) as possible for those who weren't playing, we would often divvy up the characters and melodramatically read their lines aloud; to this day, I cannot imagine the famous "You spoony bard!" line in *Final Fantasy IV* without hearing my friend Paul's attempt at a Scottish brogue.

The summer after graduation we were all set for a marathon session of a new release for the Sony PlayStation: *Lunar: Silver Star Story Complete*. (I didn't know at the time that this was a re-rereleased version—more on that later.) When we started the game, we were blown away by the introduction, which featured a CD-quality pop song set to impressive anime-style visuals. When we started the game, expecting business-as-usual text boxes, we were further amazed to hear dialogue performed by voice actors. Although the voice acting only ever lasted a minute or so at a time—there's about 15 minutes total in a 30-ish hour game, while the remainder of the dialogue is presented in text boxes—the effect was profound. Every time we started our usual practice of performing the text ourselves, we were interrupted, and the carefully constructed personas we had created were put on the backburner. As I recall it, after a second pop song made an appearance part way through the game, we gave up trying to read the lines and simply let the game tell its story.

This experience stuck with me long after my adventuring party disbanded. Years later, it came to mind when I had the occasion to read, of all things, Michel Chion's *The Voice in Cinema*. Chion notes that early film "talkies" did not so

10 William Gibbons

much introduce the voice as concretize it, depriving the listener of their imagined vocalities: "This spectator who is forced to be deaf cannot avoid hearing voices—voices that resonate in his or her own imagination ... So it's not so much the *absence of voices* that the talking film came to disrupt, as the spectator's freedom to imagine them in her own way."[1] As with Chion's cinematic example, in *Lunar*, the uncanny intrusion of voice into a genre that was previously powered by text and imagination left a lasting impression. And, although this kind of "part-talkie" format has become common in JRPGs in the years since, the point of transition in the 1990s still feels unsettled and remarkable. In this chapter, I explore the connection between the transitions to voice in 1990s JRPGs like *Lunar* and the "part-talkie" era of film in the late 1920s and 1930s, with particular emphasis on the role that song plays in both transitions. Performed (that is, diegetic) song was crucial in popularizing sound film; starting with *The Jazz Singer* (1927), the sung voice eased the transition from "silent film" to "talkies." To a surprising extent, that holds true of JRPGs in their transition to voice acting, as well. In contexts that are strikingly similar to their cinematic forebears, *Lunar* and several other prominent JRPGs released around the same time feature singing characters.

Transitioning to Voice

Although the history of film includes some earlier efforts at synchronized audio, we usually mark the coming of sound film with the intrusion of the human voice in *The Jazz Singer*. The film critic Andrew Sarris sums up the prevailing viewpoint in his 1998 book on the first decades of sound film, proclaiming that the premiere of *The Jazz Singer* on October 23 is "a date enshrined in film history, with all the dread decisiveness of Waterloo, Sarajevo, and Pearl Harbor. On this date the death knell of the 'silent' movie was sounded, and the 'talkies' were born."[2] The evocation of these decisive historical moments suggests an immediacy of change—a sudden earthquake rather than a slower tectonic shift. However, although the success of *The Jazz Singer*—and even more so its sequel, *The Singing Fool* (1928)—proved that American audiences were interested in hearing film, the transition to sound was a much longer process than is typically acknowledged.

For one thing, there were a number of technological and logistic speed bumps on the way: not all theaters had the technology necessary for sound film, for instance, and in other cases silent films were too far into production to make the change. Furthermore, not all studios were convinced that "talkies" were the future. As Douglas Gomery notes in his study *The Coming of Sound*, "In July of 1928 came the first complete 'talker,' *The Lights of New York. The Singing Fool* in the fall proved a bonanza. Yet Warner Bros. was surprisingly cautious. It continued to release part-talkies until April of 1929. Moreover, Warner Bros. released a silent version of each of its sound films throughout the 1929–1930 season."[3] Many films were advertised by their inclusion of different amount of sound: some were "all dialogue," while others were "part dialogue," with only select scenes fully

Transition to "Part-Talkie" Japanese RPGs   **11**

voiced.[4] In those cases, although different films might have different amounts of synchronized sound, the text of each film was fixed: Film X is silent, Film Y is a sound film, Film Z is a part-talkie, etc. But sometimes the situation was even more complicated. In the late 1920s and early 1930s, a single film might be released in multiple versions simultaneously, each containing different amounts of synchronized sound. In these cases, the idea of a text is more fluid; whether the film was silent, sound, or hybrid depended on where and when it was viewed.

As my initial anecdote from *Lunar* suggests, the complexities of the transition to sound film have a number of parallels to the video game market in the 1990s.[5] In fact, the addition of the human voice was a major goal of video games prior to the introduction of CD technology in the mid 1990s.[6] Some 1980s games, particularly arcade cabinets, went to impressive lengths to digitally synthesize voices—two notable examples are *Sinistar* (1983) and *Gauntlet* (1985)—yet by and large the human voice remained elusive, a technological milestone that hardware makers were desperate to reach. During the so-called "console wars," Sega was particularly eager to illustrate that their hardware was more advanced than its competitor Nintendo; "Sega does what Nintendon't," the advertising campaign promised potential buyers.[7] Capturing the human voice was part of that plan, even if it came at a cost. Reportedly one eighth of the total memory on the cartridge for the Sega Genesis's flagship title, *Sonic the Hedgehog* (1991), was the now-iconic two-note "Se-ga" tag that played when the game booted up.[8]

Theoretically, the introduction of CD-ROM technology removed those memory limitations, allowing for a significant (though by no means unlimited) amount of recorded audio. Yet, much as film histories tend to do, histories of game audio (including, in fairness, some of my own writing) tend to introduce the coming of CD audio as an overnight revolution.[9] According to such narratives, games suddenly went from featuring no voices to those of star-studded casts, and music went from synthesized MIDI to acoustic orchestras or pre-recorded popular music. Here I suggest, however, that, as with film, the transition for both music and voice was much less clear cut—especially in the early 1990s. For example, in much the same way that many film theaters lacked appropriate sound technology, not all computers were equipped with CD drives. As a consequence, to maximize their audience, developers simultaneously released versions of games on (perhaps many!) floppy disks. Likewise, releasing games on multiple 1990s consoles—say, the Super Nintendo and the Sega CD—required different versions for each system's unique audio (and video) hardware. Just as film studios created a messy range of solutions to these problems, including "part-talkie" films or multiple simultaneous releases, game developers employed multiple strategies.

Some games were issued in multiple versions more or less simultaneously, such as *The Adventures of Willy Beamish* (1991), which appeared in both floppy disk and CD formats, only the latter of which was voiced.[10] Others, however, were released in multiple versions in quick succession, with each iteration adapting to the rapid-fire changes in the latest technologies. The popular PC space sim

12 William Gibbons

Wing Commander II: Vengeance of the Kilrathi (1991) was initially released with only small amounts of voiced text, for example, but eventually players could purchase the "Speech Accessory Pack," which added full voice acting to the title. Other cases are even more drastic. Consider the LucasArts adventure game *Loom* (1990), for instance. Initially released on floppy disk, the game contained a large number of text-heavy dialogues and cutscenes. Its release as a CD "talkie" two years later, however, dramatically trimmed these cutscenes to allow for the memory demands of full voice acting.[11] That's especially remarkable given that, when games are remastered or re-released, the justification is usually the inclusion of more content. Such was the importance of voice acting, in other words, that developers were willing to *remove* a significant amount of the game's content to accommodate it.

So far, when discussing both film and games, my focus has been on techno-logical advancements and impediments related to the transition to "talkies." Yet technology is not the only factor at play. As Hubbert points out regarding early film, "The revolution was also an aesthetic one … Dialogue, sound, and musical accompaniment needed to be made audible, but they also needed to be made believable."[12] In other words, there needed to be a *reason* to include the voice—a necessity to overrule the spectator's dreamed voices, to use Chion's metaphor. In film, that impetus came from song. The prominence of singing characters in early sound film provided an aesthetic justification for the transition to sound; such a dramatic change was necessary not only because the technology meant that film-makers *could* do it, but that the narratives of the films themselves demanded it. In Hubbert's words, the recurring narrative element of the musician in late 1920s films "allowed and eventually demanded that characters sing or perform."[13] It worked, and audiences not only embraced the new sound technology, but they couldn't get enough of the singing. The ultimate result was that, for several years, it was a *de facto* requirement for sound films to include musical numbers. On the one hand, this development eventually led to the establishment of the film musical as a genre.[14] On the other hand, this tacit requirement also resulted in nonsensi-cal musical elements, as money-hungry studios began requiring the insertion of diegetic popular songs into films regardless of whether their inclusion followed any kind of narrative logic.[15]

The *idea* of song has long been central to RPGs of all kinds. As Karen Cook explores in her chapter in this volume, the bard as a character archetype has been a mainstay of fantasy RPGs since *Dungeons & Dragons* tabletop gaming, and made the transition to video games soon after. Moreover, as Ryan Thompson's chap-ter in this book illustrates, diegetic song plays a crucial role in *Final Fantasy VI* (1994), in which a main character performs a scene from an opera, complete with synthesized voice. Prior to CD audio, representations of song in games required a significant degree of musical abstraction. Sometimes that representation could be as simple as music-note icons on the screen, or a single short melodic motif or strummed chord, as was common to depictions of bards in some early games. *Final Fantasy VI* illustrates a somewhat less abstracted performance—the music

Transition to "Part-Talkie" Japanese RPGs **13**

imitates the timbre and vibrato of human voices—but the synthesized "ooh" and "ah" sounds still require a suspension of disbelief on the player's part.[16]

As with early sound film, CD audio offered a new musical possibility: "live" song—or, rather, the illusion of live song via pre-recorded acoustic music. Despite this new ability, however, diegetic song never became quite so rampant in video games as in film. Yet these types of scenes are nearly always significant; as William Cheng points out, given the rarity of diegetic song in video games, it's "likely to command significant attention, taking center stage and marking out a self-important space of performance."[17] Moreover, there are still some notable parallels between the two media, particularly with regard to the inclusion of popular song in JRPGs. I have argued elsewhere that the inclusion of song, especially popular song, is a stylistic trait common to JRPGs (as opposed to their Western counterparts)—a trend that began in the mid-1990s shortly after the introduction of CD technology.[18] For one thing, JRPG composers tended to come from pop music backgrounds (Nobuo Uematsu, for example, was—and still is—a prog rock musician), and furthermore were influenced by the music of anime films and television programs. However, I would also like to suggest that the trend of including song began for reasons similar to cinema: bridging the gap between silence (or text) and speech. To put it another way, diegetic song could smooth over the bumpy transition between unvoiced and fully voiced games—a sonic buffer that allowed for a more seamless gameplay experience.

Consider, for example, *Grandia II* (2000), a "part-talkie" JRPG originally released for the ill-fated Sega Dreamcast console and later given a second life on the much more successful Sony PlayStation 2. The plot revolves around the relationship between Elena, a "Songstress" (priestess) and Ryudo, a mercenary hired to protect her on a dangerous journey. As with *Lunar*, while most of the dialogue is presented via text, important cutscenes also include voice acting. At one such moment quite early in the game—Elena and Ryudo's first meeting—the switch to spoken dialogue is articulated by Elena's diegetic singing, which Ryudo (and the player) hear before entering the church to begin their escort job. The sound transitions from synthesized music to a pre-recorded "live" performance with singing first, easing the player into the spoken dialogue that follows soon thereafter (and continues for the next several minutes). The same pattern is repeated several times throughout the game, particularly using Elena's voice. Her identity as a Songstress provides the narrative justification for the song, which in turn provides the aesthetic justification for the voice. Significantly, in that first scene players *hear* Elena's song in the game before they see her; the mystery of her unseen voice lures players in and imbues the moment with a special gravitas. As Chion reminds us, the unseen voice—the *acousmêtre*—"becomes invested with magical powers as soon as it is involved, however slightly, in the image."[19] Chion is being metaphorical when he refers to "magical powers," but in *Grandia II* his assessment is entirely on point. Elena's music, the "Song of Light," becomes in all senses a recurring theme in the game. She sings it repeatedly, and it eventually makes its

14 William Gibbons

way into the underscore. Towards the end of the game, the "Song of Light," sung by Elena along with a large group, ultimately provides the psychological and magical energy necessary to defeat the game's villain and save the world.

The same conceit occurs in several other games as well. *Final Fantasy X* (2001)—the first game in the series released on the PlayStation 2 and the first to feature partial voice acting—prominently features popular song both non-diegetically and diegetically. Like *Grandia II*, it also features a recurring diegetic song, the "Hymn of the Fayth," which reveals magical powers towards the end of the game when sung in unison by the world's population.[20] Once again, though here the Hymn does not necessarily lead into the voice acting, the two remain connected; typically, where one appears, the other is not far behind, and appearances of the song are marked as particularly important to the narrative. Other subsequent games have followed a similar path, linking diegetic song with partial voiced dialogue—as in the *Ar Tonelico* series of PlayStation 2 and 3 games, which feature "Song Magic" as a central gameplay element.[21] With this context in mind, I'd like to return to *Lunar*. Both because of its narrative design and the circumstances of its release, *Lunar* offers a clear example of the complexities of voice and song in "part-talkie" JRPGs.

Video Games and the *Lunar* Phase

As we've already seen, one strategy that both films and games employed to navigate the technological challenges of transitioning to voice was the release of multiple versions. Films might have existed in silent, part-talkie, and full-talkie versions depending on the theater; games might be published on CD-ROM and floppy disk, or in PC or multiple home console formats, often with significant differences between the versions. *Lunar* is a case in point: I didn't know it at the time, but the game I played on my PlayStation back in high school was actually a remake. *Lunar*—originally subtitled *The Silver Star*—first appeared in 1992 on the Sega CD, a peripheral that attached to the Sega Genesis and allowed the console to take advantage of the enhanced capabilities of CD-ROM technology. After a successful Sega CD sequel in 1994 (*Lunar: Eternal Blue*), the developers decided to remake *The Silver Star*, citing the availability of new technology, the sequel's improved game mechanics, and a desire to flesh out aspects of the original's characterization and narrative.[22] *Lunar: Silver Star Story Complete*—effectively the "definitive" version—was the result. *Silver Star Story Complete*, originally released on the Sega Saturn console in 1996, was ported two years later to the PlayStation (which is where I encountered it). It has since been re-released on a variety of consoles, including an iOS version (2012), which I replayed for reference while writing this chapter.[23]

Lunar thus exists in a panoply of formats, with some significant differences between them. For one thing, there are major plot changes between *The Silver Star* and *Silver Star Story Complete*, which tidy up some inconsistencies and weaknesses in the first version. But equally important were the changes to the game's video and audio. The 1996 remake incorporated almost an hour of new animated video (in an anime style), as well as re-recorded and much-expanded voice acting. It also featured a completely new soundtrack by Noriyuki Iwadare, who had collaborated on the Sega CD version, including two songs featuring a pre-recorded singer: a title song ("Wings") and the quasi-diegetic song "Wind's Nocturne." The rapidity of multiple remakes and reissues of the game on a wide range of formats is strikingly similar to the situation with film during the transition to sound. As a result of the messiness of its release(s), it's difficult to speak of a fixed "text" when dealing with *Lunar*, but I'm most interested in the inclusion of song in *Silver Star Story Complete*, and how its inclusion enhances the transition to sound.[24]

In any of its incarnations, *Lunar* is in many ways an archetypical JRPG. It features all the trappings of the genre: turn-based battles against a variety of fantasy monsters, menus and stats galore, and a high-fantasy narrative centered on a brave group of teenagers (and the obligatory talking animal) thrown together to save the world. In this case, the two primary protagonists of this *Bildungsspiel* are Alex, a smalltown boy who dreams of being a great warrior, and Luna, his childhood friend who turns out to be the reincarnation of the goddess Althena [sic]. For much of the game Luna is blissfully unaware of her incipient divinity, preferring instead the simple pleasures of village life, including her music.

As the game opens, in fact, Luna and Alex are working up a duet for the town festival. In the Sega CD version, Alex plays the lyre, but he exchanges it for the more portable ocarina in *Silver Star Story Complete*. In both versions, of course, Luna sings (see Figure 1.1). When players first meet Luna in an animated cutscene, she sits in a forest singing a wordless, *a cappella* vocalise to herself. The Orphic beauty of her song is evident immediately; nearby birds have stopped their own activities to perch and listen. Like Luna's avian audience, the players were no doubt amazed by Luna's song—its apparent acoustic "liveness" contrasting with expectations for

FIGURE 1.1   Luna singing, *Lunar: Silver Star Story Complete*

what video game song could be. Significantly, as we saw with Elena in *Grandia II*, it is only after she sings that we hear Luna speak; the music creates a sonic segue to her spoken voice. The scene creates the first of many "musical moments," to use Amy Herzog's term—instances when film scores come to the forefront of the viewer's attention, rather than remaining in the background.[25]

In more ways than one, Luna's song, and the musical moments it creates, become an important recurring motif in *Lunar*. For one thing, this melody will become her musical calling card.[26] For another, her song becomes a source of divine power. Whereas other party members yell out the name of their special attacks in battle (using voice actors), Luna simply sings a fragment of her melody when she uses her healing magic. The implication seems to be that the song itself creates the magic, or is in some other respect a manifestation of her abilities. This power first manifests in the narrative early in the game, after the first major dungeon. To begin their journey to the distant metropolis of Meribia, Alex, Luna, and their friend Ramus must pass through a dense and dangerous forest, blanketed in an impenetrable fog. Faced with a sudden dead end on their path to adventure, Luna pipes up (via text box) that "there's something I'd like to try." The background music stops, and Luna's dialogue box reads "………."—and then she sings, her melody suddenly introducing the human voice where only text had existed before. The fog dissipates, prompting Ramus to remark: "Your voice, Luna … it's magic!" (see Figure 1.2). Thus the magic of Luna's voice exists on two levels. In the gameworld, its magic is literal; it clears the fog and enables the party to continue their journey. But, in the real world, the song's very existence seems magical, a jaw-dropping marvel of technology akin to Al Jolson's songs in *The Jazz Singer*. Also like voice in early film, however, it is an uncanny intrusion of liveness that leaves only stunned silence in its wake: the background music remains absent during the subsequent conversation, resulting in an uncommonly

FIGURE 1.2   Luna's song clears the forest

long diegetic and musical silence. In multiple ways, then, Luna's song is marked as an unusual, significant moment in the game.

Once the group reaches their next stop on the path to glory, Luna's voice makes another dramatic appearance. After some trials and tribulations, the group brokers passage on a ship headed to Meribia. At this point in the original version, Luna returns home to their village, and drops out of the plot until much later in the game. In the *Silver Star Story Complete* version, however, she remains with the party on the ship.[27] This version of the ocean voyage includes an extended cutscene: unable to sleep, Alex takes a late-night stroll on the ship's deck. He soon notices Luna in the crow's nest, at which point the screen transitions to an animated interlude. As fireflies swirl around her, Luna performs the wistful pop song "The Wind's Nocturne" (sometimes identified by the less picturesque title "The Boat Song").[28] This sudden transition to a musical interlude is unexpected, even in light of Luna's previous performances. Instead of an *a cappella* song, here we have a fully staged musical number, complete with orchestral accompaniment. As Herzog points out, this type of sudden transition has a profound effect; these "musical spectacles … are marked by excess, rupture, fluidity, and the dissolution of the space-time continuum that orders the reality of our everyday existence."[29] In other words: music spectacles are magical. Just as Luna's song alters the diegetic reality by clearing the fog from the forest, it transforms the gameworld—and the player's perception of it—by suddenly introducing a musical number.

Less charitably, however, we might also think of this unexpected, unexplained, and arguably unnecessary musical moment as a parallel to the early days of film "talkies." Those films were often logically dubious in their use of diegetic music, justifying the inclusion of diegetic music through flimsy plot devices. One could reasonably argue that Luna's magical voice—and the justification it provides for songs like "The Wind's Nocturne"—falls into the same category. Her songs, however lovely, exist only because they *could*, not because they contributed meaningful to the narrative. Only so many RPGs could use the same trick, however. Consequently, although popular song has certainly found a place in more recent JRPGs, especially in title sequences, diegetic musical numbers like "The Wind's Nocturne" never quite caught on.[30]

Nevertheless, in its various versions, *Lunar* offers an intriguing look at a pivotal moment in game audio history. Looking back, we can find early instances of audio practices that have become staples of the genre—most notably the "part-talkie" format and inclusion of popular music, which persists today despite the capabilities of modern hardware.[31] The perennial *Tales* series, which began around the same time as *Lunar* (in 1995), has for some years now included both voice acting in selected scenes and popular songs in title sequences.[32] In that way, the voice has retained its "specialness" in a way that quickly disappeared from most other game genres (including Western RPGs). At the same time, however, the foregrounding of music found in games like *Lunar*, *Grandia II*, and *Final Fantasy X* points to a future that might have been—one filled with musical interludes, or at least

18 William Gibbons

more "musical moments," in JRPGs.[33] As it is, however, *Lunar* vividly illustrates the importance of music, and specifically of song, in the transition to "part-talkie" games. More broadly, however, *Lunar* clearly illustrates both how the technological transitions of the late 1990s and early 2000s affected game audio, and how the impact of that historical moment continues to affect games decades later.

Notes

1 Michel Chion, *The Voice in Cinema*, trans. Claudia Gorbman (New York: Columbia University Press, 1999), 8–9.
2 Andrew Sarris, *"You Ain't Heard Nothin' Yet": The American Talking Film, History & Memory, 1927–1949* (Oxford and New York: Oxford University Press, 1998), 31.
3 Douglas Gomery, *The Coming of Sound: A History* (New York: Routledge, 2005), 111.
4 Jessica Taylor: "'Speaking Shadows': A History of the Voice in the Transition from Silent to Sound Film in the United States," *Linguistic Anthropology* 19 (2009): 5. As Julie Hubbert writes, "between 1926–1928 studio production was incredibly diverse. Each studio was offering films in an array of formats, some mixing as many as four different approaches at once." Julie Hubbert, *Celluloid Symphonies: Texts and Contexts in Film Music History* (Berkeley and Los Angeles: University of California Press, 2011), 114.
5 I am not unique in pointing to parallels between games and cinematic strategies. On parallels between early games and early cinema, see Neil Lerner, "Mario's Dynamic Leaps: Musical Innovation (and the Specter of Early Cinema) in *Donkey Kong* and *Super Mario Bros.*, in *Music in Video Games: Studying Play*, ed. K.J. Donnelly, William Gibbons, and Neil Lerner (New York: Routledge, 2014): 1–29; and Neil Lerner, "The Origins of Musical Style in Video Games, 1977–1983," in *The Oxford Hand Book of Film Music Studies*, ed. David Neumeyer (New York: Oxford University Press, 2014): 319–347. On the uses of pre-existing music to emulate film scores (including early cinema), see William Gibbons, *Unlimited Replays: Video Games and Classical Music* (New York: Oxford University Press, 2018), Chapter 4. For a brief exploration of the addition of voice to games, see William Cheng, *Sound Play: Video Games and the Musical Imagination* (New York: Oxford University Press, 2014), 59–61. Finally, on the general relationship between Hollywood scoring practices and game scores, see Tim Summers, *Understanding Video Game Music* (Cambridge: Cambridge University Press, 2016), Chapter 6.
6 Aside from video game applications, synthesized speech was a major selling point for other computer-based technologies in the 1970s and 1980s, as in Texas Instruments' well-known Speak & Spell line of educational computers.
7 For a summary of the rivalry in the 1980s and 1990s, see, for example, Blake J. Harris, *Console Wars: Sega, Nintendo, and the Battle that Defined a Generation* (New York: Dey St., 2014).
8 This historical tidbit comes by way of an interview with the former director of Sega's Sonic Team, Yuji Naka. Heidi Kemps, "Sega's Yuji Naka Talks!" *GameSpy* (September 30, 2005). http://xbox.gamespy.com/articles/654/654750p1.html (accessed August 3, 2018).
9 On the transition to CD-ROM technology in games, see, for example, Tristan Donovan, *Replay: The History of Video Games* (Lewes, East Sussex: Yellow Ant, 2010), Chapter 19. Notably, Donovan presents CD audio as an instant godsend for composers fed up with prior audio technologies: "CDs allowed video game musicians … the freedom to concentrate on music rather than programming. Instead of having to write music in machine code they could now write complex scores, record real-life musicians, sample sound and use voice actors" (239).
10 *The Adventures of Willy Beamish* was also ported to the Sega CD in 1993, in further evidence of Sega's commitment to voice acting in its games.

Transition to "Part-Talkie" Japanese RPGs **19**

11 Tim Summers has discussed in some detail the importance of sound and music design in *Loom*, although he does not to my knowledge address the differences in the two versions of the game. Summers, *Understanding Video Game Music*, 77–83.

12 Hubbert, *Celluloid Symphonies*, 111.

13 Hubbert, *Celluloid Symphonies*, 114. Hubbert goes on: "[Many other films], like *The Jazz Singer*, Al Jolson's second feature *The Singing Fool*, Fox's *Mother Knows Best*, First National's *The Divine Lady*, and Pathé's *Show Folks*, from 1928 as well, used synchronized sound to highlight musical performances, making music a central feature not just of the soundtrack but of the visual action on the screen" (114–115).

14 I don't mean to suggest that there was no connection between popular song and early cinema long before the late 1920s. Indeed, there is a long history of aesthetic and financial liaisons between these industries. See, for example, Rick Altman, "Cinema and Popular Song: The Lost Tradition," in *Soundtrack Available: Essays on Film and Popular Music*, ed. Pamela Robertson Wojcik and Arthur Knight (Durham, NC and London: Duke University Press, 2001): 19–30.

15 Hubbert, *Celluloid Symphonies*, 121.

16 As Cheng notes regarding the "pseudo-vocal" musical performance of the opera scene in *FFVI*, "Singing voices in the performance are simulated by synthesized tones, with each note enunciated as (what sounds like) an open-vowel … phoneme. Rapid pulsations within individual tones impart the effect of heavy vibrato. Progressions from note to note occasionally match up with the opening and closing of the performers' mouths, shoring up the impression that this music is indeed sung." Cheng, *Sound Play*, 64.

17 Cheng, *Sound Play*, 62.

18 William Gibbons, "Music, Genre, and Nationality in the Postmillennial Fantasy Role-Playing Game," in *The Routledge Companion to Screen Music and Sound*, ed. Miguel Mera, Ron Sadoff, and Ben Winters (New York: Routledge, 2017): 412–427.

19 Chion, *The Voice in Cinema*, 23.

20 On the "Hymn of the Fayth," see Stefan Xavier Greenfield-Casas, "Between Worlds: Musical Allegory in *Final Fantasy X*" (MA Thesis, University of Texas at Austin, 2017).

21 The games in the series—the titles of which indicate the centrality of song in their narratives—include *Ar Tonelico: Melody of Elemia* (2006), *Ar Tonelico II: Melody of Metafalica* (2007), and *Ar Tonelico Qoga: Knell of Ar Ciel* (2010).

22 *Lunar: Eternal Blue* was itself remade as *Lunar 2: Eternal Blue Complete* (1998) for the PlayStation.

23 In researching this chapter, I also watched YouTube playthroughs of the original Sega CD title, as well as selected scenes from the PlayStation version for reference.

24 Summers has explored the slippery notion of the "text" when analyzing video games in his *Understanding Video Game Music*, Chapter 1. See also Steven Reale's chapter in this volume.

25 Amy Herzog, *Dreams of Difference, Song of the Same: The Musical Moment in Film* (Minneapolis, MN: University of Minneapolis Press, 2010).

26 I would argue against calling the melody a leitmotif, in that it always appears in the same form rather than adapting to new circumstances.

27 Evidently the game developers felt delaying Luna's departure until later in the game would help players develop more attachment to her character before her divine origins were revealed.

28 In the English version of *Silver Star Story Complete*, the title song and "The Wind's Nocturne" are performed by Jennifer Stigile (who, confusingly, contributes the voice acting for another character, Royce), rather than Luna's voice actor. In the Japanese version, the songs are performed by Kyoko Hikami.

29 Herzog, *Dreams of Difference*, 7. In games we might also think of the kinds of musical time dilation described in Julianne Grasso's chapter in this volume.

30 One exception would be the scenes of diegetic song in *Final Fantasy X-2* (2003), in which the three protagonists perform as a girl group. One might also point to the inclusion of diegetic music for ambiance in games like *The Elder Scrolls V: Skyrim*

20 William Gibbons

(2011) or *Dragon Age: Inquisition* (2014), but I would argue that these performances do not foreground the music in the same way as *Lunar*, *Grandia II*, or *Final Fantasy X*.

31 Although she does not single out the genre by name or dwell on the topic, Collins notes the trend of "part-talkie" JRPGs in her discussion of voice acting: "Some games jump back and forth between text and voice, depending on whether the material is interactive or presented in a cinematic sequence … Some other games have relied primarily on text for dialog but have added a few exclamatory voice clips to give the characters a hint of voice." Karen Collins, *Playing with Sound: A Theory of Interacting with Sound and Music in Video Games* (Cambridge, MA: MIT Press, 2013), 68–69.

32 More recent series like the two *Ni no Kuni* games (2011/2018), for example, likewise reserve voice acting for important moments. In terms of Western RPGs, "part-talkies" have become synonymous with the 1990s style of extremely text-heavy computer RPGs (cRPGs), such as the *Baldur's Gate* series of *Dungeons-&-Dragons*-themed titles.

33 Although game musicals did not become a prominent genre as in film, I would be remiss here if I didn't mention the fascinating *Rhapsody* trilogy of RPGs, which appeared on the PlayStation and PlayStation 2 from 1998 to 2000. In addition to standard RPG gameplay, the games feature full diegetic musical numbers in the manner of a stage or film musical, complete with choreography. Although by and large the musical numbers are separate from the action and narratively unjustified (as in most musicals), the main character, Cornet, does have a magical horn. Only the first game, *Rhapsody: A Musical Adventure* (1998), was released in North America.

2

"THE THINGS I DO FOR LUST ..."

Humor and Subversion in *The Bard's Tale*

Karen M. Cook

> In a legend of the Orkney Islands, take the role of the Bard—a sardonic and opportunistic musician and adventurer, driven by carnal rather than noble pursuits. Forget your quest to save the world; you are interested in just two things—coin and cleavage![1]

Alongside other similarly worded advertising blurbs, this is the player's first introduction to The Bard, a nameless rogue who uses his musical and military prowess to woo barmaids, stockpile gold, and eventually save the world ... if he feels like it. The Bard is, as one website calls him, an "Anti-Hero Jerkass"; he is cynical, lusty, and deeply apathetic to anything that does not serve his desires.[2] It likely goes without saying, but The Bard is the central character in *The Bard's Tale*, released by InXile Entertainment for the PlayStation 2 and Xbox in 2004.[3] Only loosely related to the fantasy role-playing game (RPG) and book franchise of the same name (Interplay Production/Electronic Arts, 1985–2018), *The Bard's Tale* is an action role-playing game set in a medieval fantasy version of the Orkney Islands off the northern coast of Scotland.

The game was designed to poke fun at the more clichéd elements of RPGs, comically exaggerating or subverting them. Yes, The Bard must kill a rat in a pub's cellar, as RPG protagonists often do early on in their adventures—but it's a giant, fire-breathing rat. He must rescue a princess from atop a far-off tower, but he does so for the cause of lust, not honor, and she appears just as lusty as he is. Moreover, she turns out to be no damsel in distress, after all.

The player begins in the village of Houton, where The Bard's early-game abilities are put to the test when buxom barmaid Mary MacRary asks him to rid her cellar of a pesky rat. The Bard encounters an unnamed man in the cellar

22   Karen M. Cook

who teaches him his first magical spell, which is necessary to kill the rat and thus win Mary's favors; afterward, the same man instructs The Bard further in magic, playing to his ego and greed to talk him into rescuing the imprisoned princess Caleigh. The Bard only agrees to take on this quest once he realizes that he might both win the beautiful princess's favors and get rich along the way. However, when he finally reaches Caleigh, he discovers that she is in fact a demon who has been imprisoned for the good of the world; the player can then choose one of three different ways to end the game.

The Bard's Tale's humorous, parodic take on RPGs has been well explored by the game's designers, critics, and fans. (Since the term "parody" has multiple meanings, my use of it here echoes scholars such as Wes D. Gehring, who defines film parody as a "comic, yet generally affectionate and distorted, imitation of a given genre, auteur, or specific work."[4]) Often included in this discussion are some of the more overtly humorous uses of music in the game, especially a series of interjected songs that make fun of The Bard. I propose here, however, that music assists in reading the game as a parody in more subtle ways, as well. Unlike most earlier RPGs, there is no musical underscoring here to speak of. The interjected songs are humorous both textually and musically, as they are out of tune and sound stylistically and chronologically out of place in the medievalist game world. The musical spells that The Bard casts in order to summon his magical minions are also sonically incongruous, and neither do they function the way such spells typically do in other RPGs. While a cadre of non-primary characters sing in cutscenes throughout the game, The Bard himself never sings. Nor does he play the traditional bardic harp, which we hear performing the opening title theme; instead he plays the lute and recorder, and when the recorder joins in the title theme, it is performed painfully out of tune.[5] Lastly, while the brash English and Scottish accents reinforce the game's general location in the Orkney Islands, some of the characters are barely comprehensible. In this fashion, I argue, not only does sound play a significant and as yet unexplored role in the game's subversion of RPG tropes, but it also subverts The Bard as both heroic protagonist and bard, adding further layers to the parodic nature of the game.

In a typical role-playing game, the player directs a character through a well-defined game world to complete a series of quests, solve puzzles, or achieve a central goal—usually saving the world (or the kingdom, and/or a particular person, frequently a princess). In action RPGs, battle sequences require the player's real-time input as well. One or more AI-controlled party members might accompany the main character, who is typically controlled by the player, and all will improve their strengths and abilities as the game progresses. The player will collect money, weapons, armor, and other items during play, carrying such things in their inventory until they can be traded, sold, or discarded. Such games tend to have detailed storylines; they often offer a variety of optional side quests and locations to which a player might return, and use dialogue and voiceover narration to suggest to the player different options for story advancement, all of which create myriad replay experiences.

The Bard's Tale is in many ways a typical action RPG.[6] The player controls The Bard through the various towns and towers in the fantasy Orkneys on a quest to save the princess Caleigh. Along the way, he must search for money, better weapons and armor, new magical tunes, and clues to the princess's whereabouts, all the while fighting off the minions of her abductor. The more he fights, the more his skills and strengths grow, including his ability to summon a variety of magical companion creatures. As he travels, he learns local history and gets pointers to his next steps by talking to the various people he encounters. At times, the manner in which The Bard chooses to respond will have an effect on subsequent game options or outcomes. Lastly, he is accompanied at all times, albeit invisibly, by an unseen Narrator who fleshes out knowledge of the game world and comments on The Bard's progress.

However, the game is missing a few standard elements. There is no inventory for a player to manage, since all types of loot are automatically turned into cash at the moment of their discovery. There are only a few small side quests, so it is unnecessary to backtrack into most of the previously explored locations. Moreover, aside from the final battle, there are few opportunities to really change the course of the storyline; for the most part, each player experiences the same streamlined linear narrative and game options in each playthrough.

In these respects, *The Bard's Tale* does not always follow the expected RPG rules, and in fact creatively breaks them to parody the genre, most conspicuously by lampooning its main character. Our Bard is not the typical RPG protagonist, motivated by honor or chivalry, but is instead an anti-hero; he takes on this quest solely for booty, in every sense of the word, and cares not a whit for the world at large. The fact that The Bard cannot carry an inventory but instead exchanges every found item immediately for cash is a pointed commentary on his character. There is little need to program an array of side quests or different progressions through the game, as he will simply do the bare minimum to get to the princess Caleigh; what few side quests exist lead simply to more largely useless loot and some inessential improvements to The Bard's statistics. And, in keeping with his focus on self-preservation—yet perhaps with a subtle jab to his ego—the magical creatures he summons can only either heal him (and in some cases each other) or do his dirty work for him, at their own expense, of course, since they will dissipate as they accumulate damage.

While a convention of RPGs is that their protagonists end their quests as heroes, The Bard can actually choose at the end of the game to destroy the world and stay with Caleigh, or even to walk away and party with the undead as the world burns. His mocking tone and derisive attitude pervade both his personal asides and his conversations with others in the game. During such dialogue, the player can choose either a "nice" or a "snarky" response—although, in another twist to RPG standards, the "nice" responses are only slightly less snarky. Similarly,

24 Karen M. Cook

while a narrator (of some sort) is an RPG convention, this Narrator, voiced by character actor Tony Jay, expresses his weariness and utter contempt for The Bard, breaking the fourth wall (and thus disrupting the ludic illusion, to tweak a phrase from Dan Harries) to convey his discontent directly to The Bard, who responds in equally scornful tones.[7] Even one of the higher-level weapons, appropriately called the Ego Sword, joins the fray, denigrating The Bard and extolling its own virtues at every opportunity.

Other aspects of the RPG genre are also subject to parody here. In many RPGs the player can create any or all of the playable characters, yet here not only are all such characters pre-programmed but they are not even given so much as a name. The Bard is only ever The Bard, the Narrator is both anonymous and invisible, and the magical creatures are nothing but musically animated golems; the only characters with names are those with whom The Bard interacts throughout the game, and even some of those names have humorous overtones. While many of the characters have names rooted in Scots-Orkney heritage, at one point there is a mention of a "great highland warrior" named Duncan MacClaidh (MacLeod), whom some perceptive players might recognize as the main character in the long-running fantasy television series *Highlander*. Also, in most fiction media it is rare for more than one character to share the same name—yet in one chapter here The Bard must search for a man named Bodb only to discover that there are in fact five brothers by the same name, all of whom he must find to advance in his quest.

The plot device of saving a princess (and thus saving the world, or earning her hand in marriage, or receiving a reward from her father, the king, etc.) is certainly not unique to RPGs. The earliest adventure games, such as *Wizard and the Princess* (1980), and arcade games such as *Donkey Kong* (1981), feature characters battling the forces of evil to rescue a damsel in distress. This device has since been perpetuated in numerous genres, including graphic adventure games, RPGs, and many action/platform games, most famously *Super Mario Bros.* (1985), where the well-known trope "your princess is in another castle" originated. While several games, such as *Max Payne 2* and *Final Fantasy X*, invert this plot device by having the female character rescue herself or even save the hero, *The Bard's Tale* turns it completely on its head when the princess Caleigh is revealed to be instead an all-powerful demon who perhaps should remain imprisoned instead of rescued.

The parody inherent in some of these elements might only be obvious to gamers already well versed in the conventions of the action RPG genre. Others, such as the sharply witty, often risqué dialogue and even the attire some of the characters wear (in particular the incredibly skimpy outfit worn by barmaid Mary MacRary), play to an earthier sense of humor, but require no particular literacy in game genres to be perceived as funny. The pop culture references scattered throughout the game—such as the aforementioned *Highlander* reference, the fact that some of the wolves drop red cloaks à la "Little Red Riding Hood," and allusions to films such as *Monty Python and the Holy Grail* (1975), *Willy Wonka & the*

Humor and Subversion in *The Bard's Tale*   **25**

Chocolate Factory (1971), and *You Got Served* (2004)—also mark the game's irreverence, while also grounding their humor in more familiar sources.[8] The game is still playable and enjoyable, even if its player is not aware of its manipulations of RPG clichés. If the player does happen to be familiar with RPG conventions, though, then such manipulations become doubly humorous. The Narrator's droll jabs at The Bard are already funny, for example, but a knowledgeable player will notice that a good part of the humor in his commentary is due to his incredulity at standard but unrealistic RPG elements, such as slain foes leaving behind treasure to be picked up.

Much of the music in *The Bard's Tale* is also explicitly humorous, either due to lyrical content or to quirky musical gestures. In particular, fans and critics routinely point to the humor in a series of musical cutscenes. The first occurs quite early in the game; after flirting with Mary MacRary and clearing her basement of rats, The Bard can decide to listen to a group of singing drunks in the corner of the pub.[9] Their ditty is actually a real-life folk song, "Beer, Beer, Beer." A lowbrow ode to beer and its fictional creator, it is also known as "An Ode to Charlie Mopps," and is rumored to have originated somewhere in early nineteenth-century Ireland or England and has been recorded a number of times since the folk music revival of the 1960s. The out-of-tune enthusiasm of the pub drunks is a bit too much, even for The Bard, and so he rolls his eyes and walks away.

This tune aside, the rest of the game's songs specifically poke fun at The Bard, often using mean and even vulgar language to do so. For example, should the player decide to complete a side quest to Finstown, The Bard will there encounter a group of Vikings who sing a tribute to him, including lyrics such as "Here's to The Bard, and his scab of a brain" and "Here's to The Bard, and his knob of a head."[10] In another instance, The Bard has the option to participate in a jam session in a different pub; the singer tells the tale of the Nuckelavee, a horse-demon of Orkney mythology whom The Bard has accidentally released into the world. The singer, unaware of The Bard's involvement, sings: "Nuckelavee! Oh Nuckelavee, you're big and evil and heinous. Who could it be who set you free? He really must be an anus."[11]

One song reoccurs throughout the game: at six different points, a group of trow (a short, ugly, mischievous creature of Orkney legend) materializes to sing directly to The Bard in a manner reminiscent of the Oompa Loompas in *Willy Wonka & the Chocolate Factory*. In each instance, the trow inform The Bard of just how terribly he is doing and how little hope there is for his success, closing with the following refrain:

> Oh, it's bad luck to be you.
> Don't think for just a second it's not true.
> When your life has run amuck,
> You'll see that you're the schmuck.
> Oh, it's bad luck to be,

26 Karen M. Cook

> Really bad luck to be,
> Nobody could disagree,
> It's a freaking guarantee.
> Oh, it's bad luck to be you.
> Diddly doo.[12]

Other humorous musical examples are integrated into the gameplay. In the later stages of the game, The Bard can upgrade his weapons to the aforementioned Ego Sword or the Shadow Axe. When the Bard wields the Ego Sword, the sword itself casts the magic music used to summon the creatures, but it does so by singing in an overly confident manner, often after making some sort of snide comment to The Bard such as "Need me again? I thought so."[13] The Shadow Axe, though, introduces another absurd interjection: punning on the word "axe," The Bard plays the glowing purple weapon like an air guitar, and the tunes that formerly conjured a quasi-Renaissance aesthetic emerge fuzzily amplified in a manner more akin to Prince than bard.[14]

Each of these examples is funny on its face. The lyrics provoke shock, laughter, and even schadenfreude, the vocals are awkward and humorously out of tune, the Ego Sword slights The Bard, and the Shadow Axe incorporates humor through absurd anachronism. Yet each of these examples also plays subtly with preconceived expectations about RPGs, and other less overt sonic and musical elements act toward the same end. In a recent article, William Gibbons explores musical trends in fantasy RPGs since 2000.[15] He observes that soundtracks in Western RPGs resemble those of epic films scored by composers such as John Williams or Howard Shore: bombastic, orchestral, and consisting of a generally Romantic harmonic language filled with leitmotifs. In Japanese RPGs (JRPGs), however, composers draw equally on rock and popular music. Musical tracks in such recent fantasy RPGs are used as cues, designating location (town, dungeon, castle, etc.) or situation (peace, battle, cutscenes, etc.); in JRPGs these cues are fairly pervasive, but in Western RPGs, often much less so.

Not every RPG follows this musical schema, of course. Giles Hooper identifies several more recent Western RPGs that use silence throughout game play, such as *Dragon's Dogma* (2012) and the *Sacred* (2004–) and *Souls* (2009–) series.[16] Yet the prominence of the silence heightens the salience of the musical elements, which usually accompany major boss battles or provide an indication of location. *The Bard's Tale* employs none of these approaches, as there is no real musical soundtrack at all. This aspect of the game received some criticism in the press; one reviewer stated that "the sound effects and music … are pretty standard. The ambient sounds never really draw you into this otherwise fully-formed world."[17] In one or two of the towns that The Bard must explore, there are brief musical cues: a bagpipe draws you nearer to certain buildings in the village of Houton, for example. But such cues perform no ludic function aside from providing the player with a small bit of musical reinforcement as to the game's location in the Orkney Islands.[18]

This lack of musical underscoring is strategic, though, for the presence of a typical epic, heroic score would have been completely at odds with the anti-hero that we find The Bard to be. In that respect, the lack of such music subtly undergirds his character. Furthermore, the absence of a soundtrack, continuous or otherwise, focuses the player's attention on the other sonic elements in the game: the narration and dialogue, the sounds of battle, ambient diegetic environmental sounds, The Bard's magic music, and of course, the musical cutscenes—at no point is the game truly silent.[19] As critic Hilary Goldstein stated above, the sound effects and ambient sounds are fairly standard; there is little to comment on with regard to the sounds of The Bard battling his enemies, or the movements of the characters through different kinds of terrain. The short tunes that The Bard uses to call forth his magical companions reoccur ad nauseam throughout the game. The largely stepwise, modal, dance-like melodies and the instruments upon which they are played impart a general Celtic, Scots-Irish, or Elizabethan character that offer the player what Kendra Leonard calls "aural geo- and chronolocation"—in other words, a sense of place and time.[20] In that respect, the magical tunes perform a service to the gamer that is typical of music in RPGs, at least until the Shadow Axe undermines that sense of place and time, thrusting The Bard forward into a modern rock-and-roll era. But the other categories of sound and music, like the lack of underscoring, offer their own commentaries on both The Bard's anti-hero status and the game's subversion of RPG characteristics.

Meriting closer attention is the voice acting, especially that for The Bard, who is voiced by actor Cary Elwes, well known for his leading roles in medievalist fantasy films *The Princess Bride* (1987) and *Robin Hood: Men in Tights* (1993).[21] Despite both being comedies with strong parodic elements, each in their own way, in both movies Elwes plays a heroic straight man and, as such, he speaks with an impeccable, posh British accent. In *The Bard's Tale*, Elwes's typical elocution is gone, replaced by a much thicker drawl. This accent not only marks The Bard as a person of likely lower class—or at least someone unconcerned with the frivolities of elite diction—but it also acts as another of the aforementioned pop culture references. Those players who recognize Elwes's voice will also recognize The Bard as an inversion of the characters for whom the actor is best known. In similar fashion, Tony Jay was well known as a character actor who often portrayed villains on the one hand, and on the other provided narration for more conventional video games. While narrating *The Bard's Tale* is thus apropos for Jay, the dry wit, sarcasm, and general despondence that he communicates might be unexpected for the gamer familiar with his other voiced personas.

The expectations of casting aside, other voice work also suggests a parodic twist on the typical RPG dialogue. Given that the game is set in the Orkney Islands, it stands to reason that many of the characters would have a Scottish brogue or other such suitable accent.[22] However, some of the characters have such a thick accent, or use such unfamiliar idiomatic turns of speech, that their words are nigh on incomprehensible, a trait that The Bard doesn't hesitate to remark

28 Karen M. Cook

on.[23] Moreover, at times the dialogue is lengthy but pointless, or is deliberately raunchy, absurd, or otherwise humorous, which could be considered a parodic twist on the often lengthy but overly serious, more plot-driven dialogue choices in conventional RPGs.

While I have already discussed the interjected songs and musical cutscenes from the perspective of their lyrical content, their music also suggests a parodic take on RPGs. Hooper observes that musical cutscenes in games tend to serve one or more basic purposes: to pause and perhaps recapitulate the game narrative to that point, to enhance the player's understanding of the game world and setting, or to further advance the game narrative.[24] The music in such cutscenes specifically aids in these tasks, then, by connecting to other music used in the game and offering potential insight through lyrics, much like songs interspersed throughout an operetta that might develop a romantic agenda.[25] Yet, in *The Bard's Tale*, the interjected songs serve little such purpose; they are non sequiturs.

To be sure, certain elements of the game's plot are summarized or mentioned in the various iterations of the "It's Bad Luck to Be You" trow song, but these cutscenes do not affect the narrative moving forward. Moreover, the music of this song does not really fit with the vaguely medieval Scots-Orkney game world, as it is much more reminiscent of stereotypically Indian or Middle Eastern music, once again bringing to mind the Oompa Loompas from *Willy Wonka & the Chocolate Factory*. Even more jarringly out of place is the last cutscene, in which two rival zombie dance crews battle in an overt nod to the film *You Got Served* (and with a fairly obvious reference to John Travolta's famous disco moves in *Saturday Night Fever* [1977]).[26] The music here is quite clearly an example of what Harries would call an "extraneous inclusion," a generic imitation of twentieth-century trance or drum-and-bass genres that totally destabilizes any sense of geo- or chronolocation.[27] The "Beer" and the "Nuckelavee" songs are more aligned with the generic setting, the former being an actual folk song from the general region and the latter a sort of Celtic rock-inspired ditty; both songs support a general geographical location but are rather chronologically anachronistic. The cutscenes thus have little bearing on narrative recapitulation and none on narrative progress, they do not connect to any other musics used throughout game play, and actually disrupt, rather than bolster, a sense of game setting.

Lastly, there is the matter of the title track. In most RPGs, the theme song will connect, either thematically or in general style, with the music that occurs throughout the rest of the game. However, since *The Bard's Tale* has no soundtrack of which to speak, there is nothing for its theme song to connect to in that regard. The title track here does reoccur once in the game; in the aforementioned side quest to Finstown, the tribute song that the Vikings sing to The Bard is a texted version of the theme song. But if the player chooses not to complete that side quest, then the title track will not otherwise be heard again. Nor are there really any other songs within the game that sound similar to this track. As mentioned at the beginning, this theme is played by a harp, an instrument that makes no

Humor and Subversion in *The Bard's Tale* **29**

other appearance within the game, despite it being the instrument most closely associated with bards. The harp is later joined by other instruments, including a quite noticeably out-of-tune recorder. Having a title track that is, to say the least, somewhat painful to listen to is certainly the earliest indication the player has that the game is atypical, even comedic.

I have posited that these musical examples subvert typical characteristics of RPGs; they also do the same for the character of The Bard. The trope of the bard dates back centuries, in particular to the eighteenth-century antiquarian conflation of numerous earlier types of bards and bardic activities. While earlier bards would have been responsible for functions such as playing the harp, composing and performing elegies, eulogies, and epic sagas, as well as maintaining genealogies and histories, the concept of a bard as a type of wandering minstrel, singing love songs to the sounds of their harp, became firmly embedded in the Romantic popular imagination.[28] Consider, for example, the character of Allen-a-Dale, often portrayed as a wandering minstrel, who first joins Robin Hood's band of merry men in the late seventeenth-century Child Ballad 138 and later joins the list of characters in Sir Walter Scott's *Ivanhoe* (1819). Writers in particular focused on the bard as a nationalist Irish, Scottish, or Welsh emblem, as opposed to that of a unified "British" identity.[29] Collections of nationalist poetry and song capitalized on that image, linking minstrel-bard figures in both text and imagery to a wild, naturalistic past now endangered by the twinned rampages of technology and tyranny. These figures stood as mythical reminders of an equally mythical past and thus were emblems of rebellion against despotic, i.e., English, oppression.[30]

This predilection for linking the bard or minstrel with the grim wildness of the Irish or Scottish countryside, with its heaths and cairns, crumbling castles, abbeys, and other ancient landmarks found a comfortable home in Gothic literature's "yearning for a romanticized past."[31] So too did the bard's traditional role as lore-keeper, and in subsequent literature a bard figure is often a repository of knowledge both practical and arcane; their music and verse frequently also have magical or supernatural agency in fantasy fiction. J.R.R. Tolkien, for example, draws heavily on Anglo-Saxon and Norse cultures to construct his minstrel figures, who recite epic poems that convey to the reader the heritage and history of their peoples and even prophesy future events.[32] Drawing on Tolkien, but also legends such as the Greek myth of Orpheus or the Pied Piper of Hamelin, later fantasy authors continued to develop bards or minstrels as an array of stock characters, ranging from storyteller and historian to outlaw to musician to magician.[33]

Like other elements of Gothic and fantasy literature, such bard figures quickly crossed over into modern film, television, and games. In *Dungeons & Dragons*, the bard was fashioned from several historical personas: the Celtic bard, the Norse skald, and the Southern European minstrel or French jongleur. A player could then build their bard to draw on any of the various traits of those historical personas such that the bard could be a traditional storyteller, a fighter, a thief, and/or a mage, with the power of "Magic Music."[34] Later tabletop and computer games

30 Karen M. Cook

expanded the role of the bard; in addition to their knowledge of lore, they often acted as a morale-booster or source of healing for those around them, they might serenade the game's hero with praise, or they could attack enemies with their musical skills. However, in many cases the bard was more a hindrance than a help, their ability to do many things leaving them good at none. In the *Baldur's Gate* series, bards are jacks-of-all-trades, able to cast lower-level magical spells and perform some of the same tasks as thieves. Their real assets are the Bard's Song, which renders their party immune to magical fear and gradually restores morale, and their knowledge of lore, which allows them to identify most newly discovered items. Another example is Edward Chris von Muir, the famous "spoony bard" in the *Final Fantasy IV* (1991–2011) games; at first a physically weak character, he is nevertheless able to use his magical harp to strike at opponents and heal companions.[35] The games in which the bards played the most important roles, and which were also fundamental to the development of the RPG genre, were the original *Bard's Tale* series, where the bard could boost the strength and speed of his party members and use his songs to solve various puzzles.[36]

But, unlike bards of history, myth, and game legend, this Bard does not narrate his own or anyone else's story, he knows precious little lore, he praises no one, and he boosts literally no one's morale. Instead, the Narrator narrates his story for him, and in doing so provides The Bard and the player with the kind of information about the game world that one might expect a traditional bard to already know. Not only does the character of the Narrator thus undermine The Bard as a bard, but the cantankerous relationship that he has with The Bard also insinuates that The Bard is well aware of his shortcomings, perhaps holding the Narrator in some contempt as a result. Both The Bard's actions and his speech are in consistent opposition with the idea of praise, either with regard to extolling the virtues of his friends and comrades (which are all but nonexistent) or simply to acting nicely to others; in fact, the only character in the game to whom The Bard might express genuine affection is his dog, but even that is not guaranteed.

With regard to musical expectations of bards, our Bard does not sing. He could have the opportunity to do so, for example, in the various "jamming with drunks" cutscenes, but instead he walks away disgusted. He also scorns several of the characters for their terrible, out-of-tune singing, such as the Bodb brothers, informing them that "if this were a stage, I'd boo you off." Yet he never once attempts to show any of them that he can in fact sing better than they can. In fact, having all of the vocal songs be sung by anyone *but* The Bard is a clever bit of game design, in that it subtly suggests throughout that our Bard is not much of a musician, not even able to outperform such dreadful singers.

Nor does he play the harp. Instead he is restricted, at least at first, to the lute and recorder. While bardic characters certainly do play the lute in some post-Romantic films and video games—for example, *The Sims Medieval* (2011), *Shovel Knight* (2014), or *Darkest Dungeon* (2016), all of which significantly postdate *The Bard's Tale*—these instruments are often more closely associated with a stock troubadour or wandering minstrel figure who is focused on simpler entertainment or wooing fair ladies, rather than on the loftier bardic ideals of praise and historical preservation. Moreover, The Bard's performances on these instruments tell the player a great deal about his character. Again, he only plays his magic music in order to summon the aforementioned host of creatures who can then heal, attack, scout, or defend on his behalf; this in and of itself is at odds with his bardic game predecessors, who could through music have a direct impact on enemies or fellow party members. But significant here as well is that, in order to call forth these creatures, The Bard must sheathe his weapon and take out his lute or recorder. This is all well and good when recharging after a battle, or in preparation to enter a new area. In a combat situation, though, this means that The Bard is left defenseless for the duration of the musical spell, and so typically the player will have to choose either to take direct hits or to turn and flee from the battle—a very anti-heroic activity.

In hindsight, the wonky out-of-tune recorder in the opening title track takes on new significance, and I suggest it symbolizes The Bard himself attempting to join in the typical bardic activities of storytelling and praise song—and failing. However, the one instance in which The Bard does seem to succeed musically is in the cutscene with the song of the Nuckelavee. Here, The Bard actually joins the merry Celtic band, complete with lead singer, fiddle player, and recorder.[37] Unlike in the title song, this recorder performs perfectly in tune, implying once again that The Bard is perhaps not the best musician. But The Bard holds his own on the lute, playing loud, strong, and, most importantly, in tune. Perhaps this instrument, then, is his particular forte. This idea is further played out by The Bard's excitement upon receiving the glowing purple Shadow Axe later in the game, upon which he can unleash a torrent of electric guitar riffs. His apparent aptitude for the lute, combined with his boyish delight at the phallic axe/guitar, suggests that, at heart, The Bard would be happier playing *Guitar Hero* than actually being a hero.

In conclusion, the parodic, lampooning nature of *The Bard's Tale* was made clear long before the game itself was ever released. Its humor is blatant, and fans and critics alike also identified many of its features that were intended to spoof, as well as celebrate, the RPG genre. In doing so, most people have focused on elements of gameplay and narrative, while including only the most obvious of the musically humorous moments. I argue here, however, that sound and music play a far more crucial role in the game's parodic design than previously recognized. The outright absence of the typical continuous or intermittent soundtrack, the choices made in voiceover casting and accent, and the uncharacteristic kinds of music present in the form of non sequitur cutscenes, a strangely out of tune and disconnected theme song, and vaguely Elizabethan-cum-hard rock magical spells, work subtly throughout the game to subvert expectations of typical RPG sonic behavior. This subversion acts on multiple levels, for, in addition to manipulating expectations for the RPG genre, it strikes at the heart of the two primary

32 Karen M. Cook

identities of the main character. Through sound and music, The Bard is revealed to be both an anti-hero and an anti-bard.

Notes

1 From "The Bard's Tale for Android (2012) Ad Blurbs," *MobyGames*, www.mobygames. com/game/bards-tale/adblurbs. Unless otherwise noted, all links were last accessed April 28, 2018.
2 "The Bard's Tale [Video Game]," *TV Tropes*, http://tvtropes.org/pmwiki/pmwiki. php/VideoGame/TheBardsTale.
3 The game was later made available on Steam and other platforms beginning in 2009; a "Remastered and Resnarkled" version was also released on PlayStation 4, PlayStation Vita, Steam, and mobile platforms in 2017.
4 Gehring's definition also allows for the parody to be humorous in and of itself, regardless of the audience's literacy in the object being parodied. As Dan Harries points out, it also allows for the parody to retain characteristics of the object it parodies. Elements of *The Bard's Tale* might also be properly viewed as satire, which turns a humorous lens back on its audience to critique perceived personal or social ills; I refrain here from entering that discussion. Wes Gehring, *Parody as Film Genre: "Never Give a Saga an Even Break"* (Westport, CT: Greenwood Press, 1999), 1ff.; Harries, *Film Parody* (London: BFI, 2000), 23; see also Linda Hutcheon, *A Theory of Parody: The Teachings of Twentieth-Century Art Forms* (New York: Methuen, 1985). Lastly, it should be clearly stated that, while I describe the game as intending to be humorous, not every critic/ player reacts in such fashion, finding instead that the hypermasculinity of The Bard and the overly sexualized treatment of the female characters fail to overturn problematic misogynistic game tropes; for example, see Act, "*The Bard's Tale* (2004), or, What is Parody?" *Dragon Quill: Writing with Scales*, September 30, 2015, www.dragon-quill.net/ the-bards-tale-2004-or-what-is-parody.
5 A succinct and detailed overview of the harp as the main traditional instrument of the bard, alongside similar earlier stringed instruments such as the lyre or crwth, is given in Peter Crossley-Holland, John MacInnes, and James Porter, "Bard," *Grove Music Online*, ed. Deane Root, accessed April 23, 2018, www.oxfordmusiconline.com.
6 On musical elements of action RPGs, see Tim Summers's chapter in this volume.
7 Harries, *Film Parody*, 63. Other RPGs that make use of a narrator include Wizardry VII: Crusaders of the Dark Savant (1992), *Final Fantasy Tactics* (1997), *Dragon Age: Origins* (2009) and *Dragon Age II* (2011), and *Bastion* (2011); narrators are also used in other game genres, such as the action-adventure game *Prince of Persia: The Sands of Time* (2003).
8 Gehring points out that parodies routinely incorporate numerous "eclectic references to other structures or texts," such that in so doing *The Bard's Tale* marks itself as a parody even further, regardless of whether the player is aware of the references being made. Gehring, *Parody as Film Genre*, 13.
9 Mal Plays, "The Bard's Tale—Beer, Beer, Beer!" YouTube video, 2:12, April 15, 2011, www.youtube.com/watch?v=SrEFWv8aSQ8.
10 Mal Plays, "The Bard's Tale—Here's to the Bard—Viking Mix," YouTube video, 1:31, May 15, 2011, www.youtube.com/watch?v=wbsNlHANRbI.
11 Mal Plays, "The Bard's Tale—The Tale of the Nuckelavee," YouTube video, 2:51, April 26, 2011, www.youtube.com/watch?v=1JQpE7n6eUk.
12 Mal Plays, "The Bard's Tale—The Chosen One #4," YouTube video, 1:34, April 30, 2011, www.youtube.com/watch?v=FjeKjzn5Jvk.
13 StabbeyTheClown, "Bard's Tale—The Ego Sword's Summoning Music," YouTube video, 3:53, April 23, 2011, www.youtube.com/watch?v=s7o-Hfs2a20&t=90s.

Humor and Subversion in *The Bard's Tale*   **33**

14 StabbeyTheClown, "Bard's Tale—Shadow Axe Summons," YouTube video, 3:30, April 23, 2011, www.youtube.com/watch?v=_jmoNao90kI. Dan Harries discusses these types of puns as examples of parodic literalization; see Harries, *Film Parody*, 74.

15 William Gibbons, "Music, Genre, and Nationality in the Postmillennial Fantasy Role-Playing Game," in *The Routledge Companion to Screen Music and Sound*, ed. Miguel Mera, Ronald Sadoff, and Ben Winters (New York: Routledge, 2017): 412–427.

16 Giles Hooper, "Sounding the Story: Music in Videogame Cutscenes," in *Emotion in Video Game Soundtracking*, ed. Duncan Williams and Newton Lee (Cham, Switzerland: Springer International Publishing, 2018): 115–141.

17 Hilary Goldstein, "Review: *The Bard's Tale* (PS2)," *IGN*, October 21, 2004, www.ign. com/articles/2004/10/22/the-bards-tale?page=1.

18 This use of the bagpipe resembles James Cook's description of the "Celtic"-influenced music heard as part of the diegetic soundscape of the Skellige Island area in the game *The Witcher 3* (2015); Cook, "Playing with the Past in the Imagined Middle Ages: Music and Soundscape in Video Game," *Sounding Out!*, October 3, 2016, https:// soundstudiesblog.com/2016/10/03/playing-with-the-past-in-the-imagined-middle-ages-music-and-soundscape-in-video-game/.

19 William Gibbons discusses the rarity of extended game silences in the game *Shadow of the Colossus*, noting in particular that, due to advancements in technology, games began to shift away from a constant soundtrack in favor of a more cinematic, shifting use of music in the early 2000s, especially to heighten the emotional or narrative affect of the music that is present. Gibbons, "Wandering Tonalities: Silence, Sound, and Morality in *Shadow of the Colossus*," in *Music in Video Games: Studying Play*, ed. K.J. Donnelly, William Gibbons, and Neil Lerner (New York: Routledge, 2014); see also Devin Raposo, "In Praise of Silence in Videogames," *Kill Screen*, June 22, 2015, https://killscreen. com/articles/praise-silence-videogames/.

20 Kendra Leonard, "The Use of Early Modern Music in Film Scoring for Elizabeth I," in *Gender and Song in Early Modern England*, ed. Leslie C. Dunn and Katherine R. Larson (Burlington, VT: Ashgate, 2014): 169–183, esp. 173.

21 Similar to *The Bard's Tale*, both of these films also feature either a narrator figure or a main character who breaks the fourth wall to provide commentary on the action, which adds another layer of meaning to Elwes's vocal performance in the game.

22 Again similar to other games in which vocal accent add to a sense of geolocation; see Irish accents in *The Witcher 3* in Cook, "Playing with the Past in the Imagined Middle Ages: Music and Soundscape in Video Game."

23 This type of inscrutable accent is a common comedic gesture. See, for example, the minor character of Michael Moon on the television sitcom *Frasier*, played by Robbie Coltrane (two episodes, 2004); he mumbles so quickly in a part-Lancashire, part-generically British accent that no one but his siblings can understand him, much to the embarrassment of others and the amusement of the audience. Fortunately for the player, the subtitles can constantly run throughout the game; however, they are written in a somewhat curly Shakespearean font that can itself, like the accent, be difficult at times to decipher.

24 Giles Hooper, "Sounding the Story: Music in Videogame Cutscenes," 128.

25 See Raymond Knapp, "Music, Electricity, and the 'Sweet Mystery of Life' in *Young Frankenstein*," in *Changing Tunes: The Use of Pre-existing Music in Film*, ed. Phil Powrie and Robynn Stilwell (Burlington, VT: Ashgate, 2006): 105–118.

26 MadAsMoody, "The Bard's Tale Cut Scene—Dancing Undead! (Funny)," YouTube video, 1:17, October 28, 2012, www.youtube.com/watch?v=sP_7nFldRtY.

27 Dan Harries, *Film Parody*, 77ff. This kind of anachronistic clash between modern times and historical or fantasy pasts is discussed in Caroline Jewers's study of films such as *A Knight's Tale* and *Black Knight* (both 2001), and various settings of *A Connecticut Yankee in King Arthur's Court*, for example. Jewers, "Hard Day's Knights: *First Knight*,

34 Karen M. Cook

A Knight's Tale, and *Black Knight,"* in *The Medieval Hero on Screen: Representations from Beowulf to Buffy,* ed. Martha W. Driver and Sid Ray (Burlington, VT: Ashgate, 2014): 192–210; see also discussions of jazz, rock, or other anachronisms in modern film in John Haines, *Music in Films on the Middle Ages: Authenticity vs. Fantasy* (New York: Routledge, 2014), and Alison Tara Walker, "Towards a Theory of Medieval Film Music," in *Medieval Film,* ed. Anke Bernau and Bettina Bildhauer (New York: Manchester University Press, 2009): 137–158, or various musical references in *Young Frankenstein* in Raymond Knapp, "Music, Electricity, and the 'Sweet Mystery of Life' in *Young Frankenstein."*

28 Peter Crossley-Holland, John MacInnes, and James Porter, "Bard."

29 Sarah Prescott, "'Gray's Pale Spectre': Evan Evans, Thomas Gray, and the Rise of Welsh Bardic Nationalism," *Modern Philology* 104 (2006): 72–95.

30 Karen E. McAulay, "Minstrels of the Celtic Nations: Metaphors in Early Nineteenth-Century Celtic Song Collections," *Fontes Artis Musicae* 59 (2012): 25–38.

31 Fred Botting, quoted in Isabella van Elferen, *Nostalgia or Perversion? Gothic Rewriting from the Eighteenth Century Until the Present Day* (Cambridge: Cambridge Scholars Publishing, 2009), 4.

32 See in particular J.R.R. Tolkien, *The Silmarillion* (New York: Mariner Books, 2014).

33 A small list of fantasy fiction containing bard or minstrel characters would include Anne McCaffrey's *Dragonriders of Pern* series, Katharine Kerr's *Deverry* series, Stephen R. Lawhead's *Pendragon Cycle,* Mercedes Lackey's *Bardic Voices* series, Patricia McKillip's *Riddle Master* trilogy, Robert Jordan's *Wheel of Time* series, and J.K. Rowling's *Harry Potter* series.

34 "Magic Music," TV Tropes, accessed January 11, 2018, http://tvtropes.org/pmwiki/pmwiki.php/Main/MagicMusic. See also Doug Schwegman, "Statistics Regarding Classes: (Additions)—BARDS," Strategic Review 2(1) (February 1976): 11.

35 On *Final Fantasy IV,* see also Julianne Grasso's chapter in this volume.

36 For a short overview of bards in RPGs, see Michael J. Tresca, *The Evolution of Fantasy Role-Playing Games* (Jefferson, NC: McFarland, 2011), especially 39–40 and 139ff.; for a discussion of the original *The Bard's Tale* series, see Matt Barton, *Dungeons and Desktops: The History of Computer Role-Playing Games* (Wellesley, MA: A K Peters, 2008), 92–98.

37 The construction of "Celtic" music as an authentic folk music often finds it linked to traditional settings such as pubs and taverns. Interestingly, here the "Celtic" folk nature of this tavern tune, as well as the generally "Celtic" uses elsewhere of the lute and recorder, actually undergird the setting of this game in a quasi-traditional medieval fantasy version of the Orkney Islands. See Nugent, "Celtic Music and Hollywood Cinema: Representation, Stereotype, and Affect," in *Recomposing the Past: Representations of Early Music on Stage and Screen,* ed. J. Cook, A. Kolassa, and A. Whittaker (London: Routledge 2018): 107–123.

3

MOTHER/EARTHBOUND ZERO AND THE POWER OF THE NAÏVE AESTHETIC

No Crying Until the Ending

Tim Summers

The conventional history of the Japanese role-playing game situates the genre's ascendancy in the mid- to late 1980s.[1] During these years, primarily through the popular early entries of the *Dragon Quest* (1986–) and *Final Fantasy* (1987–) series, the JRPG firmly established itself within the Japanese video game landscape. These games reached huge audiences and, as such, became both commercially and creatively influential.[2] Riding the wave of the blossoming JRPG, Nintendo developed a Famicom game, which, while inheriting the gameplay mechanics from the antecedent JRPGs, clothed it in a distinctly different aesthetic style.

Mother (1989) was the brainchild of Shigesato Itoi, a well-known media personality and advertising copywriter.[3] Inspired by *Dragon Quest*, Itoi approached Nintendo with his own idea for an RPG.[4] Unlike its generic kin, the *Final Fantasy* and *Dragon Quest* series, which had taken their cue from fantasy literature of the Tolkienian flavor, Itoi opted for a radically different setting: the small towns and frontier landscapes of modern America. Though the game was popular and successful in Japan, and an English translation of the game was produced (renamed *EarthBound*), it was not ultimately released in the West, partly because of uncertainties about the game finding an audience.[5] The success of *Mother* in Japan prompted a sequel, *Mother 2* (1994), which was given an English-language SNES release as *EarthBound*. This game gained an avid fan following in the West, prompting interest in the original *Mother* game, which fans retrospectively retitled *EarthBound Zero* to distinguish it from *Mother 2/EarthBound*.[6] Though *Mother* was successful, its popularity in the Anglophone world was limited. Then, a copy of the unreleased *Mother* English-language prototype cartridge was unearthed in the late 1990s and its data was uploaded to the internet. *Mother* had a symbiotic relationship with the burgeoning online emulation community. As the internet came of age, fan communities began to coalesce, discussing and disseminating

36 Tim Summers

the game. *Mother* benefited from the increasing interest in online and emulation culture, and, simultaneously, the mythic and cult status of the game drew players to those online communities and activities. While *Mother* would eventually find an English release in 2015 on the Nintendo Virtual Console (under the title *EarthBound Beginnings*), it remains best known outside Japan in the form of the leaked prototype.[7] The game and its music have gained an extended life inside and beyond Japan, aided by emulation practice and internet fandom.

More than anything else, Itoi wanted the experience of playing *Mother* to be emotionally significant: the Japanese advertising for the game famously used the tagline "No Crying Until the Ending."[8] *Mother*'s appeal lies not in its gameplay mechanics, which represent no great change from the *Dragon Quest* model, but instead in its striking and unusual aesthetics. It was this style that distinguished *Mother* from its RPG siblings—and raised concerns about the game's financial viability in the West.[9] Foremost among Itoi's arsenal for achieving this affecting style is the game's music, composed by Keiichi Suzuki and Hirokazu "Hip" Tanaka.

In this chapter I argue that *Mother* uses music, and particular qualities of musical style, to exert emotional-affective influence over the player. *Mother*'s plot depicts music as extraordinarily potent: in a world of psychokinetic abilities, giant robots, and Earth-threatening aliens, it is music that is shown to be the ultimate source of power. Beyond the narrative, the game also wields this same force over its players, using music (in tandem with other aspects of the game's style) to induce the kind of affecting experience Itoi sought to generate.

Music in the World of *Mother*

Mother begins with a brief non-interactive prologue set in the early 1900s. In a "small country town in rural America" (as the game puts it), a young married couple (George and Maria) is abducted by an alien force. George returns to Earth after an absence of two years, but Maria is never seen again. The action leaps forward to the 1980s, where the rest of the game takes place. The player's primary character is George's young great-grandson. Though the game allows players to rename playable characters as they choose, this main character is conventionally called Ninten.[10] The game begins with Ninten investigating supernatural happenings in and around his hometown. Animals are misbehaving, inanimate objects appear to be possessed, and citizens are disappearing. Ninten discovers that he has psychic powers, which include psychokinesis and the ability to talk to animals. He teams up with other youngsters to forge a party of adventurers who seek to solve the mysterious occurrences.

As the story progresses, Ninten encounters objects and characters associated with the supernatural forces that play or sing distinct, short monophonic musical phrases to him. His mission, it becomes apparent, is to find all eight of these melodic fragments, which combine to form one complete melody. For clarity, the individual melodic fragments will hereafter be referred to as "phrases," while the complete eight-measure passage will be referred to as the Melody or "Eight Melodies," which is the name given to the piece by the game's creators. Whenever one of the phrases is found, the contextual environment disappears and is replaced by black and blue/purple strobing horizontal lines, isolating Ninten's party and the source of the sound from the world. All other audio is silenced so that the music may be heard clearly. The different sources of the phrases use slightly varying timbres, though they are all played at an andante tempo and typically use some form of vibrato and/or reverb effect. This arresting audiovisual presentation of the phrases implies their significance to the plot of the game, and encountering each phrase is marked as a major event in the experience of the game.

Mother allows players to check the status of their adventuring party through a menu. Here, statistics about each character are shown (experience points, equipment, etc.). Amongst the menu is a section labeled "Melody" (Figure 3.1). As Ninten uncovers the constituent phrases, that part of the field is populated with icons shaped like eighth notes. This screen indicates that there are eight phrases to find, with yet-to-be-identified phrases indicated by dots. It also implies that these phrases constitute a complete Melody. Early in the game, Ninten can obtain an ocarina; when directed, Ninten will play what he has learned of the Melody on the instrument. As Figure 3.1 shows, the phrases may not necessarily be discovered in the order they occur in the Melody. In these cases, the ocarina will play a short high-pitched "blip" to indicate the absence of a phrase, before continuing to play the rest of the phrases. Players must find the entire Melody to complete the game. To aid the player in uncovering the phrases, a friendly bard character will (if prompted) sing a song to Ninten with lyrics that allude to the location of each part of the Melody (Table 3.1).

FIGURE 3.1 Status screen in *Mother*

TABLE 3.1 The "Eight Melodies" in *Mother*

Melody (mm. = 75)	Location	Hint Text from the Bard's Song
1	Upon defeating a possessed doll, a music box is revealed that plays the first melody.	• Listen to my song! Oh music-loving adventurer Ninten! • Why do you cry, oh Cupid-Doll?
2	Reuniting a lost canary chick with its mother causes the mother to sing in joy at the reunion.	• Canary sings so sadly.
3	After defeating an alien that is causing distress to the zoo animals, the "amazing Singing Monkey" will perform this phrase for Ninten.	• Monkey sings,
4	A piano, deep inside a haunted mansion, plays this phrase upon inspection.	Piano plays, • maybe there is a ghost?
5	Using his telepathic abilities on a desert cactus, Ninten hears this phrase.	• Desert Cactus so alone, • every night his sad, sad tone.
6	A dragon says that the children "Must defeat [him] to earn his musical note." After doing so, the dragon "croon[s] his tune without much hesitation."	• The Dragon sleeps, the note remains.
7	A robot (Eve), programmed by George to protect Ninten, sacrifices herself in eliminating a dangerous foe. Examining the wreckage of Eve causes music to play.	• Eve's last song has no refrain.

Melody (mm. = 75)	Location	Hint Text from the Bard's Song
8 (Variation as heard on soundtrack album and in schoolbook.)	At the grave of Great-Grandfather George on Mount Itoi, Ninten is able to telepathically communicate with his great-grandfather, who teaches him the final part of the melody.	• On the Mount named Itoi, • you must climb high young boy. • See the XX stone, for the last tone, • then do not leave Queen Mary alone! • La la lullaby … Strange lullaby … • Bye bye bye … Goodbye. • Sure is a nice song, isn't it?

Upon discovering the phrase that concludes the melody, Ninten communicates telepathically with his great-grandfather, who explains the significance of the piece. We are told that "[Ninten's] Great-Grand Mother Maria's love was scattered, scattered in the form of melodies." The Melody, then, is not simply representative of love; it *is* love.

It is eventually shown that the supernatural occurrences are the result of an alien threat to the Earth, linked to the events described in the prologue. After being abducted, George and Maria became adoptive parents of an alien called Giegue.[11] George, however, stole information from the aliens, who are now attacking Earth, with Giegue serving as the vanguard of the offensive. At the end of the game, after collecting all of the phrases, Ninten and his party come face to face with Giegue. In this final battle, players notice that a new option has been added to the menu system for the battle mode: the characters may now "sing" (Figure 3.2). Singing is the only way that Giegue may be defeated; all other attacks are fruitless.

The complete Melody, it is revealed, is a lullaby that Maria sang to Giegue as an infant. To defeat Giegue, and win the game, players must direct the characters to "sing" the now-complete Melody. The piece is deployed like the "Fight" or "PSI" attack options: rather than using psychic power or physical force, a party member can choose to "sing" on their turn instead. The act of singing the Melody is presented as though it depletes the enemy's hit points; the Melody-as-attack depicts emotional power and physical power to be the same. The piece is so powerful that it is the only form of attack that is effective against the otherwise invincible alien. When the heroes sing, Giegue counterattacks with the aim of silencing the characters, all the while exhorting Ninten and his friends to stop singing. Each time, however, more of the Melody is able to sound before Giegue can silence

FIGURE 3.2 Final battle with Giegue

the performance. After 11 attacks, the party finally sings the Melody in its entirety and the battle ends. On realizing that he has been bested, Giegue remarks, "How could I be defeated by a song like that?"

The game's plot is centered, at least in part, around music and its power. Players must assemble the whole Melody to reach the final battle. The process of collecting the phrases structures the game: players may consult the status screen to learn how many phrases remain to be collected. Nevertheless, because Ninten does not acquire the phrases at regular intervals during the playing time of the game, the progress through the Melody does not directly correlate to progression through the game. One may know that to complete the Melody is to approach the end of the game, but how far away that conclusion is remains unclear.

When the game presents the option and act of "Singing" in the same way as the choices for psychic and physical actions of the heroes in battle, it implies equivalence between the musical material of the lullaby and the other forms of attack. Players choose to "Sing" this Melody, just as they would deploy a "Fight" command, or use one of the many PSI offensive or defensive options. The Melody is shown to have a visceral effect upon the alien, and is superior to any conventional combat.[12] It is the only way to respond to Giegue's psychic power. Perhaps, however, it is not only within the narrative construct of the game that the music is able to exert its influence.

Foregrounding Music

Itoi's agenda was, above all, to produce an emotionally impactful experience for players. His approach was not through innovations of gameplay mechanics, but rather through using aesthetic strategies to create a connection between players and the fiction of the game. Upon watching a film that featured a staged diegetic performance, Itoi was struck by how music may transcend levels of narration and link the world of the audience with the world on screen.[13] In such cases, the same music sounds in both realities; listeners in the fiction and listeners in our world are united by the communal experience of the music.

In a similar vein, musicologist Ben Winters has described the importance of moments in films when the viewers and the fictional characters listen to the same music. He writes,

> Perhaps only when character and audience are offered the chance to share the same musical experience—or to conceptualize the experience as one that might be shared—is music's power in cinema realized (as an emotional tool that helps us engage with fictional characters).[14]

Itoi deploys the same technique in *Mother* through the device of collecting and performing the "Eight Melodies." Compared with a typical filmic situation in which an audience shares in the listening experience of diegetic music, perhaps the player is even more invested in "Eight Melodies" in *Mother*, having participated as an agent in the discovery of the tune by the protagonists and prompting their performance.

In addition to the central role the "Eight Melodies" piece plays in the game, *Mother* consistently highlights and foregrounds music in other ways, too. There are several non-interactive moments that appear distinctly "staged." These are ostentatiously performative sequences with limited interactivity, but which seem to encourage the player to listen to the music, especially when characters appear to be singing or dancing. In these sequences when player agency is reduced, gameplay action is halted, and sound effects are absent, music has a very significant weight in the makeup of the medium. Even the animation is limited or repetitive, and the backgrounds sparse and plain. By reducing other components of the medium, the music stands out and commands the player's attention.

Sometimes this staging is explicit: during one sequence, the children perform a musical number on a stage in a nightclub (Figure 3.3). At other times, the staging is more private. Towards the end of the game, Ninten finds himself alone with Ana, his romantic interest. She suggests they dance, and then declares her love for Ninten. Though there is no diegetic source of music, the underscore changes to a new cue that accompanies Ninten and Ana's simple halting romantic dance, choreographed to the music (Figure 3.4). Though Ana and Ninten are alone, they share their dance with the player, who is also sonically privy to the music. Winters suggests that we could challenge the conventional idea that non-diegetic music is separated from the world of the characters, in order to recognize the power of music to connect viewers and fictional characters.[15] This is certainly supported by the dance sequence where music is apparently audible to the characters and player, but not given an explicit source within the diegesis.

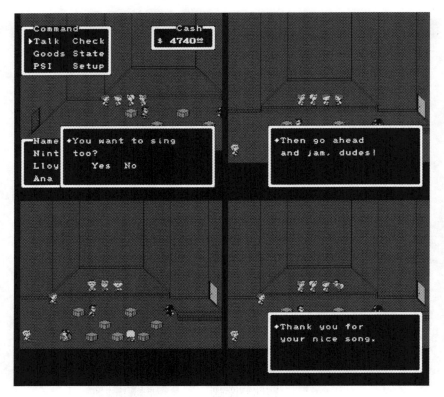

FIGURE 3.3 Ninten and his party perform a musical number at a nightclub

Even the end of the game adopts aspects of a staged performance. After the epilogue cutscene that concludes the narrative, the game finishes with each of the main characters taking curtain calls as though they were members of a theatrical cast.[16] Individually, or in small groups, the "principals" walk on from the left-hand side of the screen, stop midway across the screen, face the player and pause for a moment, before exiting "stage left." In keeping with tradition, the final call is reserved for those with the top billing: our four party members. Though these episodes stylistically adopt aspects of a staging, the game's prioritization of music is evident throughout, from the prologue (comprised only of text and music) to the epilogue preceding the "curtain call," and in between, such as train travel sequences that serve as additional opportunities to force players to listen to a musical cue for a few moments, while watching repetitive scenes of a train traversing the countryside.

The game's prioritization of music and the performative framing of particular sequences encourages players to understand the game's music as closely anchored to the characters and world. Though Winters discusses film, his view accords with Itoi's practice when he claims that music (explicitly diegetic or otherwise)

Mother/EarthBound Zero **43**

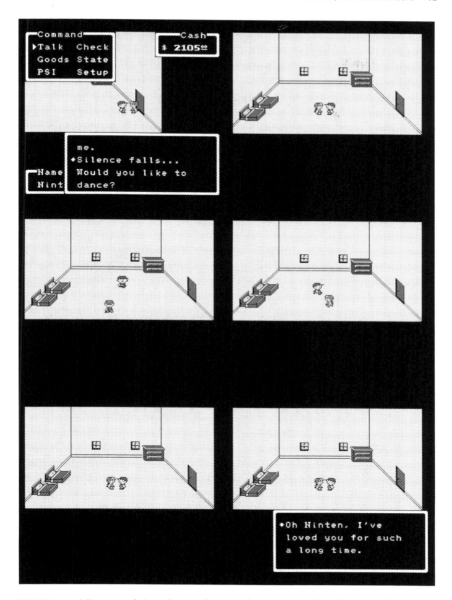

FIGURE 3.4 Ninten and Ana share a dance before Ana confesses her love for Ninten

may suggest a common shared identity with the characters and milieu of a film's world … Music is not a conveyer of cold narrative information and it does not (usually) narrate. It may allow us to feel what other characters feel in a way that is peculiarly affecting, leads to greater understanding of others, and is based on a shared experience of the music.[17]

44 Tim Summers

This connection between viewer (or player) and characters has been understood by practitioners as well as theorists. As Bernard Herrmann describes it, "[Music on the screen] is the communicating link between the screen and the audience, reaching out and enveloping all into one single experience."[18] This perspective that emphasizes the connection between viewer/player and character is particularly apt for the RPG genre, which is concerned with creating a compelling fiction and characters with which the player can invest. Music is one of the ways that players connect to, and identify with, the universe and characters of *Mother*.

Musical Traditions of the JRPG and *Mother's* Aesthetics of Naïveté

Like many JRPGs, *Mother* is accompanied almost continuously by music—silence is used either conspicuously for dramatic effect, or otherwise as momentary pauses between cues. Just as *Mother* replicates the interactive mechanics of the *Dragon Quest* games, for all the stylistic difference and emphasis on music in the plot, it draws on the precedent of musical implementation established by earlier JRPGs. William Gibbons has outlined how Japanese RPGs musically conform to a "core concept" of musical placement. In this general pattern, an RPG game's score primarily

> consists of eight loops, each attached to a particular type of location or game state. Location-based cues, all of which occur during the player's exploration of the game world, include (1) castle, (2) town, (3) field, and (4) dungeon – aurally indicating the nature (and relative safety) of each setting. Game-state cues, tied to a type of situation, rather than a specific location, include music for the (1) introductory title screen (when the game is first turned on) or opening expository cut scene, (2) the end of the game (victory screen and credits), (3) the standard combat state, and (4) the final battle.[19]

This basic pattern has its own ancestry in the antecedent *Ultima* series of Western RPGs (1981–1988), though its influence in the JRPG stems from codification in the first *Dragon Quest* game. It is so ingrained in the JRPG identity that even modern games deploy musical strategies based on this foundation.[20] *Mother* elaborates upon this model of musical implementation: it has a variety of battle themes, a plethora of location cues, and we have already noted the addition of other musical set pieces. Nevertheless, the game retains the principle, identified by Gibbons, of musically articulating a spectrum between danger and safety. *Mother,* however, does so using a distinctly different musical style to its generic forebears.

The *Dragon Quest* and *Final Fantasy* games preceding *Mother* exhibit a diversity of musical styles, but they both draw on two identifiable musical models. One the one hand, they emulate a nineteenth-century orchestral idiom of the kind

Mother/EarthBound Zero   45

used by Erich Wolfgang Korngold and his contemporaries to forge the sound of the 1930s and 1940s Hollywood action-adventure film. Here we find the well-worn musical signifiers of hunt topics, heroic fanfares, judicious dissonance for threat, and expansive textures that aspire to the symphonic. On the other hand, the games also invoke Baroque chorales and keyboard music. Toccata figurations, fragmented sequences, Alberti bass accompaniments, ornamented melodic lines, unusual chromaticism, dance topics, scant percussion, melodies with a wide tessitura, intricate melodic articulation and contrapuntal textures are all signifiers of historical "art" music, as contrasted with modern popular music.

Rather than employing a Baroque or Hollywood musical language, *Mother* develops a different style. It creates what might be called an "aesthetic of naïveté." This approach aims to create an affecting emotional experience, connecting players with the human characters while contrasting those humans with the alien "other." The style is most prominent in moments of significant plot development, during the sequences of musical foregrounding discussed earlier, and for the safer areas of the world. It is also clearly evinced in "Eight Melodies."

The naïve aesthetic is characterized by an emphasis on song-like melodic lines, played legato by one of the Famicom's square wave generators within a comfortable tessitura for a human voice. These melodies are primarily conjunct, diatonic, and feature a regular periodic frame with balanced, often repeated, phrases. Texturally, such cues are clear and distinctly stratified: the console's harsher-timbred triangle wave is segregated to form a bass part with distinct acoustic registral space between the triangle bass and the rest of the texture. The other square wave generally harmonizes the melody or provides an accompaniment pattern that repeats and alters to adjust to the chord pattern of the piece (in the process, clarifying the harmonic structure of the cue). The harmonic structures emulate a popular song style, with a regular harmonic rhythm and repetitive chord patterns that periodically cadence neatly on the tonic. The percussion parts normally maintain a steady tempo in a regular pattern resembling pop drumming styles.

The counterweight to this "naïve" style is found in music accompanying the dangerous areas in the game, which features more very high or low pitches, fragmented phrasing, emphasis on aurally uncomfortable timbres, and unclear harmonic definition (Ex. 3.1).[21] Though similar qualities of musical "danger" may be found in antecedent JRPGs, the stylistic contrast is significantly more striking when they are put alongside the "naïve" style forged by *Mother*. There is no clearer illustration of this musical discourse than in the final battle with Giegue, which (apart from the sound effects for attacks) is accompanied only by a throbbing wail in extremely high registers, and the increasingly lengthy performances of the "Eight Melodies." The game articulates a musical-stylistic spectrum, from the powerfully human "Eight Melodies" to the alien musical sound of Giegue.[22]

I have used the term "naïve" to describe the "human" musical style of *Mother* because of the way that it appears to deploy signifiers of musical simplicity.

EX. 3.1 Underground theme from *Mother*, showing the "alien" musical style

Mother's music is the product of much careful planning and technical mastery. Yet, by adopting a musical style for its humans that emphasizes textual clarity, bold and song-like melodic lines, moderate tempi, concordant pop-song-like harmonies and much repetition, it invokes a vernacular directness of communication. This style contrasts with, on one hand, the ostentatious musical complexity of styles that emulate art-music traditions (*Dragon Quest* and *Final Fantasy*) and, on the other, the fragmentation and dissonance of dangerous places in the game.

As the screenshots in Figures 3.3 and 3.4 illustrate, *Mother* is visually sparse and minimal in design. The extensive reuse of character sprites and scenic objects can make moving through the landscapes of the game feel uncannily familiar. Outside battle mode, the game uses an art style derived from Japanese anime and manga often referred to as "chibi" (little), where characters have large round heads, small bodies, and a childlike appearance. Even the dialogue in the game prioritizes brevity, though it remains evocative and allusive. Partly, of course, the plain design and repetition are prompted by the technological restrictions of the platform—but they also speak to a broader approach to such limitations. The game's music reflects the visual clarity and simplicity. Rather than aspiring to complex textures and topoi established in symphonic or instrumental music, as in *Final Fantasy*/*Dragon Quest* (which both use a more densely ornamented visual style), *Mother* appears to embrace its technological limitations. The game opts

Mother/EarthBound Zero **47**

for an aesthetic of simplicity for its human-associated cues, with aurally clear and consistent textures, steady rhythms, and regular song-like melodies.[23]

The repetitiveness of the game assists the impact of music: even more than most RPGs, *Mother* requires a lot of grinding. The game's length and the repetition of grinding means that players will hear some cues repeatedly for a great deal of playing time. As Gibbons notes, the "model of endlessly looped, location- or game state-based cues is deeply embedded in players' horizon of expectations" of the genre.[24] With such extended musical repetition, the contrast articulated with the introduction of new material, such as through encountering a new area or finding a new part of the melody, is made all the more striking. Whether through the signifiers of musical "simplicity" or the repetitive aspects of the musical deployment in the game, *Mother* revels in its own naïve style, apt for its thematic focus on children and small-town life.

The "Eight Melodies" serve as the site when this connection between musical simplicity, childhood, and affective power are made most explicit. Our young heroes learn a purely diatonic melody that is segmented into short phrases, is at a steady andante tempo, maintains a tessitura of an octave and a half, avoids significant syncopation, and prioritizes arch-shaped or descending melodic contours. Yet, despite its "simplicity," it is the "Eight Melodies" that ultimately hold the key to defeating the powerful alien.

Academic treatment of music in Japanese role-playing games has often mentioned the significance of nostalgia. Jessica Kizzire has noted how nostalgia has been used as a way to appeal to JRPG players, and William Cheng describes how nostalgic reactions can be prompted by the music long after playing has finished.[25] *Mother* requires many hours of playing time to complete, which is typical of role-playing games, but it accentuates retrospectivity through two aspects of the music. First, by using a naïve style with youthful associations, it inherently implies a degree of looking toward the past, as we are reminded of our own musical histories and childhoods. Second, the mechanic of the "Eight Melodies" embeds a musical retrospectivism into the game, whereby the lengthy playtime is charted by discovering the melodies. Whereas the long playing time of the game is spent discovering the phrases, rehearing the fragments encourages the player to reflect on their own journey through the game, projecting a framework for nostalgic reminiscence upon the play experience, and reminding them of the contexts in which each phrase was discovered and the places and characters with which they have interacted on their quest. The final cue of the game (the epilogue) illustrates this musical charting of the game's progression when it presents the "Eight Melodies" theme several times with different accompaniment patterns, interspersed with melodic material from the cue that opened the game (for the prologue and initial menus).

In his discussion of post-millennial JRPGs, Gibbons notes musical qualities that are bound up with the identity of the genre. Two are notably evident in *Mother*, despite the relatively early date of this JRPG. The first is stylistic diversity

48 Tim Summers

within the scores: "Japanese composers often pull from a larger and considerably more varied stylistic pool [than Western RPG composers], encompassing classical and popular musics."[26] *Mother* demonstrates a greater contrast of musical style within the game than the preceding *Dragon Quest* and *Final Fantasy* games, especially the mixing of classical and popular traditions. Gibbons also notes that JRPGs often include non-interactive moments that foreground music: what he calls "essentially music videos at emotionally significant moments—popular songs underscoring an animated cutscene."[27] Again, *Mother* includes such sequences. While it might be an overstatement to claim *Mother* as the origin of the musical traditions Gibbons identifies, their prototypical presence here testifies to the nascence of these musical trends of the genre. Ironically, then, a game that contrasted with its contemporary genre siblings evinces musical traits that would become central to the genre.

The Soundtrack Album

The associations of the music of *Mother* with naïveté are further illustrated by the game's soundtrack album, released in the same year as the game. The majority of the album consists of arrangements of cues as songs or pop instrumentals. While this is not the first album of game music arranged for performance by live musicians, such records were hardly commonplace in 1989.[28] We might take the existence of this project as an affirmation of both Nintendo's faith in Itoi's celebrity to attract listeners as well as the immediate appeal of the music. Unexpectedly, given the game's limited Japanese release, the album's main language is English: lyrics for the cues and the liner notes are all in English, and the album was partly recorded in the UK.[29] The album was no mere afterthought: the lyricist for the album, Linda Hennrick, reports that she was involved early in the game's production process, and devised the lyrics after discussing the game and its music with Itoi.[30] The decision to emphasize English likely stems from the intended worldwide release of *Mother*.

That a good number of the cues are straightforward adaptations to the song format with little change to the melodic/harmonic/rhythmic identity of the pieces indicates the extent to which these cues already approximate a popular song idiom. The album primarily consists of cues from the "safer" spaces of the world, or musically-significant moments: Ninten and Ana's dance, the nightclub number, and, of course, "Eight Melodies."

As befits the most narratively significant cue in the game, "Eight Melodies" is the most striking recording on the album. It is performed by choir (St Paul's Cathedral Choir), boy treble, and small orchestral ensemble in an arrangement by composer Michael Nyman. Both the lyrics and instrumental arrangement testify to the image of childhood naïveté that the score aims to project. While the track begins with a brief introduction by the strings, the first sounding of the melody is performed by the boy soloist simply using the non-lexical syllable "la," suggesting a preverbal mode of communication. On repetition of the melody, the choir begins singing lyrics that emphasize the notion of powerful simplicity:

Take a melody
Simple as can be
Give it some words and
Sweet harmony
Raise your voices
All day long now
Love grows strong now
Sing a melody of love, oh love.

Concerning the instrumental arrangement, Nyman's musical style combines the repetition and textual clarity of the so-called "minimalist" school of composition with rhythmic influences from popular music, both of which are characteristically evident here. As Pwyll ap Siôn notes,

> the techniques of layering, stratifying, reordering, and superimposing that Nyman uses to transform his material more closely resemble those of film and popular music production … the prominence of the bass in his music, as well as suggesting the influence of rock, creates a harmonic stability and rootedness more characteristic of the European tonal tradition than of American minimalism.[31]

Thus, though it may be unexpected to see his name attached to this project, Nyman's own musical priorities of harmonic stability, pop influence, traditional tonality, and melodic clarity mesh well with *Mother*'s aesthetic style.

The album serves as a paratextual interpretation of cues from the game. That is to say, it is an auxiliary product—separate from, but related to, the main text.[32] The album can influence how we might engage with the game. For gamers familiar with the album, it also acts as an agent for influencing their understanding of the music in the context of gameplay. Whether through intertextual dialogue, or just as an interpretation of the game's music, the album highlights and reinforces the musical agenda of the game.

The lyrics, instrumentation, and arrangements of the cues on the record illustrate the kinds of musical meanings that those creating the album see as central to the game's score. Given how heavily involved Itoi and the composers were in the production of the album, we might even reasonably consider the album cues as representing their artistic intention. Judging from the album, we can see that naïve simplicity has been identified as an important part of the musical discourse of the game. If the album and game assert connections with childhood and youth, elsewhere the link was actually forged.

A Lesson in Music?

The "Eight Melodies" device, both in musical content and presentation, explicitly engages with traditions of music instruction. Music chosen for novice musicians typically avoids technical demands like complex rhythmic patterns, extreme pitches, or chromaticism. Slow tempi and short, segmentable phrases help mitigate the musical disruption caused by the halting performance of an unsure beginner musician. Even if the aim of the game's creators was not to emulate the style of a childhood song or a pedagogical piece per se, so appropriately does "Eight Melodies" fit the mold of such music that it was included in a music curriculum for Japanese schools.

Textbook-centered education plays a large part in Japanese pedagogy.[33] Before a textbook may be adopted for use in schools, it must undergo a review and approval process by the government. The volume that features "Eight Melodies" belongs to one of two approved music curricula for elementary school (the particular book in question is for the 10–11 age range). It seems likely, then, that a significant number of schoolchildren will have encountered "Eight Melodies" as part of their musical education.

In the book, the piece is named as "Eight Melodies" and arranged for a flexible seven-part small ensemble.[34] The arrangement is for melody part (recorder or piano), two other keyboard parts, two vibraphones, glockenspiel, and bass. It is presented in F major, with each phrase lasting a measure (as in Table 3.1). The eight measures are marked to repeat, and the performance instructions indicate that the texture should be gradually built up as performers enter in stages, looping their parts. The melody is nearly identical to that in the game, though the second beat of the final measure is subtly altered (as it is in the soundtrack album). The arrangement bears little resemblance to the presentation of the "Eight Melodies" in the game, partly because of the greater number of parts used here. While the composers are listed, the piece's origin as music from a video game is not indicated.[35] Itoi had conceived of music crossing planes of reality; another dimension has been added here. The process of learning and performing the piece has moved from the context of the virtual world to the classroom. For students who encounter both the game and the music in school, a curious parallel will be drawn between the musical educations in both realms of reality.

To my knowledge, this is a singular example of video game music being included as part of the performing repertoire of a widely adopted music curriculum. Quite how the piece came to feature in the curriculum is not easily established, though perhaps its connections with youth culture, and the straightforward adaptation to classroom arrangement (without significant alteration to its distinguishing musical material) were factors in its selection. While the themes from *Super Mario Bros.* (1985) or *The Legend of Zelda* (1986) may be more famous than the music of *Mother*, these pieces would be far more difficult to adapt to a suitable format and difficulty for children to play in the classroom. The appearance of "Eight Melodies" in the book indicates its appropriate level of challenge for young players, as it would not have been included if it had been deemed unsuitable for young players (especially given the scrutinization that such volumes undergo to gain governmental approval). The schoolbook reveals that the game convincingly approximates youth music: The traits identified earlier as part of the "aesthetics of naïveté" are the same features that make the piece well suited to the use in the school textbook. Through successful deployment of a musical style that brings to mind childhood, the game's music was not only able to use the association for emotional power to affect players, but it actually becomes music for (and played by) children.

Mother takes as a central theme the idea of music as emotionally and viscerally powerful. In the game's story, music is presented almost as one of Ninten's psychokinetic powers—the secret to defeating the otherwise invincible alien. At the same time, this power extends beyond the boundaries of the fictional game world: just as Ninten uses music on Giegue, the game also seems to "use" music to affect its players, to prompt an emotional response. This is particularly notable in the non-interactive performative sequences and the "Eight Melodies," where the inescapable scenes encourage the player to attend to the music. Kevin Donnelly has characterized film music as a "subtle medium of manipulation," and here we see such agency both within, and outside, the universe of the game.[36]

Mother's musical strategy, then, reveals the significance of music for the aesthetic style and experience of the game. Nevertheless, in prioritizing musical "naïveté" for the humans, the game embraces its own technological limitations, aspiring not to emulate a cinematic style, but to forge a musical language of simplicity born out of those same technological limitations. In that sense, just as *Mother* expands the possible fictional settings of JRPG games, so the music demonstrates potential alternative approaches to musical style. It is non-cinematic game music, created on its own terms and tailored to the musical strengths of the technology at hand (here, the Famicom).

Ultimately, *Mother* is a testament to the power of music, within and outside games. It also shows that musical profundity is not tied to specific notions of musical complexity. The game uses music to enrapture players and provide them with a way of sharing subjectivity with the characters. We may not all "cry at the end" of *Mother*, but we do sing a simple melody of love.

Notes

1 Tristan Donovan, *Replay: The History of Video Games* (Lewes, East Sussex: Yellow Ant, 2010), 159–163; Chris Kohler, *Power-Up: How Japanese Video Games Gave the World an Extra Life* (Indianapolis: BradyGames, 2005), 84–88. I am very grateful to Lyman Gamberton for their assistance with Japanese translation. Thanks are also due to Pwyll ap Siôn for his valuable thoughts on Michael Nyman.

2 Donovan, *Replay*, 163.

3 Writing in 1989 for a Western audience, anthropologist Marilyn Ivy described Itoi as "one of the most famous media stars in Japan today with his own television show,

52 Tim Summers

numerous publications, and seemingly nonstop appearances in the popular press." Marilyn Ivy, "Critical Texts, Mass Artifacts: The Consumption of Knowledge in Postmodern Japan," in *Postmodernism and* Japan, ed. Maso Miyoshi and H.D. Harootunian (Durham, NC: Duke University Press, 1989), 35.

4 Kohler, *Power-Up*, 88–89.

5 The other reasons for *Mother*'s lack of a Western release included the lack of popularity of JRPGs in America and the chronological proximity to NES's successor, the Super Nintendo Entertainment System.

6 James Newman, *Playing with Videogames* (Abingdon, Oxon: Routledge, 2008), 77, 156–160.

7 There are some subtle differences between the localized version and the original Japanese edition of the game. This chapter primarily draws its conclusions from the English-language prototype of the game.

8 Keiichi Tanaka, "Shigesato Itoi," *Wakage no Itari*, episode 5 (Japanese version October 26, 2017, English version January 8, 2018). http://news.denfaminicogamer.jp/manga/171026 (Japanese) and http://news.denfaminicogamer.jp/english/180109 (English). Accessed January 23, 2018. Though presented pictorially, a tweet from Itoi confirms he was interviewed about *Mother* by Tanaka: https://twitter.com/itoi_shigesato/status/890407693118078976. Accessed January 23, 2016.

9 Kohler, *Power-Up*, 245.

10 The specific relationship between *Mother* and its sequel, *EarthBound/Mother 2*, is ambiguous. *EarthBound* has a similar protagonist (Ness) and villain (Giygas). While Giygas and Giegue are generally understood to be the same character, Ness and Ninten are not related, although they look similar and have names with similar Nintendo puns.

11 The final battle with Giygas in *EarthBound/Mother 2* features a similar conceit to *Mother*'s "sing" attack, in which "praying" exploits the enemy's weakness.

12 Many games present musical performance as having the ability to influence reality: *Loom* (LucasArts, 1990) and *The Legend of Zelda: Ocarina of Time* (Nintendo, 1998) are prime examples of the same trope. See also the chapters by Karen Cook and William Gibbons in this volume.

13 Tanaka, "Shigesato Itoi."

14 Ben Winters, *Music, Performance and the Realities of Film* (New York: Routledge, 2014), 66.

15 In using location-dependent music, games often encourage us to hear assumedly nondiegetic music as emitting from the environment of the characters.

16 On the incorporation of theatrical aspects into RPGs, see also Ryan Thompson's chapter in this volume.

17 Winters, *Music, Performance and the Realities of Film*, 186, 188.

18 Quoted in Winters, *Music, Performance and the Realities of Film*, 186.

19 William Gibbons, "Music, Genre, and Nationality in the Postmillennial Fantasy Role-Playing Game," in *The Routledge Companion to Screen Music and Sound,* ed. Miguel Mera, Ronald Sadoff, and Ben Winters (New York: Routledge, 2017), 418.

20 Gibbons, "Music, Genre, and Nationality," 418.

21 These are common musical semiotics of "alien" others; see, for example, my "Star Trek and the Musical Depiction of the Alien Other," *Music, Sound, and the Moving Image*, 7 (2013), 25. This example is adapted from a transcription by Ellie McEla (aka Dalisclock), *EarthBound Beginnings: An Accurate Transcription of the Original Soundtrack 2nd Ed.* (c. 2016).

22 For more on Tanaka's music for alien creatures and environments, in a similar style, see William Gibbons, "The Sounds in the Machine: Hirokazu Tanaka's Cybernetic Soundscape for Metroid (1986)," in *The Palgrave Handbook of Sound Design and Music in Screen Media: Integrated Soundtracks*, ed. Liz Greene and Danijela Kulezic-Wilson (New York: Palgrave, 2016), 347–359.

Mother/EarthBound Zero **53**

23 There are moments in the game that do seek to distinctly emulate another musical style: for example, one of the battle cues, for a less dangerous foe, clearly copies 1950s rock'n'roll in a Chuck Berry-like style.

24 Gibbons, "Music, Genre, and Nationality," 419–420.

25 Jessica Kizzire, "'The Place I'll Return to Someday': Musical Nostalgia in *Final Fantasy IX*," in *Music in Video Games*, ed. K.J. Donnelly, William Gibbons, and Neil Lerner (New York: Routledge, 2014), 183–198; William Cheng, *Sound Play* (New York: Oxford University Press, 2014), 74–79.

26 Gibbons, "Music, Genre, and Nationality," 418.

27 Gibbons, "Music, Genre, and Nationality," 417.

28 The tradition of "arranged" albums extends back at least to the 1986 *Dragon Quest* album using orchestral musicians.

29 Liner notes for *Mother* (Tokyo: CBS/Sony 32DH 5285, 1985).

30 Ron DelVillano, "Interview: Aaron Hamel," *Nintendo Life* (March 27, 2015), www.ninten dolife.com/news/2015/03/interview_aaron_hamel_on_bringing_the_mother_original_arranged_soundtrack_to_the_west. Accessed January 24, 2018.

31 Pwyll ap Siôn, "Nyman, Michael." *Grove Music Online* (January 1, 2001), www.oxford musiconline.com/grovemusic/view/10.1093/gmo/9781561592630.001.0001/omo-9781561592630-e-0000045776. Accessed April 18, 2019.

32 See Gérard Genette, *Paratexts: Thresholds of Interpretation*, trans. Jane E. Lewin (Cambridge: Cambridge University Press, 1997).

33 Masafumi Ogawa, "Music Teacher Education in Japan: Structure, Problems, and Perspectives," *Philosophy of Music Education Review*, 12(2) (2004), 139–153.

34 Tokuhide Niimi et al., 音楽のおくりもの 5 (Tokyo: Kyoiku Shuppan, c. 2015), 64–65.

35 This longstanding scheme of work is regularly revised, and there is evidence to suggest that "Eight Melodies" has featured in the schoolbook since the 1990s, though I have only been able to access the more recent edition. It seems plausible that its introduction into the curriculum would have been broadly contemporary with the game's popularity, rather than a retrospective rediscovery. The melodic alteration that the book shares with the album implies that the transmission may have come via the soundtrack record.

36 Kevin Donnelly, *The Spectre of Sound: Music in Film and Television* (London: BFI, 2005), 1.

PART II
Mystical Metaphors

4

ALIEN WAVES

Sonic Reverberations of the RPG Interface in *Lagrange Point*

Kevin R. Burke

At the dramatic sound of a diminished seventh chord, the bunny-clad child Tum in Konami's *Lagrange Point* (1991) is suddenly struck to the ground by the claws of the bio-mutant and mini boss General Oregi (see Figure 4.1).[1] For nostalgic fans of RPGs in the West, the swift slash of randomized noise and hollow thud of 8-bit square waves that accompany Tum's assault and fall are familiar sound effects. The non-diegetic signal of the surprise encounter and song of mourning that follows the boy's death, however, emit timbres different from any heard in the *Dragon Warrior* and *Final Fantasy* titles released for Nintendo's 8-bit consoles. Frequency Modulation (FM) synthesis, enabled by a custom chip inside the game cartridge, is as alien to the core sound of the Nintendo Family Computer (Famicom) as the non-player character (NPC) Tum is to the story's main party.[2] The relationship between alien timbres and alien beings is an example of the core focus of this chapter: the symbolism of sound. The music of role-playing games is assuredly an emotive and expressive medium for exploring the depths of storytelling and characterization. While thematic, harmonic, and timbral qualities often demarcate key points of understanding, I consider the irregular architecture of Konami's sound design in *Lagrange Point* as a point of correlation to the unique makeup of this sci-fi RPG. The qualitative lag in 8-bit audio technology opens up an extradiegetic space between actual and implied sound—one that reflects the suspension of disbelief essential to immersive RPG experiences. I argue that this interpretive field is further enhanced by the discrepancy between the sound expected from a Famicom and the sound emitting from a Famicom (by way of external audio sources). The liminal space gamers occupy in RPGs depends on a degree of reconciliation between the game's structural makeup and the immersive agency of the character roles in the narrative. That space constitutes a state where analogies like the one drawn above abound. Just as a game reflects the materials of

58   Kevin R. Burke

FIGURE 4.1 The death of NPC Tum in *Lagrange Point*

its construction, so can the game guide our understanding of the building blocks. From this point of inquiry, I argue that the music and sound of *Lagrange Point* is as reflective of its RPG design—its maps, weapons, and characters—as it is symbolic of its narrative.

My approach to presenting the music and sound of *Lagrange Point* within the framework of an 8-bit RPG is guided by theories of human-computer interaction. In *Computer as Theatre*, virtual reality pioneer Brenda Laurel describes an "interface" as a complex nexus of human-computer interaction. She posits theatrical design and its representation of worlds as reality as a metaphor for interface design and its representation of reality to extend the faculties of the interactor.[3] Laurel's consideration for the audience as user—or interactor, as she prefers—replaces a model of interface design as a toolset for accomplishing gameplay tasks. Rather, interface design, like theatre, leverages established relationships between representation and reality to simulate what "cannot exist in the real world, in ways that invite us to extend our minds, feelings, and senses to envelop them."[4]

Interface designer Noah Wardrip-Fruin establishes a concept of "expressive processing," an overshadowed parallel he identifies to the non-process output of creators. For Wardrip-Fruin, the computational processes of creation are as significant a form of expression as the work itself. When one authors a new form of digital media, one also defines the rules for what is possible and what is left out.[5] While the soundtrack to *Lagrange Point* is a primary subject of study for this chapter, the unique components of its development are a reflection of the overall game mechanics of this RPG.

In returning to the vantage point of the audience, expressive processing finds mediation in a layer that Wardrip-Fruin identifies as the "surface." Put another way, the surface encompasses the physical hardware and the environment where audience interaction takes place. He extends this analogy to video games, in which the surface constitutes everything tangible that the audience experiences, such as the controller and its buttons, the sound hardware and sound produced, and the display monitor and images.[6] The outlandish vibrations of *Lagrange Point's* external sound source draw attention to the space where the game master and the gamer connect—the platform. At this critical nexus, the RPG's narrative functions and structural mechanics serve as roadmaps for exploring how Konami developed and implemented the Famicom's most otherworldly soundtrack.

Maps

The spatial layout of the Isis Cluster, the advanced human space colony where *Lagrange Point* is set, is as important to the game's premise as it is to the game's mechanics. Two cylindrical colonies ("Land 1" and "Land 2"), as well as a satellite base that operates the asteroid mining group Vesta, are anchored in the gravitational harbor of one of the five libration points theorized for orbital space missions.[7] However, notwithstanding the colony's gravitational balance, its societal balance is awry. A biohazard on Land 2 has fragmented the colony's leadership and led to the outbreak of an alien force: an army of bionoid mutants, who begin to overtake the residents of the other colonies. An investigation of the path and source of these alien waves is key to defeating the Bio Corps army, but, surprisingly, provides a compelling analogy for *Lagrange Point*'s unique sonic makeup (compare Figures 4.2a and 4.2b).

The source of the audio outbreak is Konami's custom Memory Management Controller (MMC, or "Mapper"), the VRC7.[8] While mappers primarily extend the capabilities of the Famicom by enabling memory bank switching and mirroring, a few provided a second audio source to expand the overall sonic palette.

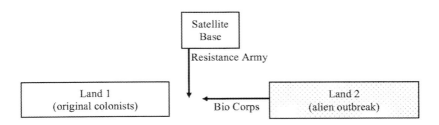

FIGURE 4.2a   Mapping the Isis Colony Cluster in *Lagrange Point*

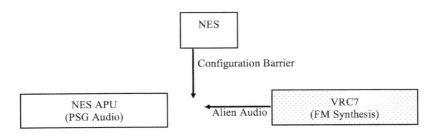

FIGURE 4.2b   Mapping the audio in *Lagrange Point*

The VRC7, in particular, included an integrated derivative of the YM2413, the cheapest member of the "L" family of Yamaha sound chips (OPLL), which was known for 2-operator FM synthesis as opposed to the more common 4-operator FM synthesis found in the other chip families.[9] Mapping external audio from a game cartridge into the Famicom's audio processing unit, however, was not an easy endeavor, and remained rare. The revisions Nintendo made for the NES, for example, eliminated the necessary signal path. External audio remained the privilege of the Japanese market until the fan community developed tools for acquiring it either with emulation or by console modification.[10]

Weapons

Unlike modern RPGs, which might lead players into the game's mechanics through storytelling or dedicated tutorials, *Lagrange Point* left players directionless to navigate complex networks of gaming elements and optimize use of spells, magical items, and of course weapon and armor.[11] A unique mechanic of *Lagrange Point*'s gameplay is the ability to fuse two weapons into more advanced artillery (see Figure 4.3a).[12] Character advancement is aided by strategic upgrading as much as the traditional combat grind.

Tables 4.1, 4.2, and 4.3 illustrate the complex system of weapon fusion. For example, fusing a Battle Knife (Electric, R1, One) with an Ice Rifle (Freeze, R3, All) will create a Corrode Sword, which is the Rank 3 "Chemical" weapon that can target a single enemy, whereas fusing a Sol Bazooka (Plasma, R4, All) with a Sonic Bazooka (Sonic, R4, All) will yield a Luft Cannon, which is the Rank 5 "Chemical" weapon that can target all enemies. The weapon created by the fusion

FIGURE 4.3a The process of weapon fusion in *Lagrange Point*

TABLE 4.1 Weapon fusion chart by type, *Lagrange Point*

	Electric	Plasma	Sonic	Freeze	Chemical	Special
Electric		Plasma	Sonic	Freeze	Chemical	Special	Electric
Plasma			Sonic	Chemical	Electric	Special	Plasma
Sonic				Freeze	Special	Electric	Sonic
Freeze					Chemical	Plasma	Freeze
Chemical						Special	Plasma
Special							Electric

TABLE 4.2 Weapon fusion charts by rank and number of targets, Part 1

	R1	R2	R3	R4	R5	R6
R1	R2	R2	R3	R3	R4	R4
R2		R3	R3	R4	R4	R5
R3			R4	R4	R5	R5
R4				R5	R5	R6
R5					R6	R6
R6						R1

TABLE 4.3 Weapon fusion charts by rank and number of targets, Part 2

	One	All
One	All	One
All		All

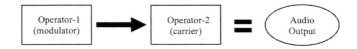

FIGURE 4.3b The resulting synthesis of 2-operator FM

process, in theory, is more advanced than either of the original weapons, but fusing weapons of a higher rank does come at a greater cost.

In a parallel fashion, the resulting waveforms of FM synthesis, such as that contributed by Konami's VRC7, attain greater complexity than the core periodic waveforms—usually sine waves.[13] In typical, 2-operator FM synthesis, each oscillator generates a sine wave and are cast in the role of a "modulator" and in the role of a "carrier" (see Figure 4.3b). The modulator influences the carrier's harmonics at levels determined by the modulator's own amplitude level and envelope of attack, sustain, decay, and release (ADSR). The relationship is similar to the effects of the low frequency oscillator (LFO) found on many synthesizers.[14] Even the basic fusion of two sine waves will begin to yield other waveform types common in sound synthesis.[15]

Tables 4.4a and 4.4b identifies some basic waveform techniques for 2-operator FM synthesis—the same type available on the VRC7 in *Lagrange Point*. In the first example, a low frequency oscillator (LFO), which exists outside the audible range, modulates the carrier waveform to produce vibrato, although the waveform shape is unaltered by the slight deviations in frequency. The remaining three examples demonstrate the output of a modulator and carrier sine wave at some fundamental

TABLE 4.4a Fusing weapons in *Lagrange Point*

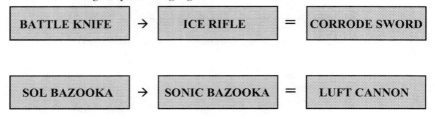

TABLE 4.4b Fusing sine waves in 2-operator FM synthesis

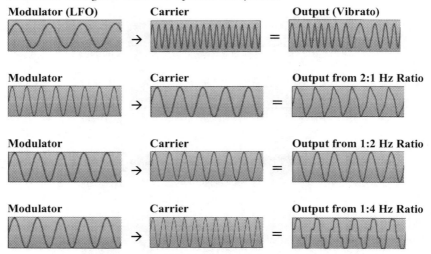

frequency ratios—2:1, 1:2, and 1:4—which will impact the harmonic sidebands (as opposed to inharmonic sidebands) in shaping new timbres.

Characters

RPG games of the 8-bit generation commonly involve three functional character types. Protagonist(s), or essential playable characters, are the controllable centerpieces of the party. The rest of the active party may comprise a variety of playable characters who may be rotated in and out for strategic purposes. Last, non-playable characters often join the party to carry out an essential, fixed, and predetermined role. The number and distribution of these functional types, as well as the degree of variability, will differ from game to game, and some characters may operate as more than one type over the course of the game. As a sci-fi RPG, *Lagrange Point* already stands as a unique offering for Konami and for the Famicom.

Alien Waves: *Lagrange Point* **63**

TABLE 4.5 The three functional character types in *Lagrange Point*

Playable Characters	Protagonist	Non-Playable Characters
Humans: Dennis, Chris, Astro, Rita	*Human*: Jin	*Humans*: Tum, Morita, Dan
Cyborgs: Pamil, Ryu, Kiesa		
Robots: Tic, Tac		*Robot*: Piko

While the influence of Sega's *Phantasy Star* series is evident, the key players in the game's genesis and design are the product of multifaceted collaboration that included elements from enthusiastic fans as well as from renown artists outside of the video game industry. The *Geiyume Kōbō* (Dreamwork Studio, 芸夢工房) competition took place in 1990, while *Lagrange Point* was in development. Commemorating the 100th issue, the *Family Computer Magazine* (or *Famimaga*) announced its partnership with Konami to provide "readers a glimpse into the production process" of game development. The new monthly feature invited magazine readers to submit ideas for several areas, initially with the title and event, but later with some music tracks. Konami's decision to incorporate a YM2413 variant in the VRC7 mapper was made by the time of the competition, and the *Famimaga* authors advertised the FM enhancement directly to entice would-be submitters.

When the development team solicited ideas for the game's audio, they expressed particular interest in music that would accompany gameplay, and announced that the selected submissions would be arranged by the Konami sound team. Much like a gamer's ability to control actions of playable side characters as it pertains to gameplay, Konami staff were able to select and choose to use from a large pool of content generated outside the company. Three songs from the competition made it into the final game, though additional winners were also named in the announcement.[16]

Like the party of characters in the game, the audio production staff enlists both fixed and indeterminate characters. Composer credits for *Lagrange Point* remain difficult to uncover. Konami, like many Japanese game developers in the 1980s and early 1990s, did not credit individual staff members to ensure that ownership of the music was retained by the company.[17] This practice is maintained with *Lagrange Point*: the only composers credited in-game were external contractors: Noriyuki Takahashi and Akio Dobashi, both of the J-Pop band Rebecca, who hold attribution for the tracks "Tum's Boogie" and "The Resurrection of Sabbath—Ending Theme," respectively. The only other in-game credit is to Konami's *Ku-kei-ha* (Square Wave) Club, an umbrella term for the music staff and occasional in-house band. Given the size of the game and growth in company size by the year 1991, any number of active Konami staff could have contributed music to the game; only one, the prolific anime composer Aki Hata, can be

64 Kevin R. Burke

identified, and then only because she included nine of the game's music tracks among the composition credits listed on her website.[18]

While the identities of the other composers for the game remain shrouded in mystery, the Konami staff working on the game's sound design is more readily identified. Both Atsushi Fujio and Katsuhiko Suzuki receive in-game credit for sound design and both are credited composers for other Konami games at that time.[19] Fujio joined in Konami in 1987 and figured heavily in the development of titles for the Famicom Disk System (FDS), a peripheral upgrade with extra data storage and audio channel that was released in Japan. His FDS sports titles *Exciting Billiards* and *Exciting Basketball* were among the first to exhibit differential pulse-width modulation (DPCM), a digital-to-analog conversion initially tapped for the occasional speech or sound effect sample, as an extra music channel. Consequently, Fujio likely played a large role in the development and integration of the YM2413 derivative into the VRC7.[20] Suzuki was part of a subset of the Konami sound team that later formed the offshoot company Treasure in 1992. *Lagrange Point* was the last of five games on which Fujio and Suzuki worked together for Konami; the other four, *Twin Bee 3* (1989), *Rollergames* (1990), *Mōryō Senki MADARA* (1990), and *Laser Invasion* (1991), bear the footprint of their collaboration by some idiomatic design features of the games' sound engine.[21] While there is no certainty without more information, it would not be surprising if they composed some of the BGM for *Lagrange Point* in addition to their roles supervising and implementing the game's audio components.

Finally, three winners of the Dreamwork Studio competition, Makoto Kawamoto, Kenji Nakamura, and Tadashi Sawashita, though absent from the game's ending credits, are identified in the original soundtrack release for the tracks they contributed.[22] Table 4.7 provides the full list of the music tracks in *Lagrange Point* and their corresponding track numbers in the three soundtracks released to date.[23] Permissions to include the winning tracks of the competition were not secured for the latter two releases, and thus those tracks and credits are provided only in the original 1991 soundtrack.[24] Almost 30 years later, the external contributors are all known: both those Konami recruited directly, the J-Pop artists as determinate collaborators selected by solicitation, and the Dreamwork Studio fans as indeterminate collaborators selected by means of a competition. While the in-game credits are incomplete and vague, the character roles of the sound and music team are reflected in the treatment of the external creative property in the various soundtrack releases (see Table 4.6).

TABLE 4.6 The three collaborator types in *Lagrange Point*'s music and sound creation

Indeterminate Collaborators	Konami Sound Team	Determinate Collaborators
Makoto Kawamoto	Atsushi Fujio	Akio Dobashi
Kenji Nakamura	Aki Hata	Noriyuki Takahashi
Tadashi Sawashita	Katsuhiko Suzuki et al.	

TABLE 4.7 Music track list for *Lagrange Point*

Name	1991	2015	2016	Credit
Theme of Isis	7	1	1	KKC
Searching for Stolte—Start Town	8	2	2	KKC
Wandering Journey (LAND 1 Dungeon)	9	3	3	KKC (Aki Hata)
Awaken into Warriors (Battle)	10	4	4	KKC
VESTA'S WALL (Vesta Outer Wall Dungeon)	11	5	5	KKC
Satellite Base (Satellite Base, Vesta Town)	12	6	6	KKC
Music Box of Sadness (Gin Faints)	13	7	7	KKC (Aki Hata)
City of Birthday (LAND 1 Town)	14	8	8	KKC (Aki Hata)
Searching for the Promise Land (LAND 1 Map)	15	9	9	KKC (Aki Hata)
Relaxed Atmosphere (Relaxation Room)	16	—	—	Makoto Kawamoto
Machine City (Robot Factory, Ironworks)	17	10	10	KKC
TUM'S BOOGIE (Electric City)	18	11	—	Noriyuki Takahashi
Bubbles of Light (Tum's Death)	19	—	—	Tadashi Sawashita
Warriors of Sorrow (Mid-Boss Battle)	20	12	11	KKC
Departure and Arrival (Port Tower, Point)	21	13	12	KKC
AQUEDUCT (LAND 2 Map)	22	14	13	KKC (Aki Hata)
Physical Energy (LAND 2 Town)	23	15	14	KKC
Fortified Zone (Bio Laboratory, Base, Fortress)	24	16	15	KKC (Aki Hata)
Within the Deep Darkness (LAND 2 Dungeon)	25	—	—	Kenji Nakamura
Silent Alarm (Metallic Dungeon)	26	17	16	KKC
Orange Party (Orange Camp Town)	27	18	17	KKC
Bio Paradise (Bio Paradise Map)	28	19	18	KKC (Aki Hata)
Last Fortress—Bio Palace—(Bio Palace)	29	20	19	KKC (Aki Hata)
Broken Replicaizer (Fake Biocaizer Battle)	30	21	20	KKC
Fight to the Death—Biocaizer—(Biocaizer Battle)	31	22	21	KKC (Aki Hata)
THE RESURRECTION OF SABBATH (Ending)	32	23	22	Akio Dobashi
Defeated—Defeated in Battle	—	24	—	KKC
Weightless (Colony Outer Wall)	—	25	—	KKC
Level Up	—	26	—	KKC
Good Night	—	27	—	KKC
Bad Luck	—	28	—	KKC

The trifold character types in *Lagrange Point* form a framework for the immersive experience of the RPG. Jin, the protagonist, is an extension of the player and thus Jin's ability to carry out the narrative is dependent on the gaming mechanism. The non-playable characters are embodiments of the setting and mood. The tragedy of the boy Tum advances the story, not achievement in the game. Finally, the other playable characters are a bridge between this agency and determinism that blurs the distinction between fantasy and reality.

Much like an RPG character party, the sound chips contributing to *Lagrange Point*'s music have specialized roles. The audio processing unit (APU) of the Famicom handles the drum tracks and the VRC7 in the cartridge carries the remaining musical material, such as the lead melody, accompaniment parts, and the bassline. Although the hardware permits up to 11 independent sound channels, the Konami sound engine does not make use of all 11. The second pulse wave channel of the Famicom APU, for example, is not used in the game, and the triangle wave channel contributes only a single note (more on this later). Finally, the audio channels that are used rarely constitute independent musical lines. Consistent with Konami's efforts to produce high-quality music from the limited hardware is a variety of multi-track effects and techniques that leverage the additional channels for timbral, rather than textural, expansion. Double-tracking, layering additional audio channel of the same musical line in slight alteration, also occurred in many Konami (and Famicom) games that lacked the additional number of audio channels—in fact, two-channel echo, detuning, waveform pairing, and other types of double-tracking were staples of the Konami sound engine by 1991. The fusion of differing audio sources and forms of sound synthesis, as well as the timbral melting pot of Konami's complex multi-tracking, paint the sonic profile of *Lagrange Point* as something truly enigmatic; its instruments and expressive effects sound neither like the 8-bit Famicom nor like quintessential FM presets, rendering the soundtrack as something of a chimera.

The same can be said for the architects of the Bio Corps Army in *Lagrange Point*. The Board of Five, former leadership of the colony gone savage, are the embodiment of an unnatural fusion between human and beast. Each of them stands as a boss during the course of the game, the last, chief scientist Stolte, revealed as the identity behind the dreaded Biokaizer. The physical forms of the

FIGURE 4.4 The Bio Corps boss Ledesma

bosses are distinct from the random encounter monsters in the game. Rather than taking on a singular, new form, the Bio Corps bosses are also a type of chimera. The boss Ledesma, for example, takes the shape of a bird of prey with reptilian wings and a parasitic humanoid growing from the back (see Figure 4.4). The abomination is a perverse merging of human with beast. Only by wounding the enemy are Jin and other members of the party able to uncover Ledesma's true human form and acquire another clue in revealing the Corps' chief motive to mutate and then rule the people of Earth.

While the VRC7's audio unit is an almost identical twin of Yamaha's YM2413 sound chip, its behavior in terms of technical capabilities as well as performance are notably different. As is common in most of the "L" family of FM chips, the oscillators can function as either nine channels of 2-operator FM synthesis or as six channels of 2-operator FM synthesis with five drum sounds that occupy the six registers normally reserved for the last three FM channels. The schematic of the YM2413, however, requires two pins for outputting audio: one for the FM sounds and the other for the drum sounds. The VRC7, on the other hand, has only one pin for outputting audio and thus does not contribute any drum instruments to the music. Those sounds emerge from another source.

The PSG within the main console's APU emits many sounds familiar to Konami games for the Famicom; however, it has lost its identity as the primary voice of the game's soundtrack. Only three of the five core audio channels even play a part in *Lagrange Point* and they are limited to the drum sounds, unable to carry the soundtrack alone. One of the two pulse wave channels, the noise channel, and the DPCM sample channel shape the drum patterns for most of the BGM, with the triangle wave contributing only a single sound in the entire game. Ex. 4.1 presents the typical distribution of specialized roles among the audible characters from both the Famicom's PSG sounds and the VRC7's FM sounds.

The abilities these audio roles lend to the soundtrack center around issues of timbre. The VRC7, like the YM2413, has 15 hardwired instrument patches and one customizable patch slot, which, for *Lagrange Point*, could load one of 64 predetermined instruments from RAM at a time.[25] The hardwired patches of the VRC7 and the generic YM2413, however, are different. And, of course, the user-defined custom patches will vary from application to application. However, 2-operator FM has a far more limited range of timbres than the 4- and 6-operator families of FM chips, so, while technically different, there are many audible similarities in the preset patches between the two variants. It is no great surprise that names given for the instrument presets of the generic YM2413 and the VRC7 are similar (see Table 4.8).[26]

With the melodic and harmonic roles of the soundtrack outsourced to the VRC7, the Famicom APU has some relief to maximize its sonic abilities—when the shield is abandoned, the extra hand brings more firepower. Of particular note to the percussion kit for the *Lagrange Point* soundtrack is the preponderance of waveform duality from within the regular Famicom APU. With a handful of

EX. 4.1 A typical distribution of *Lagrange Point's* audio in "Aqueduct," mm. 9–12

exceptions, the majority of the percussion sounds are a juxtaposition of sound synthesis types: pulse waveforms paired with randomized noise, in most cases, and with samples generated by differential pulse-code modulation.[27] Table 4.9 presents the full percussion kit in the sound engine for *Lagrange Point*, noting the sound channel source(s) that shape them. The single triangle wave *portamento* for a low tom hit in "Aqueduct" remains an isolated exception within *Lagrange Point*, but Konami's frequently made use of the slow pitch bend as a link between an introductory drum fill and the main section of the BGM. It began appearing with some regularity in the second half of 1988, with some examples including the First Stage BGM from *Bayou Billy* (1988) and the Street View BGM from *TMNT* (1989).

A more unusual example of the sonic juxtaposition is the pairing of the triangle wave's *portamento* in "Aqueduct" with an independent snare rhythm from the noise channel, although this snare drum's envelopes are not the same as other two

TABLE 4.8 Names given for the 15 preset instrument patches

YM2413 (Generic OPLL)		VRC7 (OPLL Derivative)
0	Custom	Custom
1	Violin	Bell
2	Guitar	Guitar
3	Piano	Piano
4	Flute	Flute
5	Clarinet	Clarinet
6	Oboe	Rattling Bell
7	Trumpet	Trumpet
8	Organ	Reed Organ
9	Horn	Soft Bell
A	Synthesizer	Xylophone
B	Harpsichord	Vibraphone
C	Vibraphone	Brass
D	Synthesizer Bass	Bass Guitar
E	Acoustic Bass	Synthesizer
F	Electric Guitar	Chorus
BD	Bass Drum	
SD	Snare Drum	
TOM	Tom-tom	
T-CY	Top Cymbal	
HH	Hi-hat	

TABLE 4.9 The Famicom APU's drum kit for *Lagrange Point*

Instrument	Pulse 1	Triangle	Noise	DPCM
Bass Drum				Yes
Snare Drum 1			Yes	Yes
Snare Drum 2	Yes		Yes	
Snare Drum 3			Yes	
Hi Tom	Yes		Yes	
Low Tom		Yes		
Hi-Hat (closed)	Yes		Yes	
Open Cymbal	Yes		Yes	

snare drum patches found in *Lagrange Point*. Much like the shocking reveal of the human behind the mutant at Ledesma's defeat, the isolated disruption of the percussion's sonic meld provides a momentary glimpse into the independent voices of the Famicom APU. But, for the rest of the soundtrack, the percussion track remains entirely monophonic. Evidence does, however, suggest that the Konami sound driver variant that accompanied Fujio's games in the early 1990s treated percussion as a single, monophonic line as well, even when drawing from multiple sound channels. In Ex. 4.2, an excerpt of the score from *Yume Penguin Monogatari* (Konami, 1991), the percussion is executed with coordination between the noise and DPCM channels: the bass drum is a single sample, the snare drum is a sampled attack with noise release, much like the Snare 2 in *Lagrange Point* (Table 4.5), and the cymbals are made from just the noise channel. Still, however, only one percussion instrument occurs at a single time; the constant hi-hats of a typical rock beat are merely implied. As a point of comparison, one also finds a monophonic drum track around the isolated beat at the end of m. 12 in "Aqueduct." Ex. 4.3 provides a score reduction of the Famicom APU, showing the similarity to the *Yume Penguin Monogatari* example. With the exception of the triangle wave hit discussed above, the specialized roles of the Famicom APU channels gravitate toward collaboration and coordination, yielding a drum kit of timbral depth and singular determination.

Lagrange Point illustrates a conflation of multiple Konami sound engine techniques, such as the famous single-channel echo, within the VRC7 as well.[28] Unlike the two-channel echo that loops the same content at a later frame, usually at a lower volume and possibly detuned, the single channel echo is more situational; it occurs only during space between melodic phrases or staccato notes, when a note is released and reattacked at a lower volume following a brief silence. The additional melodic channels afforded by the VRC7, notably, enabled Konami to extend these techniques further by chaining extra channels and even combining both echo types at once. In the track "Bubbles of Light" (Ex. 4.4), the first three channels of the VRC7 pair instances of single-channel echo at phrase endings with continual three-channel echoing, resulting in chains up to six as found (including primary note and five echo legs) between mm. 8–9 and mm. 11–12.

Perhaps the most advanced level of Konami's multi-tracking abilities is shown in Ex. 4.5. A four-channel echo chain is displaced from regular intervals; the first and second echoes are timed more closely together than the final echo. The displacement enriches the reverb with a more natural spacing. Finally, the third FM channel doubles the first FM channel, but with a harmonic rather than a doubling at the same frequency. The harmonic, therefore, fuels the overtone sideband and

EX. 4.2 Monophonic drum kit in *Yume Penguin Monogatari*, mm. 1–4

EX. 4.3 Triangle wave tom and the 2A03 drum kit in "Aqueduct," mm. 9–12

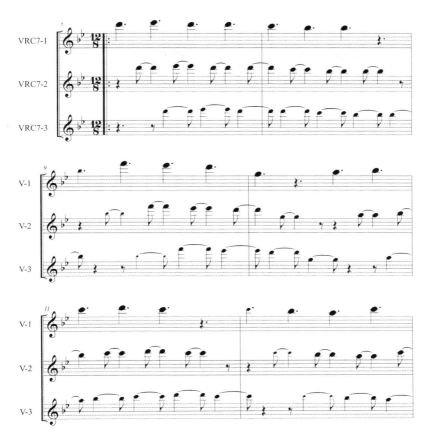

EX. 4.4 Single- and multi-channel echo in "Bubbles of Light," mm. 7–12

EX. 4.5 Four-channel echo and harmonics in "Theme of Isis," mm. 1–2

is inaudible unless isolated. Mirroring the sound engine's combinatorial aesthetic and *Lagrange Point's* gravitational balancing act, the addition upgrades 2-operator FM to a limited form of 4-operator FM in an algorithm one might find in more advanced Yamaha sound chips, such as the 4-operator YM2612 found in the Sega Genesis.

Atsushi Fujio, one of the sound designers credited in-game, reflected on the complex juxtaposition of two 2-operator FM channels in the liner notes to the *Lagrange Point Soundtracks Returns* in 2015.[29] In order to create depth like the more "sophisticated" 4-operator FM chips, Fujio cites the bell chimes in the opening to the game's ending theme, "The Resurrection of Sabbath." Following a similar technique illustrated in "Theme of Isis," the audio output of the fourth and fifth channels of the VRC7 meld into a single bell sound. Here, however, the harmonic occurs at a delay, rather than simultaneously with the fundamental tone (see Ex. 4.6). Thus the opening and ending themes, "Theme of Isis" and "The Resurrection of Sabbath" respectively, reflect the course of the game as well: Just as Jin and his party have defeated the Board of Five bio-mutants by separating the human form from the beast, so have the pair of voices that form the feigned 4-operator FM technique fallen, even so slightly, out of time to further the echo effect of the bells and enhance its timbral depth.

It is noteworthy that the most potent example of these advanced techniques, the four-channel echo and FM operator doubling in "Theme of Isis," is also the first moment the alien waveforms are heard. Only later in the song do some minor contributions from the more familiar Famicom APU appear. As the opening sequence sets the main components of the story, the soundtrack reveals the two main sound sources, first alien (VRC7) and then familiar (Famicom APU),

EX. 4.6 Two-channel echo and harmonics in "The Resurrection of Sabbath," mm. 1–4

as well as the complex juxtapositions audio channels and waveform types that occur throughout the game. *Lagrange Point* presents both an abnormal type of sound synthesis to the Famicom's APU as well as an abnormal application of the Konami sound driver to adapt to the new sound chip. Both the hardware and software constitute an interface into the RPG's central design, reflecting the game's development by characters from within and outside of the company as well as the unique weapons system. The introduction of FM synthesis into the Famicom's sonic lexicon renders it a potent expression of *Lagrange Point*'s truly unique platform.

The process by which developers fashioned games in the 8-bit era was both rapid and siloed. Conventions for video games and video game music were still in infancy. As the industry gained momentum and viability in the marketplace, technological innovation took many forms. *Lagrange Point* presents a case study that challenges the typical narratives that early video game soundtracks are (1) a reflection of the limitations in sound hardware or (2) a composer's triumph of overcoming those hardware limitations. Rather, the particular situation by which Konami made a conscious effort to build an RPG with input beyond the company and with an uncanny sound addition to the game cartridge offers a roadmap by which scholars can understand both the musical score and the game mechanics.

Notes

1　A part of this chapter was read, under a different title, at the North American Conference for Video Game Music in Austin, TX (January 15, 2017). I gratefully acknowledge the assistance of Stephen Meyerink for translating the Japanese text from the *Family Computer Magazine* (*Famimaga*) and from the *Lagrange Point Soundtracks Returns* liner notes, as well as supporting information on the VRC7 expansion chip from Olivér Kovács, Steve Lakawicz, Patrick Todd, and David Viens. Image captured by the author from gameplay. This chapter adopts "Tum" as the translation of "Tamu" (タ ム), following Konami's usage in the titles of two tracks in the original soundtrack recording (King Records, 1991). The unofficial English translation of the game implemented by the fan community Aeon Genesis, however, uses "Tam" for the character's name.

2　Nintendo adopted the Famicom for Western markets as the Nintendo Entertainment System (NES) in 1985. Both consoles share the same core architecture and sound capabilities; however, the NES is unable to route expansion audio, as found in the *Lagrange Point* cartridge, without modification.

3　Brenda Laurel, *Computers as Theatre*, 2nd ed. (Upper Saddle River, NJ: Addison-Wesley, 2014), 16.

4　Laurel, *Computers as Theatre*, 38.

5　Noah Wardrip-Fruin, *Expressive Processing: Digital Fictions, Computer Games, and Software Studies* (Cambridge, MA: MIT Press, 2012), 7.

6　Wardrip-Fruin, *Expressive Processing*, 11.

7　The published proceedings of the 2002 international conference on Libration Point Orbits and Applications details several space mission examples. See Gerard Gómez, Martin W. Lo, and Josep J. Masdemont, eds., *Libration Point Orbits and Applications* (River Edge, NJ: World Scientific, 2003).

74   Kevin R. Burke

8   Memory Management Controllers are commonly referred to as "mappers," a term originating from the iNES emulator community. For more information, refer to the article on the NESdev Wiki: https://wiki.nesdev.com/w/index.php/Mapper.

9   A thorough discussion of Yamaha's various families of sound chips is beyond the scope of this chapter; however, for more information on the adoption of Yamaha's low-cost FM chips in arcade cabinets, home consoles, and PC sound cards, see pp. 22–23 of Robert Johnstone, "The Sound of One Chip Clapping: Yamaha and FM Synthesis," *MIT Japan Program* (September 1994): 1–32.

10 I provide a step-by-step tutorial for modding a North American NES to play external audio emulated on a flash cart (Power Pak, Everdrive N8, etc.) on my blog. Further modification to the Famicom-to-NES pin adapter is required for playing expanded audio off of a *Lagrange Point* cartridge. http://curriculumcrasher.com/2017/01/24/nes-expanded-audio-100k-pot-mod/.

11 A high-definition scan of the game's guidebook is available at this link: www.video gameden.com/fc/extra/lpo.pdf.

12 A fan-developed weapon fusion guide in English is available at this link: https://vonith-ipathachai.deviantart.com/art/Lagrange-Point-Weapon-Fusion-Guide-494176870.

13 See Karen Collins, *Game Sound: An Introduction to the History, Theory, and Practice of Video Game Music and Sound Design* (Cambridge, MA: MIT Press, 2008), 38.

14 Nathan Altice, *I Am Error: The Nintendo Family Computer/Entertainment System Platform* (Cambridge, MA: MIT Press, 2015), 272–273.

15 While the product waveforms of these basic, 2-operator examples of FM synthesis resemble pulse waves and sawtooth waves, they are distinct from their PSG counterparts.

16 For example, a submission by Masashi Hamauzu, composer of *Final Fantasy XIII* (2009), was announced with the winners, but was not included in the final game. Hamauzu confirmed this in a tweet to Stephen Meyerink on February 1, 2018. https://twitter.com/MasashiHamauzu/status/959001853332615168.

17 Chris Greening's interview with *Castlevania* composer and Konami Sound Team veteran Kinyuo Yamashita offers considerable insight into Konami's management of its employees in the 1980s, including project assignments and author credits for games and soundtracks. www.squareenixmusic.com/features/interviews/kinuyoyamashita.shtml.

18 According to her website, Hata also contributed music to *Contra III: The Alien Wars* (1992) and *Senki Madara 2* (1993) for the Super Nintendo Entertainment System (Super Famicom) and to *Rocket Knight Adventures* (1993) for the Sega Genesis (Mega Drive), as a recurring fixture on the Katsuhiko (Nazo²) Suzuki team that would become the independent firm Treasure. http://akihata.jp/?p=9817

19 Credited in-game by the aliases Sukenomiya Fujio and NazoNazo (Nazo²) Suzuki.

20 The Famicom is equipped with the most basic form of DPCM, known as delta modulation, which quantizes data only one bit at a time. Still, processing a steady input of DPCM in BGM during active gameplay was not an obvious (or simple) possibility for Famicom sound programmers at first.

21 Sound engines carry macro instructions for a variety of audio details, such as volume envelopes, pitch tables, expressive gestures, and instrument timbres.

22 This information is available online at https://vgmdb.net/album/3689.

23 *Lagrange Point* (King Records, 1991), *Lagrange Point Soundtracks Returns* (Egg Music Records, 2015), *Lagrange Point* (Ship to Shore Records, 2016).

24 Haruhisa "hally" Tanaka addresses the absence of these tracks in the liner notes to *Lagrange Point Soundtracks Returns*, Konami Kukeiha Club et al. (Egg Music Records EMCA-0021, CD, 2015).

25 Altice, *I am Error*, 274.

26 Instrument names for the YM2413 are taken from *YM2413 FM Operator Type-LL (OPLL) Application Manual*, 7. Yamaha, n.d. For years, the exact settings for the VRC7's preset instrument patches were unknown, since they are hardwired to the chip and

Alien Waves: *Lagrange Point* **75**

cannot be altered by data from the CPU, as is possible with the custom patch. The NESdev and FamiTracker communities had approximated the preset settings and named them for use in emulation and chiptuning, with the most widely used one proposed by Brad Smith in 2012. *VRC7 Audio.* NESdev Wiki. https://wiki.nesdev.com/w/index.php/VRC7_audio. These preset names are provided in the instrument editor of the FamiTracker, chiptune freeware. The Retro Game Audio podcast has provided an audio comparison of the preset patches between the hardware and the emulation approximations, timestamped at this link: https://soundcloud.com/retro-gameaudio/the-vrc7-and-lagrange-point#t=14:11. Due to recent advances in reading the VRC7's internal die, however, Alexey Khokholov determined a way to dump the ROM data, and the preset instrument settings are now verified as of March 15, 2019. https://github.com/nukeykt/VRC7dump.

27 Bi-timbral instruments on the Famicom are not excusive to *Lagrange Point*, nor to games by Konami. Developer Sunsoft, for example, paired triangle waveforms with randomized noise in games like *Journey to Silius* (1990) in order to craft more complex drum sounds. But this was certainly more the exception to the rule among the library of games, as well as within the games that employed it.

28 The single-channel echo for which Konami Famicom music is famous, entered the sound drivers in an abbreviated form late in 1987 and became fully established as a signature mainstay in 1988. In an interview with Jeremy Parish, ex-Konami sound engineer and composer Hidenori Maezawa describes the technique of single-channel echo and its early use in *Contra*. The interview is available online at https://youtu.be/-Ykbfrf5uXY?t=238

29 Fujio's recollections are summarized in Tanaka, liner notes to *Lagrange Point Soundtrack Returns*.

5

THE PENULTIMATE FANTASY

Nobuo Uematsu's Score for
Cleopatra no Ma Takara

Dana Plank

The title screen of クレオパトラの魔宝 (*Kureopatora no Ma Takara*, usually translated as *Cursed Treasure of Cleopatra*, 1987) immediately sets the stage for intrigue, promising mystery and adventure in a faraway land. A sweeping script presents the title of the game, inserting two stylized eyes of Horus in the word 魔 (*Ma*).[1] The screen has a color scheme of desert sands and a deep blue reminiscent of lapis lazuli (see Fig 5.1). But far more striking is the title track by Nobuo Uematsu, with droned open fifths in the lower voices approached from below with chromatic grace note appoggiaturas, an emphasis on descending melodic patterns, a fanciful triplet flourish decorating the melodic line, and the frequent use of augmented second intervals (see Ex. 5.1). The second statement of the theme adds a fanciful scalar counter-melody and increases the harmonic motion of the bass drones (beginning at the double bar in m. 9).[2]

Cleopatra no Ma Takara was released for the Famicom Disk System on July 24, only five months before the release of another, better-known Uematsu project: *Final Fantasy*. *Cleopatra* illustrates what ultimately became established as standard role-playing game elements: turn-based combat awarding gold and experience, a gradual increase in strength and defense through "leveling up," the ability to equip various weapons and items, and so on. The plot begins when the main character, Daisuke Kusano, decides to spend his summer vacation visiting his archeologist father in Alexandria. While the two are busy excavating, evil spirits kidnap Daisuke's father; the boy must then locate a magical artifact, the Tears of Isis, to summon Cleopatra's ghost to plead for his father's life.

Uematsu's tightly constructed musical score foregrounds exoticist gestures—even at the expense of other functions music typically serves in JRPGs. I argue, in fact, that *Cleopatra no Ma Takara* complicates conventional assumptions of musical

FIGURE 5.1 Title screen of *Cleopatra no Ma Takara*

EX. 5.1 Nobuo Uematsu, "Title," mm. 1–10 *Cleopatra no Ma Takara*

78 Dana Plank

style and function in JRPGs, suggesting that conventional tropes may only apply to games with a quasi-medieval-European fantasy setting. In service of this argument, I will contrast Uematsu's music for *Cleopatra no Ma Takara* both with his own contributions to conventional JRPG scoring in the *Final Fantasy* franchise as well as with Koichi Sugiyama's score for *Dragon Quest III* (Enix, 1988).[3] Like *Final Fantasy*, *Dragon Quest III* came out within a year of *Cleopatra* and so represents another ideal point of comparison; though its music largely contributes or conforms to our modern notion of a paradigmatic JRPG score, it also presents isolated instances of exoticist scoring. These games differ both in the deployment and degree of exoticist musical gestures, illustrating how *Cleopatra no Ma Takara* falls more in line with depictions of Egypt in other media (e.g., film) than with its JRPG contemporaries. While this focus creates an evocative, compact, and iconic depiction of Egypt, it represents a marked departure from compositional practices that by the late 1980s were already in the process of solidifying into identifiable ludomusical tropes.

Japanese Exoticism(s): Orientalism, Self-Orientalism, and Occidentalism

> The word exotic, I have grown to realize, has magnetic, insidious, and sometimes explosive force.[4]
>
> *Ralph P. Locke*

Musical exoticism seeks to evoke an Elsewhere or an Other. The composer and their audiences *perceive* and *receive* certain markers of difference from normative musical practices; therefore, musical exoticism must rely on codified devices and gestures to be intelligible as such. The boundary between normative and exotic—and its rearticulation over time—is vital in the process of meaning-making between composer and audience.[5] As Timothy D. Taylor has stated, "political and geographical margins are peculiarly energetic sites where meanings are made, remade, altered, transformed, altered again."[6] Exoticist works tend to rely not on encounters with any verifiably "real" exemplar of foreign music, but instead upon a composer's impressions of a culture designated as an Other.[7] Most frequently, exoticism is an intertextual—rather than a meticulously researched—compositional technique, referring to previously encountered methods for depicting difference. The term does not simply describe mere oddities or moments of musical tension; instead, it implies a deliberate attempt to evoke that which is foreign to the composer and their audience.[8] As Matthew Head suggests, exoticism "constitutes its objects; it does not just depict them."[9]

Cleopatra no Ma Takara conjures ancient Egypt as a visual and musical object for the player, but the subjects performing this imaginative act deserve particular consideration. While the literature on musical exoticism is rich and complex, it has tended to focus on the music of colonial and imperial Europe from the sixteenth to the nineteenth centuries. Uematsu's music for *Cleopatra no Ma Takara*—a Japanese game set in ancient Egypt that was never released to Western audiences—employs exoticizing devices common in Western classical music and Hollywood film scoring, but the contextual shift is significant.[10] Does the fact that Japan represents one of the traditional Others of the West complicate, alter, or disrupt the traditional exoticist paradigm?

The relationship between the cultural actors in the case of *Cleopatra no Ma Takara* is difficult to disentangle, since they are politically, geographically, and temporally displaced. Though Japan has an imperial past, it neither colonized Egypt nor even had substantial cultural contact with it until the twentieth century.[11] Does the game then enact a *metaphorical* colonization, regardless of the actual political power differentials? In drawing on exoticist tropes from the West, does it situate Japan as an analog for Western colonial powers?

Long before the advent of the video game industry, Japan was forced to contend with Orientalized, exoticized portrayals by the West. The nation did so by translating, importing, or domesticating these representations into cultural discourse; countering them; assimilating some of them; and by representing its own Others in a constant exploration and articulation of identity.[12] This process is inherently playful, combining and recombining elements using aspects of self-Orientalism (or self-exoticism, reflexive processes that grapple with existing representations) and counter-exoticism (which challenges or subverts existing exoticist portrayals).[13] For example, Sugiyama's theme for the town of Jipang from *Dragon Quest III* uses self-Orientalist signifiers such as a pentatonic-hued melody tinged with augmented intervals, ostinato (Pulse 2) and repetitive rhythms that differentiate the track from the rest of the score (see Ex. 5.2). Koichi Iwabuchi writes that, "while Orientalism enjoys the mysterious exoticism of the Other, self-Orientalism exploits the Orientalist gaze to turn itself into an Other."[14] Cultural objects that are meant only for Japanese consumption are informed by some of these outward-facing processes, even those that participate in traditional exoticist representational strategies: negotiating, adjusting, and creatively reinventing difference while defining or reinscribing identity.[15]

Egyptomania in the West and in Japan

> The Other cannot be misrepresented, since it is always already a misrepresentation.[16]
> *Mitsuhiro Yoshimoto*

Players are unlikely to take the musical objects in *Cleopatra no Ma Takara* as literal recreations of any true music of antiquity. The musical gestures are, ultimately, stereotypes—inventions that try to distill and recreate emotional experiences evoked by coming into contact with ancient Egyptian artifacts, settings, and stories.

EX. 5.2 Koichi Sugiyama, "Jipang," *Dragon Quest III*

The representations that result from such imagined contact only seem to reinforce the unknowability and mystery of Egypt, the sense of monumentality at all there is yet to uncover and understand, all that still lies latent, buried in centuries of windswept sand.

Many forms of exoticism begin with some kind of contemporary cultural encounter—a spark that inspires artists to wonder and create. The trouble with ancient Egypt is that it is too distant in the past; a great deal of it is lost to history. Yet, most fascination focuses exclusively on the ancient and inaccessible while brushing aside the region's modern inhabitants—or, worse, conflating the two. Elliott Colla, writing on nineteenth-century European responses to Egyptian-themed museum exhibitions, found that visitors emphasized a paradoxical sense of familiarity and closeness with the objects on display, while also reifying distance in reactions tinged with "awe, marvel, even humility."[17] Despite the notion of Egypt as eternal and timeless, our imaginings of it are also always situated in the present moment of encounter.

One of the first major waves of Western Egyptomania occurred after Napoleon's African campaign in 1798 and 1799, spurred by the publication of the first volumes of *Le Description de l'Egypte* in 1809.[18] Then, in 1822, Jean-François Champollion deciphered the hieroglyphic text of the Rosetta Stone, stimulating European interest in Egyptian iconography.[19] As Diego Saglia has shown, exoticist representations since that time have had to grapple with the sheer variety and density of meanings attached to the myriad Egyptian motifs over time, ranging from the mysterious to the sublime.[20] Saglia speaks to fearful underpinnings of the nineteenth-century obsession with an Egypt that is "too vast, too grand, overflowing with signs, and too close to the otherworld and afterlife ... [Egypt] is consumed and possessed, yet it also moves, slides, threatens, proliferates, and creates."[21] Europe avidly appropriated Egypt "while, at the same time, anxiously fearing to be consumed (invaded, infected, taken over) by it."[22] Jean-Marcel Humbert describes Egyptomania in less physical terms, suggesting that fascination stems not from beauty or Saglia's notions of contagion, but from irrationality.[23] Egypt is impossible to fully assimilate, integrate, or absorb.

One of the first moments of contact between Japan and Egypt took place in 1863, when the Tokugawa Shogunate sent an ambassadorial delegation to Europe and Egypt, commemorating the trip with Antonio Beato's striking photograph of samurai warriors in front of the Great Sphinx (see Figure 5.2).[24] Japanese Egyptology began to take hold in the early twentieth century, as scholars began to participate in excavations and publish in archeological journals at home and abroad.[25] Academic articles from this period even argued that the Japanese language derived from a form of Ancient Egyptian.[26] The most significant instance of Japanese

FIGURE 5.2 Samurai warriors at Giza, photographed by Antonio Beato (1863)

82 Dana Plank

Egyptomania occurred after an exhibit toured Japan in 1965 that introduced the treasures of Tutankhamen to record numbers of museum attendees. According to Kawai, the show "brought about a fever for all things ancient Egyptian."[27] Japanese Egyptomania took the form of an increase in academic scholarship, archeological excavation projects, popular publications, documentaries, translations of books and articles on Egyptology, and even wholly imaginative musical representations in video games.[28] In the case of a Famicom game, the gameplay mechanics and graphics help to craft this representation in tandem with the music and sound, and the non-exotic moments and gestures are just as discursively productive and interesting. Whereas many of the complicated webs of meaning in the field arise from claims of inauthenticity, of imagination that creates images without fidelity to the "truth" of a particular musical culture, representation of ancient Egypt is *by necessity* cut from whole cloth—whether the diaphanous and transparent linen of court dress depicted in tomb paintings, or the opaque, resinous, protective gauze that wrapped Egypt's deceased.

Musical Exoticism and Ancient Egypt

> To reinscribe alien wonders in familiar words or notes, or to bind or embed them within safely familiar frames, was, of course, to reinterpret, to control, and to take away some of their frightening distance and incomprehensible power.[29]
> *Linda Phyllis Austern*

Musical-exoticist representations of ancient Egypt cannot be based on any "real" music from the era because no surviving notation exists. As Bellman writes, and as discussed earlier:

> The exotic equation is a balance of familiar and unfamiliar: just enough "there" to spice the "here" but remain comprehensible in making the point. Exoticism is not about the earnest study of foreign cultures; it is about drama, effect, and evocation. The listener is intrigued, hears something new and savory, but is not aurally destabilized enough to feel uncomfortable.[30]

Any musical gestures employed to represent Ptolemaic Egypt are participants in a dense web of signifiers that often reach beyond the explicitly musical; and yet, these devices are often quite clear to the listener even outside of the game context due to repeated appearances in other media.

Taylor has listed chromaticism, dissonance, avoidance of a tonal center, lack of goal orientation, and metrical changes or ambiguity (including hemiola) as characteristic markers of musical exoticism.[31] These devices are largely interchangeable, essentially equating all non-Western cultures. Augmented seconds are another common exoticist device; while the lower tetrachord of the Arabic *hijāz* mode contains an augmented second (e.g., A–Bb–C#–D), Scott, Locke, and others have demonstrated that this interval is far less common in non-Western musics than in Western representations of such musics, suggesting that the interval's use is less about fidelity to the true mode than obsession with its sound.[32] Scott establishes a large list of Orientalist devices that can serve as musical markers of cultural difference, ranging from melodic motion (arabesques, melismas, ornamented lines, "sliding or sinuous chromaticism"), intervals (whole tones, augmented seconds and fourths), and harmonic inflections (parallel motion in fourths, fifths, or octaves, drones, pedal points, chords of uncertain duration or harmonic direction), to rhythmic alterations (use of triplets in duple time, repetitive rhythms, and rapid scalar passages, especially if they employ irregular patterns such as 11 notes in the space of a half note).[33] Scott further suggests that Egypt is specifically conveyed by prominent woodwinds such as the cor anglais. However, these musical codes often overlap, and not every musical device is inherently exotic in character, especially if heard in isolation.[34] Instead, devices combine with each other and with extra-musical material (such as game graphics) to construct the exotic for the listener.

Cleo-patronizing? The Score for *Cleopatra no Ma Takara*

> And the music was not the least part of it, what with its hieratic colour.[35]
>
> *Filippo Filippi*

A composer incorporating exotic gestures must do so within the limitations of their own musical milieu, notational standards, and representational norms.[36] Uematsu is no exception. As with most composers in the 1980s, he had to contend with constraints in the mimetic capabilities of synthesized sound for the Famicom; the hardware in the 8-bit era was better suited to evoke a cor anglais than to try to sample one. Therefore, each of Uematsu's musical tracks rely on multiple exotic gestures to convey the desired effect. Beyond the constraints of relatively short development cycles and the technical and spatial limitations of the sound chip, Uematsu needed to situate his score within established tropes of "Egyptianness" that would be intelligible for his audience no matter his chosen electronic timbres. Although overt musical references to Egypt are not terribly common in early games, the few representative tracks possess remarkable similarities to Uematsu's score. Sugiyama's Pyramid dungeon theme from *Dragon Quest III* (1988) could easily have been written for *Cleopatra no Ma Takara*, with its septuplet runs, rampant augmented second intervals, and plodding, rhythmically repetitive accompaniment (see Ex. 5.3).[37] The difference is that this exoticist music is unique in the game context rather than a driving force unifying the entire score.

One of the most striking aspects of Uematsu's *Cleopatra no Ma Takara* score is how short many of the most prominent loops are. Some of the tracks are only two

EX. 5.3 Koichi Sugiyama, "Pyramid," *Dragon Quest III*

measures long, repeating ad infinitum until the player can progress to another area; this characteristic is apparent in the town theme that greets the player after the title screen (see Ex. 5.4). The track is certainly tuneful, but hardly tranquil, and this is a clue to the unusual function of this town in the game: the player encounters random battles in the streets and alleyways between shops. The player must spend a large amount of time in random encounters in town, fighting to gain enough experience and gold to upgrade weapons and take on the first dungeon.[38] And yet, the Random Encounter theme is little respite from the repetitiveness of the town theme (see Ex. 5.5). Both themes are replete with exotic signifiers: the Town theme prominently features a *hijāz*-like rising figure with the augmented second (B♭–B♮–D♮–E♭) and repetitive bass and accompaniment figures, whereas the Random Encounter theme boasts a rapid whole-tone scale, incessantly repetitive pulse, and unstable 7/4 meter.

EX. 5.4 Nobuo Uematsu, "Town," *Cleopatra no Ma Takara*

EX. 5.5 Nobuo Uematsu, "Random Encounter," *Cleopatra no Ma Takara*

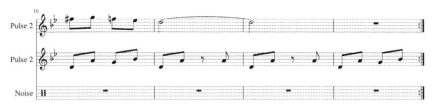

EX. 5.6 Nobuo Uematsu, "Victory Fanfare," *Cleopatra no Ma Takara*

The Victory Fanfare's opening trill-like figure seems to suggest a cue launching *into* battle rather than announcing triumph *from* it (compare Ex. 5.6 and 5.7). Rather than a victorious major-key theme in the brass, the fanfare that follows the initial sting revisits the melody of the Title track, intensifying the line by doubling its tempo and increasing the activity of the accompaniment with a relentless leaping accompaniment pattern. While providing a measure

EX. 5.7   Nobuo Uematsu, "Battle 1," mm. 1–4 *Final Fantasy II*

of thematic unity to the game, the track seems more anxious than celebratory. The Shop theme is the longest that the player hears during the initial phase of gameplay, featuring a trill-like quintuplet continuously outlining a mordant-like figure, and a quirky, plodding bassline outlining a perfect fifth followed by a tritone (see Ex. 5.8).

These themes are striking for their brevity as well as for their repetition—the player only hears these four cues for the first several hours of the game. This repetition further emphasizes the musical markers of exoticism in the score, perhaps at the expense of the other musical functions these tracks might perform. For example, rather than merely heightening the sense of urgency with percussive regularity, the Random Encounter theme seems to steep the player in dizzying confusion. It is a whirl of activity appropriate for battle, but it lacks the focus and drive of most JRPG battle themes (see Ex. 5.9).

Role-playing games typically present towns as safe spaces free from dangerous encounters, and the music reflects this with markers of safety and comfort—tonal stability in a major key, stepwise motion, pleasing melodic contours (see Ex. 5.10 and 5.11). Although there *are* "unsafe" towns in JRPGs, they are typically explicitly delineated for the player via unique music and graphics, and often appear after hours of play and experiences with "safe" villages. *Cleopatra no Ma Takara* begins the game with an "unsafe" town, immediately subverting genre expectations for the player.[39] These initial musical moments, as well as the gameplay, eschew typical JRPG tropes in service of depicting this Egyptian adventure as dangerous, mysterious, unpredictable—unlike anything else the player has known.

Other tracks share this focus on concise loops densely packed with exoticist signifiers. The track for the Goddess Temple (the final dungeon), for example, consists of a four-measure phrase which is itself a culmination of all of the exotic gestures in the game: Pulse Channel 1 establishes metrical irregularity by dividing the subdivided eighth-note pulse into groups of 3–3-2 (featuring a prominent rising leap of a fifth in each measure), and the Pulse 2 melody contains augmented seconds (between the C and D# and F and G#), ornamentation using triplet figures with "sinuous chromaticism," and a rapid scalar passage that characterizes the final flourish (see Ex. 5.12).[40] The loop also suggests a modal character. If the loop is in the key of E, then the pitches suggest a major scale with ♭2 and ♭6.

EX. 5.8   Nobuo Uematsu, "Shop," *Cleopatra no Ma Takara*

This is sometimes classified as the Flamenco mode, but it is interesting to note the similarity of this pattern to the Japanese *In* or *miyako-bushi* scales used in koto and shamisen music. Both scales use the same pitches, but *miyako-bushi* conceives of the scale structurally—built on tones a fourth apart—in this case, E to A and B to E. Though this similarity may suggest a local source for this particular gesture, it also serves as a good illustration of the notion that exoticist devices are relatively interchangeable and that their evocative power is dependent on context and interaction with other musical and non-musical devices.

D.C. Parker referred to exoticism as an "accretion" in 1917; most other authors have cited a similar process of expansion, multiplication, and absorption of formerly exotic signifiers into normative musical practices.[41] It is a process of intention, imposition, idiom, invocation, idolatry, insolence. As Taylor describes it,

> The rate of change of representations today is so rapid in large part because there are so many tropes of Otherness now available … newer ideas about Others did not eclipse older ones, but instead complicated the notions of the Other and otherness."[42]

88 Dana Plank

EX. 5.9 Koichi Sugiyama, "Battle Theme," mm. 1–8, *Dragon Quest III*

Borders expand and contract, empires rise and fall, and diverse groups encounter each other—even if one of those groups cannot respond, existing largely in the imaginative utterances of another. Uematsu's score for *Cleopatra no Ma Takara* draws upon nearly all of the Western musical markers of musical exoticism, these attempts to reanimate Egyptian antiquity. And yet, two moments complicate the notion of Japan borrowing directly from Western appropriations—moments of musical rupture rife with destabilizing potential, or exceptions that prove the rule of exoticism in this particular game.

EX. 5.10 Nobuo Uematsu, "Town Theme," mm. 1–10, *Final Fantasy II*

EX. 5.11 Koichi Sugiyama, "Village Theme," mm. 1–10, *Dragon Quest III*

EX. 5.12 Nobuo Uematsu, "Goddess Temple," *Cleopatra no Ma Takara*

90 Dana Plank

In the end credits track for *Cleopatra no Ma Takara*, the melody from the Title takes on a solemn ceremonial tone, like a military procession with the snare-drum-like rolls in the noise channel (see Ex. 5.13). Yet, the B section is more reminiscent of a rhapsody than of Ramesses (mm. 27–34 of Liszt's Hungarian Rhapsody no. 2 in C sharp minor, to be exact). This moment provides thematic contrast to the melody heard throughout the game on its title screen and in its victory fanfare, but the exoticist signifiers do not retreat entirely—the repetitive rhythms and ostinato support the melody even as it loses its emphasis on augmented seconds.

The Game Over theme could have been written for any JRPG in this era, with its straightforwardly melancholy melodic minor key and figuration in Pulse Channel 2 (an alternating, bariolage-like figure common in instrumental music of the eighteenth century; see Ex. 5.14). It is possible that Uematsu meant to evoke the antiquity of Egypt in a different way, by coding devices from the Baroque era of Western art music as temporally displaced (and thus timeless), severed from their original historical moment. Or perhaps Uematsu meant to signify sublimity, invoking a connection between religious affect, awe, and the afterlife. The notable departure from traditional ludomusical signifiers in this game makes the moment where Uematsu follows the expected trope all the more intriguing, potentially

EX. 5.13 Nobuo Uematsu, "Credits," mm. 15–24, *Cleopatra no Ma Takara*

Uematsu's Score for *Cleopatra no Ma Takara* 91

EX. 5.14 Nobuo Uematsu, "Game Over," *Cleopatra no Ma Takara*

meaningful as an instance of subtle Occidentalism or counter-exoticism coding the music of the West as antiquated, esoteric, or funereal. Whatever Uematsu's intentions or aesthetic rationales, this musical depiction of finality is one that he employs often; the association may have personal significance (see Ex. 5.15).

The ultimate musical strangeness of this 8-bit artifact, however, is not an augmented second or any other exotic devices listed in Taylor and Scott: it is the asymmetrical, computerized sweep accompanying the Underground levels of the Goddess Temple (see Ex. 5.16). The track for the interior of this final dungeon registers more as a fearful extended sound effect than a melody—a thematic fragment against an imitation of a slide figure, followed by a nervous chortle and flurry of excitement, cascading into nothingness. The approximation of a low rising glissando or chromatic ascent is unsettling; the precise, perfectly even pace of the pitch shift too exact to come across as a true glissando. The track evokes the player's descent into darkness; a loss of coherence, of geographic specificity, of intelligibility, of music itself.

As these transcriptions demonstrate, the music of *Cleopatra no Ma Takara* has a singular focus: conveying the ancient Egyptian setting. To this end, Uematsu chose to ignore or subvert ludomusical tropes that were already forming in the 1980s as games in the JRPG genre became grander, more narratively driven, and increasingly orchestral in scope. Transcriptions from *Dragon Quest III* provide representative examples of these conventional scoring techniques but also serve to suggest a more typical deployment of exoticist material in the genre. Music tinged with the exotic adds color and interest to the themes for Jipang and the Pyramid dungeon in *Dragon Quest III*, rather than serving as the bedrock for the entire score, as in Uematsu's implementation of the devices throughout *Cleopatra no Ma Takara*. Lest the reader conclude that Uematsu's compositional approach is idiosyncratic or

EX. 5.15 Nobuo Uematsu, "Dead Theme," *Final Fantasy II*

EX. 5.16 Nobuo Uematsu, "Goddess Temple: Underground," *Cleopatra no Ma Takara*

inconsequential, the examples from *Final Fantasy II* attest to his engagement with—and, indeed, formative influence upon—normative JRPG scoring practices.

One final example will serve to highlight *Cleopatra no Ma Takara*'s uniqueness in Uematsu's compositional oeuvre. Like *Dragon Quest III*, *Final Fantasy V*

(Square, 1992) contains a pyramid dungeon, an isolated instance of musical exoticism in a sweeping orchestral score. Yet, unlike *Dragon Quest III* or *Cleopatra no Ma Takara*, the track "Slumber of Ancient Earth" situates the exoticist scoring as a B section amidst a more mystical theme, complete with heroic rising gestures, harp arpeggios, and fateful chordal arrivals (see Ex. 5.17). [43]

As the writers on musical exoticism suggest, a great deal of the power in exoticist representations lies in their challenge to normative musical practices, in their very fictive and furtive processes of signifying, in their very irrationality. As Saglia suggests, representations are replete with ambivalence and slippage—appropriating, reworking, and adapting motifs and materials, and inventing the rest, accumulating signs and icons along the way.[44] These encounters with Egypt in early JRPGs may attract or repel the player, much like Egypt has done for centuries—captivating and yet capturing its visitors, instilling awe and agitation in equal measure. Like *Cleopatra no Ma Takara* itself, these tensions—between

EX. 5.17 Nobuo Uematsu, "Slumber of Ancient Earth," *Final Fantasy V*

EX. 5.17 (Continued)

knowing and unknowing, Egypt, Occident, Orient, exotic, Other, and Self—invite replay and return. Perhaps the player will find peace in the paradox, simultaneously illuminated and more deeply obscured.

Notes

1 The eye of Horus was an ancient symbol of protection linked to the cobra goddess Wadjet, who served as Horus's wet nurse in Egyptian mythology. The game is often called *Cleopatra no Mahō* (or *Mahou*) in English-language sources, but 魔宝 is written out またから (*ma takara*, literally translated as "evil spirit treasure"), not まほう (*mahō*, which would be 魔法, meaning "magic, witchcraft, or sorcery"). Indeed, the unofficial English translation of the game on romhacking.net completed in April 2018 uses "Mahou" (www.romhacking.net/translations/3534/). However, *Cleopatra no Ma Takara* is the literal Romanization of the kanji, and so I will defer to this spelling throughout. It is also more fitting to the game, in which the player seeks to recover an ancient artifact in order to remove an ancient curse.

Uematsu's Score for *Cleopatra no Ma Takara* **95**

2 The Nintendo Entertainment System used a five-channel Ricoh RP2A03 sound processor chip; two pulse-wave channels, a triangle channel, a noise channel, and a differential pulse-code modulation channel capable of limited sampling of analog sound. The Japanese Famicom Disk System's Ricoh RP2C33 had an additional channel, expanding the musical-textural capabilities of the console. All transcriptions are my own. Track titles for *Cleopatra no Ma Takara* are also my own and are purely descriptive; no official soundtrack or published score exists for the game.

3 The *Dragon Quest* series was released as *Dragon Warrior* in the US; since *Cleopatra* was a Japanese-only release, it seems fitting to refer to the Japanese version of this game as my point of comparison.

4 Ralph P. Locke, "On Exoticism, Western Art Music, and the Words We Use," *Archiv für Musikwissenschaft* 69 (2012), 325.

5 Jonathan D. Bellman, "Musical Voyages and Their Baggage: Orientalism in Music and Critical Musicology," *Musical Quarterly* 94 (2011), 420; Many writers use the terms "exoticism" and "Orientalism" as approximate synonyms (with Orientalism as more geographically specific); however, Bellman has challenged this equivalence, exploring the boundaries of the terminology.

6 Timothy D. Taylor, *Beyond Exoticism: Western Music and the World* (Durham, NC and London: Duke University Press, 2007), 71.

7 Derek B. Scott, "Orientalism and Musical Style," *Musical Quarterly* 82 (1998), 309; one need not know the legitimate musical practices of the exoticized Other; rather, "it seems that only a knowledge of Orientalist signifiers is required."

8 Locke, "On Exoticism," 322–323.

9 Matthew Head, "Musicology on Safari: Orientalism and the Spectre of Postcolonial Theory," *Music Analysis* 22 (2003), 212.

10 See, for example, the music for *The Ten Commandments* (1956) and *Cleopatra* (1963).

11 Nozomu Kawai, "Egyptological Landscape in Japan: Past, Present, and Future," *Comité international pour l'égyptologie (CIPEG) Journal* 1 (2017), 51.

12 Ofra Goldstein-Gidoni and Michal Daliot-Bul, "'Shall we Dansu?': Dancing with the "West" in Contemporary Japan," *Japan Forum* 14(1) (2002), 64–67.

13 Goldstein-Gidoni and Daliot-Bul, "'Shall we Dansu?'" 64–67.

14 Koichi Iwabuchi, "Complicit Exoticism: Japan and Its Other," *Continuum* 8 (1994), 70.

15 William Tsutsui, *Japanese Popular Culture and Globalization* (Ann Arbor, MI: Association for Asian Studies, Inc., 2010), 10; Amy Shirong Lu, "The Many Faces of Internationalization in Japanese Anime," *animation: an interdisciplinary journal* 3 (2008), 172.

16 Mitsuhiro Yoshimoto, "The Difficulty of Being Radical: The Discipline of Film Studies and the Postcolonial World Order," *Boundary 2*, 18 (1991), 257.

17 Elliott Colla, *Conflicted Antiquities: Egyptology, Egyptomania, Egyptian Modernity* (Durham, NC and London: Duke University Press, 2007), loc. 139.

18 Published by the French Government, these volumes represent the labor of approximately 160 civilian scholars and scientists who accompanied Napoleon's military expedition to Egypt; another 2,000 artists and 400 engravers helped to illustrate and compile the volumes.

19 Andrew Robinson, *Cracking the Egyptian Code: The Revolutionary Life of Jean-François Champollion* (Oxford: Oxford University Press, 2012); Jean-Marcel Humbert, "Egyptomania: Fascination for Egypt and Its Expression in the Modern World," in *A Companion to Ancient Egyptian Art*, ed. Melinda K. Hartwig (Chichester, West Sussex: John Wiley & Sons, 2015), 466.

20 Diego Saglia, "Consuming Egypt: Appropriation and the Cultural Modalities of Romantic Luxury," *Nineteenth-Century Contexts* 24 (2002), 317, 321; Writers often attached Egyptianness to Edmund Burke's notion of the sublime, emphasizing "vastness, infinity and magnitude."

21 Saglia, "Consuming Egypt," 327–328.

22 Saglia, "Consuming Egypt," 329.

96 Dana Plank

23 Humbert, "Egyptomania," 467; Colla, *Conflicted Antiquities*, loc. 3224; Colla describes Egyptomania as inherently irrational, ever in danger of contaminating "the rationality of Egyptology" as a scientific mode of study.
24 Kawai, "Egyptological Landscape in Japan," 51.
25 Jiro Kondo and Sugihiko Uchida, "Egyptology: The Land of Pharaohs from a Japanese Viewpoint," *Orient* 36 (2001).
26 Kawai, "Egyptological Landscape in Japan," 52.
27 Kawai, "Egyptological Landscape in Japan," 55.
28 It has also led to a modern internet-meme renaissance for Medjed, an obscure god associated with Osiris whose image resembles a cartoon ghost.
29 Linda Phyllis Austern, "'Forreine Conceites and Wandering Devises': The Exotic, the Erotic, and the Feminine," in *The Exotic in Western Music*, ed. Jonathan D. Bellman (Boston, MA: Northeastern University Press, 1998), 28.
30 Jonathan D. Bellman, "Introduction," in *The Exotic in Western Music*, ed. Jonathan D. Bellman (Boston, MA: Northeastern University Press, 1998), xii.
31 Taylor, *Beyond Exoticism*, 57.
32 Ralph P. Locke, "Constructing the Oriental 'Other': Saint-Saëns's *Samson et Dalila*," *Cambridge Opera Journal* 3 (1991), 267. In the words of Locke and the anthropologist Francis Affergan, the use of augmented seconds is a caricature "emphasizing the [sedimentary] residues … of what differs most" from the music of the West.
33 Scott, "Orientalism and Musical Style," 313.
34 Taylor, *Beyond Exoticism*, 70; "Sometimes a minor key is just a minor key."
35 Ralph P. Locke, "Beyond the Exotic: How 'Eastern' is Aida?" *Cambridge Opera Journal* 17 (2005): 105–139. A lovely line from Filippo Filippi's review of *Aida* from 1872, quoted on page 105.
36 Ralph P. Locke, "Doing the Impossible: On the Musically Exotic," *Journal of Musicological Research* 27 (2008): 334–358 (here 352).
37 *Zoda's Revenge: StarTropics II* (Nintendo, 1994) for the NES also includes a level set in ancient Egypt. Yoshio Hirai and Takashi Kumegawa's music for the player's conversation with Cleopatra (after a mission to fetch her a pizza from "Caesar Hut") is also replete with augmented intervals.
38 Several walkthroughs suggested leveling up before attempting the Sand Tower, at which point the player can take on a few of the smaller enemies in that dungeon in order to raise money and purchase equipment upgrades to fight the stronger enemies in the dungeon. In my playthrough, I had to run away from more difficult creatures, frequently travel back and forth to town to stay at the inn and recover health (which requires tedious flipping of the disk on the FDS, and slow load times between these two regions). It took several hours of back and forth to finish this dungeon—at which point, Daisuke was already at level 11 out of a possible 13.
39 It is beyond the scope of this chapter to explore how many games it would take to establish generic conventions. I would argue that the first two *Dragon Quest* games (released in May 1986 and January 1987, respectively) were *the* foundational JRPGs, and the source of many (if not most) of the conventions of the genre.
40 Scott, "Orientalism and Musical Style," 313.
41 D.C. Parker, "Exoticism in Music in Retrospect," *Musical Quarterly* 3 (1917), 153.
42 Taylor, *Beyond Exoticism*, 11.
43 Track title taken from the official soundtrack for the game. *Final Fantasy V* was released for the Super Famicom, whose S-SMP audio processing unit and SPC700 chip allowed for eight channels (all labeled "SPC," because they had identical capabilities).
44 Saglia, "Consuming Egypt," 318.

6

MUSIC IN THE TIME OF VIDEO GAMES

Spelunking *Final Fantasy IV*

Julianne Grasso

You find your party in a misty, damp cave, with no clear way forward. There's music playing—a dance? At a moderate pace, in triple time, a harp bubbles upward in waves as strings and flute outline a glistening melody. An easygoing strum of a bass guitar and a drum set's tapping hi-hat seem to keep it all together from disappearing in a wisp.

With trepidation, you follow random paths through the dark labyrinth, until— *RRRIPPP*, a sound slices violently through the music's shimmering veil. With the harp and flute gone, the strings ascend in a wild flourish, leaving behind a trail of minor thirds. The sleepy bass and drums now awaken to action, pulsing even eighth notes in a quicker tempo.

You are still inside the cave's maze, but this sonic intrusion signaled an encroachment of another kind—an enemy attack. Now, the party is fending off an onslaught, accompanied not by flute and harp but brass and percussion, which punctuate a kind of urgency. This is no longer the music of mystery, but rather a more imminent form of danger, starkly lit against the harmonic penumbra of that delicate dance. Indeed, as the leader of the group, you must choose *now* whether you use a sword or shield, whether your comrade casts a spell, whether another scans for weaknesses, all amidst the enemy's attempts to do the same to you.

This fight music, like the fight itself, goes back and forth: C major, A minor, C major, A minor, etc. (It maps, perhaps, onto well-worn tropes of musical signification: major and minor, light and dark, good and evil.) When the enemies are finally vanquished, so is the music. The brass, which had carried the battle's imposing melodic presence, is now repurposed for a lighter victory fanfare, an Aeolian cadence in C (bVI-bVII-I) that sheds any impression of A minor.

The whimsical waltz returns, and your party marches onward.

98 Julianne Grasso

The scene described above, also diagrammed in Figure 6.1, is a typical turn of events in the video game *Final Fantasy IV* (Square Enix, 1991).[1] As a classic role-playing video game, *Final Fantasy IV* features a fantastical adventure within a virtual world accompanied by music. Exploring this world has its dangers, in the form of spontaneous, random encounters with enemies, also accompanied by a sudden shift in music. This musical change also marks a shift in the afforded interactions of play, which take on a greater deal of urgency in battle; in place of exploration and navigation, the player is now tasked with doling out strategic commands to their characters to fight and defeat enemy monsters.

Veteran *Final Fantasy* composer Nobuo Uematsu created *Final Fantasy IV*'s soundtrack, his first for the Super Nintendo/Famicom console, charting new sonic and stylistic territories beyond the square- and triangle-wave tones of the prior three games of the series. The swirling, dance-like cue "Into the Darkness" accompanies exploration of the cave, while the eclectic pop-rock cue "Fight 1" lends its upbeat energy to the dangers of combat.[2] Musical transitions—the "ripping" sound effect at the battle's opening, and the brassy fanfare at its close—act as framing devices that further clarify a distinction between the mode of exploration and the mode of battle.

My description of the musical events that occur alongside the game events was intended to be more than mere description, thick as it was. Rather, I meant to illustrate something fundamental about music as an aesthetic element of video games: music exists through time, and time in games is organized by narrative events facilitated by play. Music, while meant to be heard in the space of the cave, is also meant to accompany the actions of the player in that space. Navigating a cave, defending against enemy attacks, and so on, are interactions with their own ludic temporality, structured by the predetermined storyline of the game. And musical changes, with whatever narratives we might assign them, commingle with these other ludic temporalities in games. This chapter explores some of that commingling, using *Final Fantasy IV* as a model to show not just how music mediates time, but also how that mediation helps us more generally conceptualize player engagement in the ludonarrative fictions of video games.

Time and narrative are particularly multifaceted in RPGs, a genre known for both strong storytelling that immerses the player in characters and plot, and its style of strategic play that keeps the player more distant from actions and events in the game world. This sense of distance refers to the relationship between a player's physical gestures on the controller and the actions of an avatar; role-playing games of the 1990s typically mediated that relationship by letting the player control and command several characters at once, often through text-based menus that more closely resemble the interface of a computer operating system than an immersive virtual world. In these RPGs, the feel of the game is developed less through precise timing and dexterity of action, and more through strategy and text-based decision-making that facilitate the progression of a story.

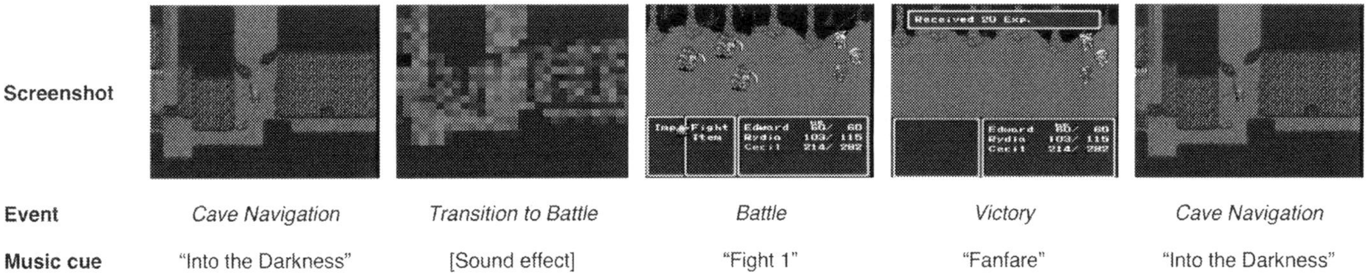

Screenshot					
Event	*Cave Navigation*	*Transition to Battle*	*Battle*	*Victory*	*Cave Navigation*
Music cue	"Into the Darkness"	[Sound effect]	"Fight 1"	"Fanfare"	"Into the Darkness"

FIGURE 6.1   A sequence of events in *Final Fantasy IV*

100 Julianne Grasso

We can thus broadly identify two timelines in video games, made clearly distinct in RPGs: that of the player's interactions (controlling characters, and so forth), and that of the embedded story those interactions facilitate. The relationship between these timelines can get quite a bit more complicated when overlaid with the various kinds of temporal distortions utilized in storytelling, such as flashbacks or momentary asides, which then require a differentiation between the temporality of *story* and the temporality of *storytelling*—not to mention the interactive role that a player brings. Such a distinction between the story and its telling is a familiar device in narratology, which delineates a *story* and a *discourse*.[3] As an example of this distinction, *Final Fantasy IV* begins with a rather cinematic, non-interactive scene in which the main character, Cecil, commands a fleet of airships returning home from a mission. Cecil is shown with his crew on deck, displaying regret for the violent actions he and his crew executed against innocent people. The violent scenes are shown as sepia-tinted flashbacks in a classic distinction of story from discourse—the events of the flashback occurred in the past with respect to the chronology of the game's fictional world, but are presented anachronistically in the present.

In importing this narrative distinction into video games with an interactive story, several scholars have found it useful to bundle together player interactions with games as a form of narrative discourse—after all, such interactions, particularly in role-playing games, facilitate a story's discursive unfolding.[4] The confounding element here is the indeterminacy of play, and thus the indeterminacy of that "discourse"—even with a rather determined story.[5] Despite the guided linear pathways that game design in RPGs often provide, a player might simply choose to meander, to pause, or to skip over one task to do another—not to mention to fail and restart over the course of negotiating progressively difficult challenges.

Indeed, temporality is malleable in the varying narrative flow of a video game, but one could easily find parallels in any kind of engagement with media, even in the form of text, where the act of reading is a kind of interactive facilitation. Consider the plot of *Final Fantasy IV*:

> After expressing regret for a devastating attack on the peaceful land of Mysidia, Cecil, Captain of the Red Wings fleet, is dismissed from his post. With his friend Kain, Cecil is now tasked by the King with delivering a package to the Village of Mist—a parcel revealed to be a bomb, which destroys the village. This explosion triggers a series of events in which Cecil wanders the world, the earthlike "Blue Planet," joined by various allies on a quest to ease his cognitive dissonance and, eventually, save the world. The main antagonist, Golbez, has since taken over the Red Wings and seeks all of the crystals of the world, including a vast underworld populated by dwarves, in order to reach the moon. Cecil and the party of characters he has met along the way aim to steal those crystals back. Unfortunately, they all fall into a literal trap set by Golbez, tumbling down into the underworld,

Spelunking *Final Fantasy IV* **101**

where learning of a legendary airship capable of lunar travel proves to be the "dwarf ex machina" they needed all along. Traveling to the moon on this ship, Cecil and company learn from a "Lunarian" sage called Fusoya that Cecil's father was a Lunarian, a race that also includes in its membership the genocidal maniac Zemus, who is hell-bent on taking over the Blue Planet. After defeating a giant robot that Zemus deployed to annihilate all life, Cecil learns that Golbez has been under the mind-control of Zemus, and is actually Cecil's brother—a turn of events not unlike the plot of a Star Wars film. Golbez and Fusoya defeat Zemus, who then resurrects in a more powerful form: Zeromus. At the moon's core, Cecil and his party, with the magical help of the thoughts and prayers of allies on earth, defeat Zeromus decisively. In a happy ending, Cecil and his girlfriend Rosa get married, becoming king and queen of Baron.

Just as a player might play through these events at an unpredictable pace, a reader might also vary their speed, reread parts, and engage with the text in otherwise inconsistent and nonlinear fashions.[6] (You might have not read it at all, intuiting that it contained no citation-worthy analysis.)

What I take to be particularly interesting about an indeterminate engagement with video games is not the effects that interaction has on the telling of a story, but rather how these different ludic temporalities shape and color the playthrough of that story. And unlike the text above, the virtual world of *Final Fantasy IV* brims with music—music for Cecil's fleet, for the kingdom of dwarves, for the desolate lunar landscape, for the antagonism of Golbez, for Zeromus's giant, and so on. Music fills the spaces of these virtual worlds, inviting players to experience a musical presence in the game's fiction.

In analyzing music in time, I take as my premise that music offers structures of temporal perception, making available to the "player-as-listener" a guide for the conscious perception of passing time as it relates to the narratives of play. Such a broad perspective necessarily draws on a rich history of theoretical conceptions of time in music, a proper survey of which lies well beyond the scope of this essay. The topic of time and narrative in music has seen a number of different approaches, from the literary (as in Byron Almén's *A Theory of Musical Narrative*) to the philosophical and psychological (Christopher Hasty's *Meter as Rhythm*), to the indefatigably taxonomical (Jonathan Kramer's *The Time of Music*).[7] Of course, much of this kind of analysis considers music-narrative perception without accompanying sensory stimuli, let alone the particular graphics and haptics of video games. Film music scholars have at least addressed the dimension of the screen, theorizing how music contributes to the creation of film worlds and their narratives.[8] Music has been empirically shown to alter or enhance the perception of a narrative scene in combination with visual input.[9] There is reason to believe this same effect exists for video games; Karen Collins has argued that the tactile-audio-visual experience in games forms a meaningful and memorable sensory

102 Julianne Grasso

fusion, which she terms "kinesonic synchresis" (after Michel Chion's term "synchresis" of audio and visual in film).[10]

In short, there's something about musical experiences that elucidates narrative experiences. I aim to keep things simple here, relying on some of the most basic concepts of both music and narrative. Much of my thinking comes from work based in cognition, as well as a somewhat phenomenological perspective of musical time, as might be gleaned from my player-centric opening descriptions that outline the experiential, moment-by-moment contexts informing the perception and prediction of musical (and non-musical) events.[11]

In the spirit of a discussion on temporality, I'll deliberately stretch out here with a longer glance at *Final Fantasy IV*'s world. Notwithstanding my evocative description of the game in my opening vignette, *Final Fantasy IV*'s 16-bit universe is actually composed rather simply with two-dimensional maps, sprite-based characters, and relatively static visual backdrops. Such evidence of its early position in the trajectory of video game technology—it was released in 1991 as a relatively early title for the Super Famicom and Super Nintendo Entertainment System (SNES)—is paralleled in the sound quality of the music. While many modern games now feature live-recorded, richly scored orchestral music, the soundtrack for *Final Fantasy IV* consists of 44 brief musical loops made with synthesized instruments over eight (at most) simultaneously sounding channels, which must also account for sound effects. These musical cues correspond to either generic narrative events, places in the game world, or both; there is rarely a moment of silence in *Final Fantasy IV*.[12]

Despite the omnipresence of music, *Final Fantasy IV* might seem to be an unremarkable choice for a chapter about time in role-playing games, particularly given some of the interesting ways that other, similar RPGs have used time thematically. Within the same series, *Final Fantasy VI* (1994) incorporated a rich use of flashbacks, timed quests, and good deal of narrative development that is reflected in the music, also composed by Uematsu. (See Ryan Thompson's chapter in this volume.) *Chrono Trigger* (1995) uses a mechanism of time travel in narratively innovative ways. Developments in gaming technology since have unleashed many creative ways of using music to outline, augment, or attenuate temporal structures of more recent games, and I could have chosen any one of those to bolster an argument about musically mediated time.

But I tread carefully here, as noting the 16-bit capabilities of the SNES as "limited" is only to participate in the same tired teleology of games as evolving alongside technological developments; it is a rhetoric wielded in capitalist aims to sell new gaming systems, forcibly deprecate the old ones, and remake the old games in "HD."[13] I focus on *Final Fantasy IV* because it demonstrates some of the basic structures that have defined the RPG genre; as the first of Square's well regarded RPG contributions for the SNES, it establishes conventions of RPG gameplay and musical accompaniment. And while even music in modern video games is repetitive and systematic, their underlying computational procedures are more deftly hidden by the sounds of "real" recorded instruments and very fine-grained musical changes. *Final Fantasy IV* and its music, on the other hand, lay bare both the constraints and the possibilities of video games as a medium of fiction.

Even if, as philosopher Susanne Langer put it, music "makes time audible," theories of time in video games typically have not made much use of music or sound.[14] As mentioned above, those interested in time usually work with the traditional story/discourse distinction to elucidate the ways that play complicates traditional narrative theory. In this vein, game scholar Jesper Juul has characterized the story/discourse distinction as Play Time (the actual clock-time it takes for a player to interact with the game) and Event Time (the in-game, narrative time that has elapsed).[15] For instance, a player may take three clocked hours of Play Time to complete a task that, in the game world (Event Time), is presumed to have taken a few minutes, or perhaps a few years, etc. Juul connects the two timelines by mapping actions and events, representing the process by which a player's actions are perceived as actions in the game world. As Juul describes, games that are more action-based—like first-person shooters or racing games—usually have a consistent 1:1 mapping between play time and event time (Figure 6.2), where the player's actions (e.g., pressing the "A" button) have a direct and immediate influence within the game world (e.g., shooting a missile at an enemy). In role-playing games like *Final Fantasy IV*, actions like choosing a command from a menu typically pause the game and render that action some time later, thereby opening up that distinction more clearly (Figure 6.3).[16]

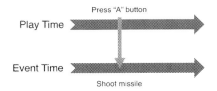

FIGURE 6.2 A 1:1 mapping between a player's action and an event in the game world. Adapted from Jesper Juul, "Introduction to Game Time" (2004)

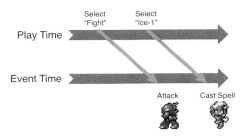

FIGURE 6.3 An approximate mapping of the delay between a player's action and corresponding event in the game world in *Final Fantasy IV*

104 Julianne Grasso

Other scholars have expanded on Juul's distinctions; for example, adding the consideration "real-world" clock-time as separate from time clocked in the virtual world.[17] Still, the distinction between play time and event time is a core governing structure to these theories, and so I'll apply it to *Final Fantasy IV* to give a context for adding music to a discussion from which it is typically absent. Figure 6.4 applies Juul's model to the formal diagram of the narrative sequence from the introduction of this chapter.

In the cave, the player's actions pertaining to roaming around and exploring have a 1:1 correspondence between play time and event time, much like the action games described earlier.[18] With every press of the control pad, the character in the game world moves in the corresponding direction. The straight vertical arrow represents a mapping from a press on the control pad to the in-game movement of Cecil's sprite. During the brief transition between cave and battle, play time is essentially "paused" as this moment is non-interactive and out of the player's control—yet, it still constitutes an "event." On the other hand, during the victory sequence after battle is completed, event time is paused as the player reads through the text denoting spoils won, pressing a button to resume cave exploration. As diagrammed earlier, the diagonal arrow mapping for battle mode reflects the temporal delays between choosing actions in a menu (play) and those actions appearing as events.[19]

To this framework, music adds an extra complication. By describing how the music sounds in the opening, I aimed to give a sense of how music simultaneously accompanies the exploration of the cave while outlining temporal structures in the form of musical metaphors of motion as change over time (ascending harps, oscillating triads). More broadly, music also signals events in the game narratives by marking those changes with musical ones. This sequence delineates two forms of musical temporality—the first, which I'll call an *affective* temporality, concerns the intra-musical workings of each cue that bestow a feeling of motion in time, and the second, a *narrative* temporality, relates to game events through synchronized musical changes.

The musical cues for both the cave navigation ("Into the Darkness") and the battle ("Fight 1") enact their own affective temporalities that shape these play modes. Time in "Into the Darkness" is markedly different from time in "Fight 1"—for one thing, the former is in triple meter, the latter in duple. Combinations of other elements of rhythmic activity, harmonic functionality, and melodic contour further contribute to an affective temporal difference between these musical tracks, which even further sets these modes of play apart as temporally unique structures. Having established that the affective differences already mark these tunes as distinct, the interruption of the battle sequence coordinates with a large-scale musical change, which further distinguishes them through the processes of narrative temporality. What follows is a descriptive analysis of these musical cues, which will further nuance our formal mapping.

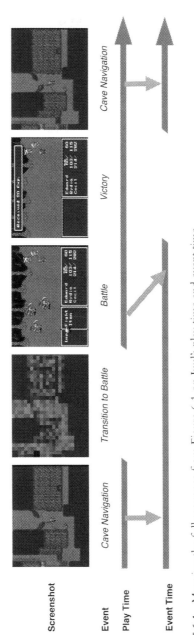

FIGURE 6.4 Mapping the full sequence from Figure 6.1 on Juul's play time and event time

106 Julianne Grasso

Cave

"Into the Darkness" is aptly named; its four measures of introduction seem to purposefully obfuscate both key and time, oscillating indistinctly between a G-flat major triad and a C major triad, sonorities a tritone apart, from keys which share only F as a common note (Ex. 6.1). While this relationship could be heard in F minor as a Neapolitan predominant chord (G flat) to dominant (C) to predict F, the oscillation attenuates any cadential pull toward F (while conveniently making the arrival of F minor aurally unremarkable). The loop proper indeed outlines F minor, with a strong pull from G flat as an upper neighbor. Bolstered by percussion, flute and strings in measure 5 evoke a clear triple time, along with the harp's ascending arpeggios that churn a flurry of rhythmic activity and motion. Beneath, the bass guitar offers rhythmic and harmonic grounding. The triple time, modal coloring, and instrumentation together activate a constellation of narrative musical tropes associated with darkness.[20]

The cave environment featuring "Into the Darkness" indeed appears to be gloomy and somewhat winding, qualities we might also broadly locate in this music as we see it on the page (if we are trained to do so). But music doesn't merely show, it also tells; the process by which we move from the first four measures of rather free-floating harmonic and metrical bounds to the relatively stable triple-meter measures in F minor tells a kind of narrative—of finding one's way, of seeing a path, and then successfully navigating contours that at first seem winding and confusing. Further, with every repetition of this loop, the player develops a memory for the music, and a set of reinforced expectations for what comes next. Such expectations effect a sense of "forward" listening that keeps the player engaged, if not fully entrained to the groove that is deepened with each loop. This "listening ahead" is implicit, especially for players whose attention is not directly on the music, but nonetheless forms a part of temporal awareness. Discussing the effects of such repetition, Elizabeth Margulis notes that "repetition makes it possible for us to experience a sense of expanded present characterized not by the explicit knowledge that x will occur at time point y, but rather by a heightened sense of orientation and involvement."[21] Music offers players a process by which they can apprehend the world around them—or, more accurately, the game world around Cecil and his party. This affective temporality thereby draws the player into the fiction of the game simply by projecting the narratives of this space—of exploring and navigating a dark and perilous cave.[22]

Battle

Margulis refers to the effect of repetition as a feeling of "inevitability" which offers a sense of "rightness" about what we're hearing.[23] In other words, repetition both creates and confirms aural expectations, which feels like a sensory affirmation.

EX. 6.1 The introduction and opening few bars of "Into the Darkness" from *Final Fantasy IV*

108 Julianne Grasso

It thus follows that, after countless cycles through the "Into the Darkness" loop, the sudden interruption of battle is *especially* jarring. As the musical accompaniment for a random encounter, "Fight 1" is named so as to differentiate it from other music that accompanies more difficult and narratively specific battles, such as boss fights. The interruptive sound effect appears suddenly and with little warning, immediately causing the ongoing loop to cease, regardless of where in the music the loop occurred (Ex. 6.2). This kind of violent musical upheaval is par for the course in 1990s RPGs. Even those that feature non-random, visible enemies—as in some of Square's other efforts like *Chrono Trigger* and *Super Mario RPG* (1996)—still use music to illustrate the effect of a sudden, surprising attack. This moment of shift is affectively charged in this call for attention, confirming for the player that something has changed.

The music that follows immediately is another sort of introduction, a wildly ascending diminished arpeggio in the strings, seemingly out of time, yet now distinctly musical. Then, just as in "Into the Darkness," some temporal clarity emerges: the two-measure pulsing in the bass, between A and G. This beat sets the tone in several ways: the pitch pattern outlines the Aeolian mode, which, along with the instrumentation, is a stylistic marker for rock music, whose generic associations with masculinity and aggression meaningfully resonate with a situation of combat.[24]

Along with an external appeal to rock genres, the opening pulse is a familiar gambit found in many of Uematsu's battle themes for *Final Fantasy,* offering another layer of meaning that draws on reference. By drawing on conventions both within and without the spheres of video game music, Uematsu's cue creates an access point for the player's musical subjectivity, not just strung along through an immediate phenomenological temporality, but in a mode of recollection that is centered in the experience of music. Lawrence Zbikowski has referred to these two kinds of hearings in terms of "embodied immersion" and "detached reflection" in works by Toru Takemitsu.[25] Being in the moment of musical time can evoke feelings of embodied immersion when the listener connects musical motion to physical motion, a sensation that is certainly possible in the percussive and tempestuous battle music. On the other hand, moments of recognized musical reference, internal or external, lead the listener into a detached reflection "away from temporal experience as it is constructed by a succession of musical events and … into time as it is constructed by the words, thoughts, and ideas that populate our recollections."[26] While video game players are likely less active listeners than Zbikowski's imagined Takemitsu listener, this "detached" experience of musical time can be useful when thinking of how the player might come to apprehend the fictional narrative in which they play. A player's recollections and recognitions of styles and references, including recognizing the cue itself, informs play and the listening process more broadly. In other words, players need not be paying much attention to the musical processes

EX. 6.2 The first half of "Fight 1," the primary battle music of *Final Fantasy IV*

of "Fight 1" or "Into the Darkness" when these cues become familiar enough to signal all of the meanings and associations that are set to unfold amongst their musical processes.

The victory fanfare that follows a successful battle also comes by way of interruption, though not surprise, occurring just as the last enemy is vanquished, no matter where in the cue the music is. The fanfare (shown in Ex. 6.3), with brass in sharp triplet rhythms, is also typical of fanfares as a musical topic with a long history in actual military trumpet and horn calls that were then referenced as a narrative device in various music genres.[27] But perhaps more salient to *Final Fantasy* series players is its consistency, as the very same victory music appears in almost every title in the franchise. In this iteration, the almost disco-like bass keeps this music somewhat more in line with the style of the battle music that came before it, but it is otherwise a clear signaling device that marks the battle's end and the

EX. 6.3 The victory fanfare cue at the conclusion of a successful battle in *Final Fantasy IV*. This loop will repeat until the player has read through the text denoting the acquisition of points and spoils

Spelunking *Final Fantasy IV*   **111**

oncoming return of the player's prior exploration. The post-fanfare loop music is short and relatively static in that it simply outlines that same Aeolian cadence over and over while the player reads the list of the party's spoils—certainly a prime case for a "detached reflection" engagement with the music. The music then returns to that whimsical opening to "Into the Darkness," and players can similarly restart where they left off.

With an understanding of how music can mediate time—and thus presence—in a game world, I turn back to Jesper Juul's model of play time and event time. As shown in Figure 6.5, I've added visualizations of both musical narrative time and affective time based on how I have thus far described the music. Musical narrativity, considered here as simply the synchronization of musical changes with changes of play mode, is represented as modular loops, a paradigm adapted from Elizabeth Medina-Gray's work on musical modularity in later games.[28] Musical affective temporality is approximated as different kinds of "wavy" arrows that signify a difference in the feeling of time, whether more winding ("Into the Darkness"), more forward-leaning ("Fight 1"), or statically looping ("Fanfare"). These affect-arrows show that the feeling of forward-moving musical time is possible despite the actuality of constant looping.

Now that the model is marvelously disorderly, we might wonder whether such visual diagramming of ludic temporalities could account for player experiences. Reducing games to play-vs.-story dichotomies obfuscates a great deal of the realities of play—how we learn the rules and controls, the feelings of being in the world, the frustrations of failures and joys of success, let alone our musical subjectivities. Play is, indeed, marvelously disorderly—a messiness that music brings to the fore. Jesper Juul's model focuses on a more objective mapping between time as a scientific, measurable phenomenon able to be deposited into minutes and seconds, and the narrative time of events happening in the story of a video game. In aiming to account for temporal experience, he appeals to Mihaly Csikszentmihalyi's concept of *flow* states.[29] In short, tasks in games can be variably challenging or boring, and such variability will alter or even eliminate our perception of time passing. (A state of flow can occur when there is a good balance between challenge level and skill level.) Juul nonetheless notes the limitations of this approach: "flow can only explain games as a challenging activity in play time but ignores the projected world, the event time."[30]

But, as I have tried to show, a player's perception of time in video games is not solely a function of their enjoyment of the tasks of play, but also mediated by the musical time that permeates the game world. It is through time that music models processes of motion and action, creating an affective temporality that plays alongside the player. Even if the random encounters of *Final Fantasy IV* become too easy for the player, the music betrays no change in urgency or intensity. "Fight 1" is just as it ever was—dangerous and imminent, and we can't help but be immersed in what Margulis calls the "expanded present" of that imminence.[31] Indeed, Csikszentmihalyi has linked musical repetition with his notion of flow,

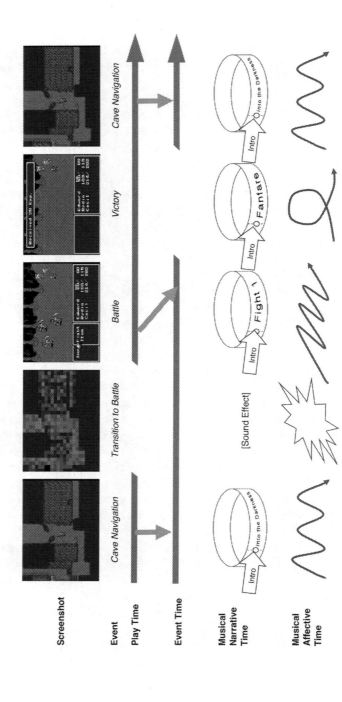

FIGURE 6.5 Messing up Juul's model with music, as promised

Spelunking *Final Fantasy IV* **113**

giving credence to the idea that these looping musical cues might indeed help modulate the challenge and enjoyment of video games.[32]

My goal is not necessarily to refute Juul's models, but rather to take seriously the interactive pretenses of video games in which the joystick seems to disappear and player actions appear to meld with character actions. In this way, musical mediation of the mapping between play time actions to event time narratives is rather a way of making *immediate* the game world and its events, allowing even the player of an RPG to feel the intensity of battle as an intensity of the relationship between self and game, character and world.

Postscript

In 2012, Square Enix released the first in a series of retrospective rhythm games called *Theatrhythm: Final Fantasy*, announced as "a celebration of the greatest musical moments from the history of the FINAL FANTASY series," promising us that the music will "reawaken the magic and memories" of games past.[33] Rhythm games involve a visual display of cues for player input, timed to the rhythm of music.[34] *Theatrhythm* merged rhythm game mechanics with the familiar gameplay from the series, including a battle mode that made rhythm tapping, rather than menu navigation, the interface of combat. Mapping musical activity directly to the timing of offensive attacks is uniquely bewildering; the act of encountering and fighting an enemy is made at once more abstracted by being musical, and more immediate. *Theatrhythm* casts the temporal nature of music as key to the "magic and memories" of the series, as if the unfolding of music itself is the story of each game—or the story of its play. Music thus no longer mediates the mapping between play time and event time, but rather collapses these timelines onto its own structure of temporality—to play is to enact the music, and the music forms the events of play. In this way, Square Enix seems to capitalize on music's ability to not just mediate the temporalities of play, but also to *inscribe* it, to link itself inexorably with a player's experience of a virtual world. By tapping along with the music, then, we find ourselves indeed revisiting a history of play, one captured by those swirling musical narratives that connected with our own.

Notes

The analyses in this chapter were first presented in a conference talk given at the Society for Music Theory's annual meeting in 2015 and the North American Conference on Video Game Music in 2016. In expanding that talk into this chapter, the author would like to acknowledge the fruitful discussions had at these conferences, especially with Jesse Kinne, Elizabeth Medina-Gray, William Ayers, and Steven Reale.

1 *Final Fantasy IV*, produced by Hironobu Sakaguchi for Square Enix (then Square) and published for the Super Famicom in Japan, was released in North America (for the Super Nintendo Entertainment System) as *Final Fantasy II*, as neither the bona fide

114 Julianne Grasso

Final Fantasy II nor *III* had yet been localized for release. For the purposes of this chapter, the two versions are essentially the same.

2 For track titles, I use the translations from one of the English-language soundtrack releases, *Final Fantasy IV: Official Soundtrack* (Tokyopop Pictures, 2002), audio CD.

3 These terms originated in Russian formalism (as "fabula" and "syuzhet"), but are also attributed to French literary theorist Gerard Genette. See *Narrative Discourse: An Essay on Method* (Ithaca, NY: Cornell University Press, 1980).

4 This includes Jesper Juul, "Introduction to Game Time," in *First Person: New Media as Story, Performance, and Game*, ed. Noah Wardrip-Fruin and Pat Harrigan (Cambridge, MA: MIT Press, 2004): 131–142; and Lluís Anyó, "Narrative Time in Video Games and Films: From Loop to Travel in Time," *GAME: The Italian Journal of Game Studies* 4 (2015). www.gamejournal.it/anyo_narrative_time.

5 To even consider games in narratological terms has been an historical source of debate. The dialectic of ludic vs. narrative in game studies is well illustrated in Matthew Wilhelm Kapell's edited volume *The Play Versus Story Divide in Game Studies: Critical Essays* (Jefferson, NC: McFarland, 2016).

6 Checking this endnote from the text proper is one method of nonlinear engagement with the text. Incidentally, such a manner of engagement forms some of literary critic Roland Barthes's ideas in *Le Plaisir du texte* (Paris: Éditions du Seuil, 1973). Various forms of narrative engagement are well illustrated in Umberto Eco's *Six Walks in the Fictional Woods* (Cambridge, MA: Harvard University Press, 1994).

7 Byron Almén, *A Theory of Musical Narrative* (Bloomington: Indiana University Press, 2008); Christopher Hasty, *Meter as Rhythm* (New York: Oxford University Press, 1997); Jonathan D. Kramer, *The Time of Music: New Meanings, New Temporalities, New Listening Strategies* (New York: Schirmer, 1988).

8 Notable examples include Claudia Gorbman's *Unheard Melodies: Narrative Film Music* (Bloomington: Indiana University Press, 1987) and Michel Chion's *Audiovision: Sound on Screen* (New York: Columbia University Press, 1994).

9 See work by Annabel Cohen, e.g., "Congruence-Association Model of Music and Multimedia: Origin and Evolution," in *The Psychology of Music in Multimedia*, ed. Siu-Lan Tan, Annabel J. Cohen, Scott D. Lipscomb, and Roger A. Kendall (New York: Oxford University Press, 2013).

10 See Karen Collins, *Playing with Sound: A Theory of Interacting with Sound and Music in Video Games* (Cambridge, MA: MIT Press, 2013).

11 In Edmund Husserl's development of phenomenology, a musical melody offered for him an example of understanding temporal perception as a consciousness of continuing "objects" (in which objects are the notes moving from one to the next). Music theorist David Lewin expanded on Husserlian phenomenology to dig deeper into music as it moves through time, aiming to account for levels of conscious awareness of various musical phenomena that influence, predict, and look back on other musical phenomena as they are iterated through time. See David Lewin, "Music Theory, Phenomenology, and Modes of Perception," *Music Perception* 3 (1986): 327–392.

12 But when there *is* silence in *Final Fantasy IV,* it opens up the potential for poignant moments. Dana Plank has investigated the role of silence in video games, presenting on the topic at the North American Conference on Video Game Music: "On Silence in Video Games," at Texas Christian University, January 17, 2015.

13 Not including its sequel, *The After Years* (2008), or the prequel-sequel that was wedged in between the two, *Interlude* (2011), *Final Fantasy IV* has been "rereleased" nine times as of writing, most recently in 2017.

14 From Susanne Langer, *Feeling and Form: A Theory of Art* (New York: Scribner, 1953), 110.

15 Juul, "Introduction to Game Time," 131–142.

Spelunking *Final Fantasy IV* **115**

16 In this mapping, I deliberately conflate the pressing of a button with the menu selection. I could have instead noted that the selection itself is a kind of game event, but, in keeping with the premise of role-playing games as being based on narrative, I've collapsed the categories to better show the delay between an action of the player and an event in the fiction of the game world. With regards to the timing of these physical gestures and music, Jesse Kinne has argued that musical groove can influence player actions in "Groove Mediates Ludo and Diegetic Temporalities in *Heroes of Might and Magic*," University of Texas, Austin, January 15, 2017.

17 For example, José P. Zagal and Michael Mateas delineated a "real time" of the player as well as a "coordination time" that marks the regulation of multiple interactive agents (as in turn-based play), in "Time in Video Games: A Survey and Analysis," *Simulation & Gaming* 41(6) (December 1, 2010): 844–868. https://doi.org/10.1177/10468 78110375594.

18 I'll note that menus are accessible in this mode, and interactions with these menus could be considered as a pause in event time while players go about the tasks of resource allocation, battle planning, post-battle restoration, etc. I nonetheless want to focus on exploration as a relatively immediate and "active" form of play (if sometimes tentative and meandering).

19 *Final Fantasy IV* introduced a mechanism patented as "Active Time Battle" ("ATB") that calculated timings for combat events based on individual character attributes, their equipped materials, incidental status effects, and other features—hence the rather haphazard mapping between play time and event time. The variability in ATB calculations causes the mappings between play time and event time to be somewhat unpredictable, which is why Figure 6.5 offers an approximation rather than a precise time delay.

20 Not least of which are the similarities to Saint-Säens's famous tone poem *Danse Macabre,* which begins with similar metrical ambiguity and dissonant tritones.

21 Elizabeth Margulis, *On Repeat: How Music Plays the Mind* (New York: Oxford University Press, 2014), 9.

22 Not every exploration or navigation-based track in *Final Fantasy IV* features this level of tonal ambiguity or metrical difference that lies in stark contrast with battle music—some explorable places sound quite brassy and percussive, closer in time, tone, and timbre to the musical materials of "Fight 1."

23 Margulis, *On Repeat,* 115.

24 For a survey of some of the modal patterns frequently found in rock music, see Nicole Biamonte, "Triadic Modal and Pentatonic Patterns in Rock Music," *Music Theory Spectrum* 32(2) (2010).

25 Lawrence Zbikowski, "Musical Time, Embodied and Reflected," in *Music in Time: Phenomenology, Perception, Performance*, ed. Suzannah Clark and Alexander Rehding (Cambridge, MA: Harvard University Press, 2016): 33–54.

26 Zbikowski, "Musical Time," 35.

27 For more on musical topics, see, for example, Raymond Monelle, *The Musical Topic: Hunt, Military, and Pastoral* (Bloomington: Indiana University Press, 2006).

28 See Elizabeth Medina-Gray, "Modular Structure and Function in Early 21st-Century Video Game Music" (PhD dissertation, Yale University, 2014).

29 See Mihaly Csikszentmihalyi, *Flow: The Psychology of Optimal Experience* (New York: Harper, 2008).

30 Juul, "Introduction to Game Time," 139.

31 Margulis, *On Repeat,* 9.

32 Asserting that "the flow experience can be found in activities other than games" (37), Csikszentmihalyi interviews music composers in one of his earlier works on the subject, *Beyond Boredom and Anxiety: Experiencing Flow in Work and Play* (San Francisco,

116 Julianne Grasso

CA: Jossey-Bass, 1975), asserting that musical activity is one of the intrinsically reward-
ing tasks that can bring about a state of flow.

33 From promotional copy on Square Enix's website. http://na.square-enix.com/us/
games/theatrhythm-final-fantasy. Accessed March 31, 2018.

34 Rhythm games have received attention in recent years from a number of scholars working from different approaches to address the coordination of the mind and body in
musical play. See, for instance, Peter Shultz, "Rhythm Sense: Modality and Enactive
Perception in *Rhythm Heaven*," in *Music Video Games: Performance, Politics, and Play*,
ed. Michael Austin (New York: Bloomsbury Academic, 2016): 251–274, as well as
Kiri Miller's monograph *Playable Bodies: Dance Games and Intimate Media* (New York:
Oxford University Press, 2017).

7

OPERATIC CONVENTIONS AND EXPECTATIONS IN *FINAL FANTASY VI*

Ryan Thompson

Final Fantasy VI (1994, hereafter *FFVI),* released at the peak of the 16-bit era for the Super Nintendo in late 1994, has long been a fan favorite, in part because of its iconic opera sequence.[1] In this chapter, I argue that the opera sequence is not merely a novelty, but rather that the entire game is organized around notions of theatrical—and especially operatic—production.[2] Opera helps differentiate *FFVI* from previous games in the series, and offers a rationale for its unique structure. While not presented as an opera directly, *FFVI* shares much in common with the art form. Specifically, the ways in which characters are introduced to the player, the leitmotivic approach to the game's score, and the game's epilogue (which hints that the entirety of the game might be a staged production) are all indebted to stage conventions. Furthermore, the game's plot broadly mirrors the structure of the in-game opera, inviting players to consider other areas of operatic influence.[3]

In exploring *Final Fantasy VI*, it is helpful to position the game within the context of the entire *Final Fantasy* series. Though each title in the series is independent (that is, world geography and individuals in one game do not exist and therefore are not referenced in sequels), there are a few connecting threads that unify the games into a cohesive franchise. The plot to most of the early titles (*I, III, IV, V*) are all largely based around protecting crystals of earth, fire, water, and wind; additionally, certain types of magical creatures recur throughout the series. Similarly, the gameplay in most of the early *Final Fantasy* titles revolves around a "job system": the first and third games allow players to select a party of four characters composed of various job classes—one such party might have a fighter, a thief, a monk, and a white mage.[4]

Final Fantasy IV places limits on this class-based model of gameplay by permanently assigning each character within the game's plot one of those job classes. The game features an ensemble cast in which characters rotate in and out of the player's

118 Ryan Thompson

party in the course of the plot; as a result, rather than having the option to select a party that suits one's own style, players must learn to manage the diverse party types scripted by the game's events. *Final Fantasy V* combines the flexibility of the third game's party system with the plot-directed system of the fourth. It boasts perhaps the most complex job system of the franchise: players may not merely switch jobs at will (as in *Final Fantasy III*), but may also learn the abilities of one job and apply them to another. For instance, a Knight may learn the White Mage's curative magic, or a Black Mage might gain the health pool of the sturdier Monk.

Final Fantasy VI differentiates itself from previous entries by significantly departing from these conventions. Though characters are all assigned a job class and a custom skill—Locke the "Adventurer" can steal, Edgar the "Machinist" can use tools, etc.—those abilities are largely rendered moot when, near the beginning of the game's second act, every character has equal access to magic and equipment choice is less tied directly to character class.[5] The result is that players can, if they choose, control a party of super wizards who are ultimately not significantly differentiated from one another—a ludic reduction that would come to define the next few games in the franchise.[6]

In another departure from the linear plots of previous games, *FFVI*'s second world map (known as the World of Ruin) is a nonlinear experiment that invites players to explore the new landscape on their own terms, without pointing players in a particular direction. This alteration of familiar JRPG plot structures (normally a linear sequence of events) allows the player to choose which characters to develop; if a player chooses not to play with a specific character in the second world, that character's personal story will simply go unresolved. Failing to recruit a character completely will cause them to be omitted from the game's epilogue. Having (mostly) done away with the job system and given the world map new context, all that remained for *Final Fantasy VI* to clearly step away from its predecessors was a new unifying aesthetic. Instead of organizing a plot around four elemental crystals, the game instead is organized in the style of its most memorable scene—an in-game opera.

About one-third of the way through *Final Fantasy VI*, the characters require the use of an airship owned by Setzer Gabbiani, known as the "Wandering Gambler." He intends to kidnap Maria, the star of the opera house's current production, and, in one of the game's more spectacular coincidences, Maria just so happens to strongly resemble Celes Chere, a member of the player's party. To orchestrate a meeting between the adventurers and Setzer, Celes substitutes for Maria as the star of the opera in the hopes of being kidnapped instead. The game's part-playable, part-cutscene opera sequence is the result. The opera sequence runs for approximately 25 minutes and consists of three major scenes: first, the protagonist Draco, champion of the West, is introduced on the field of battle, singing of his love—who is, like the original singer, also named Maria. The second scene of the opera mirrors the first; Maria's home has been overtaken by Prince Ralse of the East, and she sings of her love and longing for Draco. The final scene is intended

Operatic Conventions in *Final Fantasy VI*   **119**

to portray a duel between Draco and Prince Ralse, but the opera is interrupted by a monster attack: Ultros the octopus, who functions throughout the larger game as a recurring comedic villain, shows up to wreak havoc on the production.

The ensuing showdown between Ultros and the player's party begins on the catwalks above the production. When the player reaches the monster, everyone falls to the stage, and the battle concludes in front of the audience, with a ham-fisted attempt on the part of the Impresario to improvise it into the plot of the opera.[7] This interruption is then itself interrupted, this time by Setzer, who kidnaps Celes-as-Maria in a surprise close to the sequence. As the curtain falls, a confused Impresario tells the audience to return later for part two of this new twist on the opera.[8] This sequence of events—the introduction of main characters, showdown between main characters, and wildly unexpected departure from reasonable predictions of the outcome of that showdown—neatly mirrors the narrative arc of the whole of *Final Fantasy VI*. The game's story (which following sections summarize in more detail) is divided into three major arcs, which this chapter refers to as acts, each beginning with the same event: a character waking up in a bed, confused about how they arrived there.

Another instance of operatic structure is the way the game introduces playable characters: all but the character sprite fades to black and a textual description of the character appears beneath. These descriptions are brief—just enough to assist the player in remembering all the different members of the cast, similar to the character descriptions found at the beginning of many opera scores (see, for example, Figure 7.1).[9] The notion of these character introductions borrowing from operatic conceits is reinforced during the opera sequence, when the Impresario's sprite appears on stage in the center as the overture begins to play, despite the Impresario having just taken his seat in the rear balcony with the other characters—his sprite is used as an indication that he authored the program notes to the opera, displayed onscreen for the player's benefit before the show begins (see Figure 7.2). When new characters are introduced, the player is given the opportunity to rename them, a common convention in Japanese role-playing games of the era.[10] *Final Fantasy VI* plays with this ludic convention and ties it back into traditions of the theater as part of the game's epilogue.

At the end of the game, the camera fades to black, and an image of a book's pages turning appears and then fades. Items representing the cast are shown one at a time—a two-headed coin bearing the faces of twin brothers Edgar and Sabin Figaro, flowers from the opera sequence for Celes, etc. As each item is shown, the name for each character chosen by the player is presented with the word "as," and replaced in much larger text with the official name of the character, regardless of player choice. "Ryan as" (etc.) fades to "Locke Cole." Put another way, the game foregrounds the idea that a player names the character for their own unique staging (that is, playthrough) of the production, not for all players.[11] Maria the opera singer shares a similar ambiguity—is Maria the name of the musical performer, the character within the opera, or both? This combined with the epilogue's opening image of the turning book—representing a libretto—appears to suggest that

RINALDO

Opera in tre Atti.

PERSONAGGI.

GOFFREDO, capitano generale dell' armata Christiana.   Alto.

ALMIRENA, sua figlia, destinata sposa a Rinaldo.   Soprano.

RINALDO, heroe del campo.   Soprano.

EUSTAZIO, fratello di Goffredo.   Alto.

ARGANTE, rè di Gierusalemme, amante d'Armida.   Basso.

ARMIDA, incantatrice, regina di Damasco.   Soprano.

Mago Christiano.   Alto.

Vorwort.

RINALDO ist die erste einer langen Reihe Opern, welche Händel für die Londoner Bühne schrieb, und eine der allerschönsten. Componirt in etwa 14 Tagen, wurde dieselbe am 24. Februar vu im Haymarket.Theater mit allgemeinem Beifall aufgeführt.

Der Verfasser des Textes war ein Engländer, Aaron Hill, der Director jenes Theaters, und Giacomo Rossi übertrug das englische Gedicht in's Italienische.

Von dem Autograph ist nur wenig erhalten, aber das vollständige Werk liegt vor in Händel's Handexemplar, hin und wieder von ihm corrigirt. In dem Anfangs- und Schlussritornell der letzten Arie des 2. Acts „Vo for'guerra" (p.78.79) steht zweimal in den Linien statt der Noten geschrieben „Cembalo." Dies waren die Stellen, an welchen Händel sein glänzendes Talent für Improvisation zeigte.

Preface.

RINALDO is the first of a long series of Operas that Handel wrote for the London stage, and one of the most beautiful. It was composed in about a fortnight, and first performed on the 24th of February 1711 at the Haymarket, with general applause.

The author of the poem was an Englishman, Aaron Hill, then the Director of the Haymarket Theatre, and Giacomo Rossi translated it into Italian.

But little is extant of the composer's autograph; but the complete work is preserved in his conducting score, which is here and there corrected by him. In the concluding air of the second act "Vo far'guerra" (p.78.79) there is twice written, in the commencing and concluding ritornello "Cembalo" instead of the notes, in the lines. These were the passages in which Handel showed his brilliant talent for improvisation.

LEIPZIG, Jan. 1, 1874.

FIGURE 7.1   Front matter from score to Handel's *Rinaldo* (1711)

the entire game is actually a staged production.[12] After each name is shown, a brief vignette starring the character in question plays, in the spirit of the curtain call following a theatrical performance.

The score to *Final Fantasy VI* is highly leitmotivic—melodic fragments appearing in one cue become recontextualized and transformed by their appearance in others. Moreover, in some cases a cue referring to a character appears while that character is offscreen, encouraging the audience to recall previous events. Given the relative lack of formal training on the part of series composer Nobuo Uematsu, this scoring strategy popularized by Wagner's operas likely comes to

Operatic Conventions in *Final Fantasy VI* **121**

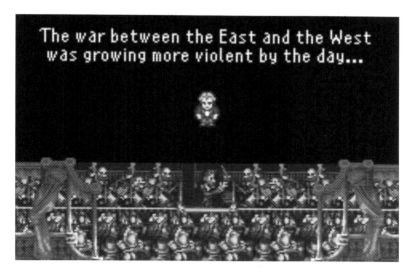

FIGURE 7.2 Impresario appearing on stage

Uematsu filtered through film composers such as John Williams—but that filtering doesn't make the technique any less operatic in nature. *Final Fantasy VI* "creates a referential musical vocabulary through leitmotifs that to the depiction of each of the game's main characters, subsequently standing as referential symbols of those characters."[13]

Theodor Adorno and Hanns Eisler rail against the use of the leitmotif outside of opera: "Cinema music is so easily understood that it has no need of leitmotifs to serve as signposts, and its limited dimension does not permit of adequate expansion of the leitmotif."[14] One must remember that this was written in an age before *The Godfather*, *Star Wars*, and *Lord of the Rings* made their way to the silver screen, but their larger point remains: applying the language of opera to other media is not without pitfalls, especially given "the conflict between opera's slow pace and film's affinity for speed."[15]

In writing on how the Godfather trilogy of films is operatic in scope, Marcia Citron describes the "epic structure" of the films, including their long runtimes, extended narrative spans, and use of themes "commonly found in nineteenth-century Italian opera: honor, loyalty, betrayal, and revenge."[16] The Japanese role-playing game might serve as a means by which to reconcile the conflict between opera and cinema described above; by the above definition and Citron's logic, *Final Fantasy VI* is certainly a game of operatic proportions. Simply listing the order of music that plays in the game alongside a four-word description of each geographic location for each new musical entrance would take 3,500 words—almost a book chapter unto itself. A single playthrough of the game takes approximately between 40 and 60 hours. Japanese role-playing games may make for a compromise between the slow pace of opera and the speed of film, to paraphrase

Citron. Instead of retreading the game's extensive plot in full, I present here only the bare minimum required to argue that the game's three-act structure mirrors that of the opera sequence (as promised a few pages ago).

Act One involves Terra (the first playable character) waking up in bed following a brief prologue during which she encounters a magical being from another realm (an "Esper"). The introductory act focuses on the relationship between Terra and the Esper, culminating in their reunion, after which Terra disappears. Act Two sees Locke (the game's thief) wake up in the immediate aftermath of that encounter (in the same bed that opens the game) and resolve with others present to find Terra and stop the evil Gesthalian Empire. In rare form for the Japanese role-playing format, this optimistic plan ultimately fails: Kefka, the Empire's second-in-command, kills the Emperor just before a climactic showdown and decimates the entire world in the process, completely changing the topography of the game and killing off a significant portion of its population.[17]

Act Three involves Celes (the general-turned-opera singer) waking up on a deserted island a full year after the events of Act Two, for a largely open-ended, nonlinear finale—this is the "wildly unexpected departure" from gaming norms referenced above.[18] It functions in some ways as a sequel to the events of the first two acts; players are reintroduced to every major character they come across (one at a time), and we learn about them in the context of the changed world. Celes (with whatever portion of the cast the player finds; as a nonlinear act, this ending can take place at almost any point) ultimately uses a new airship to infiltrate Kefka's tower. Kefka has assumed the role and visage of a god, but ultimately falls to the combined might of Celes and company.

Citron also describes an operatic approach to cinematography, favoring "a stable camera, a style that favors *mise-en-scène* over montage, and a rhythm that is slow and deliberate."[19] Compared to previous Japanese role-playing games (especially prior *Final Fantasy* titles), *FFVI* employs a very deliberate, highly complex mode of presentation with regard to its in-engine cutscenes. Consider a sequence where Setzer (the gambler, now a party member) escorts Celes into the tomb of a minor character (his ex-lover Darill), telling her the story of the deceased woman. The camera moves from being centered on Celes (the player-controlled character) upward to reveal a visual telling of Setzer's story. The effect manages to communicate a flashback while keeping the main characters in the frame the entire time—a video game equivalent of a single, long shot as opposed to simply cutting the camera between the flashback and the present. As a result, players don't simply see the flashback; we see Celes learning, as well.

Other similarly clever uses of camera movement to give a cinematic sense to certain sequences abound throughout *Final Fantasy VI*; one of the more memorable ones is when Sabin sits down on the throne in Figaro Castle, remarking that not much has changed since his last visit, only to have the camera pan down and away (but, crucially, not fade or cut) from him towards the throne room's door to show the chancellor and his aides discussing the death of Sabin's father, the king—the exact moment Sabin was reflecting upon.[20] The game has a number of technical advancements that enable these sorts of cinematic scenes, but in order to keep this chapter focused on opera, I leave further study along these lines for other scholars, and now dive more deeply into some of the game's leitmotifs that prompted this brief departure to the movies.

The theme associated with Locke (simply entitled "Locke") is initially upbeat and in a major key, befitting his job class of "Adventurer," yet returns in a minor mode (with the A and B sections reversed) via the "Forever Rachel" cue that appears during a flashback with Locke and his former lover Rachel (see Ex. 7.1 and 7.2).[21] The cue is made more complicated by its inclusion not just in the two optional sequences featuring Locke and Rachel, but also when Celes (in the game's present, also romantically involved with Locke) discovers Locke's bandana after regaining consciousness in the aftermath of her suicide attempt.[22]

The game musically situates Celes differently than most of the other characters. For the rest of the cast, their theme plays as they are formally introduced with their short programmatic note glossing who they are and what role they will play in the story. Celes's introduction reads as follows: "A Magitek knight forged by the Empire and tempered in battle. None have ever truly known the woman beneath the general's guise." The "none" of the second sentence of the description also applies to the player, who does not hear Celes's theme during the introduction; instead, "Under Martial Law" plays, the track accompanying Locke as he

EX. 7.1   Transcription of "Locke"

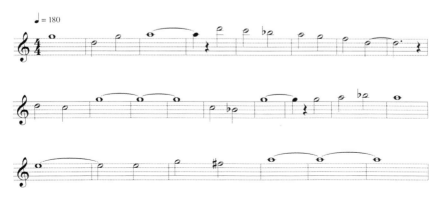

EX. 7.2   Transcription of "Forever Rachel"

124 Ryan Thompson

sneaks around a town under military occupation (meeting Celes in the process). As Tim Summers writes:

> [A]fter the opera sequence, [Celes] adopts the melody of Maria's aria as her musical theme. Celes's introductory biography refers to the enigmatic quality of the character—we hear no music to tell us more about her, until her operatic manifestation reveals "the woman beneath the general's guise." In supplying Celes with her musical identity for the game, the opera is presented as a moment of honest expression for the character.[23]

Celes's theme recurs in other cues, as is the case with many characters, often revealing their inner motivations and desires. This usually occurs as one theme being an arrangement of another, in a paired relationship: Locke's theme is developed by "Forever Rachel," the two Figaro brothers have "Figaro" and "Coin Song," and so on. I argue that the version of Celes's theme the player hears first—the opera aria she performs on the stage—is the *alternate* version of the tune. Celes, the product of significant abuse and emotional hardship, attempts to escape her troubled past by immersing herself in the present fiction of the opera (see Ex. 7.3), allowing her to project a confident persona to the other characters.

Only later, when she is alone, do players hear the piece entitled "Celes" on the soundtrack (see Ex. 7.4), an arrangement rendered less optimistic and more wistful than the version in the opera, owing to a slower tempo, a less active harp accompaniment, and the absence of the synthesized human voice (the melody instead uses a timbre approximating a music box).[24] For each of the other characters with an altered theme, the second theme reveals events of the past that drive the character in question—a secret otherwise closely guarded and rarely shared with the other cast members.

Celes's secret, inner desire is to have hope that her situation will improve, even in the face of past hardship, in the same ways that the opera character Maria maintains her hope (of a reunion with Draco) in the face of adversity. By the time we hear Celes's theme, it's clear that the two women couldn't be more different: in the words of William Cheng,

> the tune, cloaked in memories of a better past, serves as a bittersweet reminder of how Celes sang. Having lost all hope and voice, this heroine—with nothing left to live for, nothing left to sing or say—surrenders to Kefkaesque despair.[25]

Further hammering this point home is the symmetry of Celes (as Maria) throwing flowers off of the balcony (see Figure 7.3) to conclude her aria and Celes later throwing herself off of a cliff in despair, after awakening to a broken world at the beginning of Act Three; the latter is staged to evoke the former.[26] Both of the two occasions that "Celes's Theme" plays have her longing for Locke, wanting him to serve as a symbol of forgiveness for her past misdeeds. Though it goes unspoken between the pair, Locke needs her for the same reasons.

Operatic Conventions in *Final Fantasy VI* **125**

EX. 7.3 Voice and harp parts from second stanza of Celes's opera aria

Using a leitmotivic technique, the score acknowledges the intertwined relationship between these two characters twice. The first time is at the opening scenes of Act Three—when Celes sails her raft away from the island with Locke's bandanna in hand, "Forever Rachel" underscores her departure. This theme, used previously to develop Locke's character, now ties Celes to Locke directly. The epilogue further connects the two characters by pairing the two themes musically, during one of the only serious vignettes in the eight-minute curtain call sequence. We hear Celes's theme first, followed by both Celes and Locke's melodies together, and then the introduction of "Forever Rachel" in transition from Celes to Locke indicates that both characters have, at this point, finally let go of the past, embracing each other as the credits continue to roll.

If the player fails to recruit Locke in the World of Ruin, Setzer (the gambler, introduced above) saves Celes during the epilogue instead of Locke. The music doesn't change, however—listeners still hear that her theme (and, as a result,

EX. 7.4 Voice and harp parts from Celes's theme

FIGURE 7.3 Celes throwing flowers at the close of the opera scene, midway through Act II

her destiny) is intertwined with Locke's. She stands holding Locke's bandanna—before the camera fades away to the next vignette, she describes the item's emotional weight, and says a prayer for the missing adventurer.

The use of operatic conventions in *Final Fantasy VI* was relatively novel at the time, though other games have since employed opera in various ways. I argue that this novelty was, alongside the absence of the sword-and-sorcery aesthetic represented by the

EX. 7.5 Transcription of "Ending Theme (part 1)," excerpt

four elemental crystals and the near-abandonment of the job system, part of an effort to mark this game as a new beginning for the franchise. Understanding the game through an operatic lens explains a number of design decisions and departures from the practices underlying the previous titles—the often-radical shifts in tone between comedy and melodrama, the framing of certain sequences with complex cinematic techniques, and the extensive musical score. It also invites players to understand the first decade of the *Final Fantasy* franchise not as constituting three trilogies (one per generation of game hardware), but as a set of five games following a certain formula of ludic and aesthetic conventions, a trilogy of games that attempt to discard and move beyond those limitations, and a ninth game that wraps itself in nostalgia for the very conventions *Final Fantasy VI* so effectively leaves behind.[27] I offer this analysis of the game as something of an opera playbill that might accompany a critical playthrough of *Final Fantasy VI*. It is typical of the program notes that are included in a playbill to offer some reflections on the work as a whole, revealing new insights to even those audience members intimately familiar with the work. It is my hope that this chapter might serve as such a resource for future studies into the *Final Fantasy* franchise.

Notes

1. This opera sequence is also the main subject of the second chapter of William Cheng's *Sound Play: Video Games and the Musical Imagination* (New York: Oxford University Press, 2014). *Final Fantasy VI* was originally released in North America as *Final Fantasy III*, because it was the third title to be released for an American audience. The second, third, and fifth Japanese releases were unavailable in the West for many years. To avoid confusion, I will defer to the Japanese numbering.
2. The author, with the assistance of scholars and musicians Dana Plank, Julianne Grasso, Karen Cook, Doug Perry, Michael Harris, and Jarel Jones, has made available commented playthroughs of *Final Fantasy VI* and other games on his YouTube page. www.youtube.com/rtbardic/.
3. This is especially true of subsequent playthroughs, where the game's plot and structure are known to the player.

128 Ryan Thompson

4 *Final Fantasy II,* as the sole outlier avoiding both the job system and the elemental crystals, is largely not considered in this chapter's analysis, given the franchise's quick return to the stylings of the first game in subsequent entries.

5 Each character can wear a different subset of equipment, but it's rarely differentiated along class lines in the ways those divisions are made in *FFIV* and *FFV.*

6 As far as gameplay is concerned, *Final Fantasy VII, VIII, X, X-2,* and *XII* all feature increasingly interchangeable characters, with the characters in *Final Fantasy XII* having no gameplay differentiation whatsoever.

7 William Cheng hints at a notion that this fight might be staged; he notes that failure on the part of the player to win against the monster does not result in death, but merely an unsatisfactory performance of the opera sequence, which must then be repeated. See *Sound Play,* 74.

8 The so-called part two never comes to fruition – the opera house is never a required destination again and is a part of only one other (optional) event made available towards end of the game.

9 The Chrysander edition referenced in Ex. 7.2 is available in full on IMSLP: http://imslp.org/wiki/Rinaldo,_HWV_7a_(Handel,_George_Frideric).

10 This is a tradition largely made obsolete by voice acting, which necessitates fixed names so that characters may refer directly to one another.

11 This is, of course, true for every game that allows players to rename characters—but it's unique that *FFVI* calls such attention to the process.

12 William Cheng also suggests in passing that this book might be a libretto. See *Sound Play,* 83.

13 Tim Summers, "From Parsifal to the PlayStation: Wagner and Video Game Music," in *Music in Video Games: Studying Play,* ed. K.J. Donnelly, William Gibbons, and Neil Lerner (New York: Routledge, 2014), 207.

14 Theodor Adorno and Hanns Eisler, *Scoring for the Films* (London: Athlone, 1994), 5.

15 Marcia J. Citron, *When Opera Meets Film* (New York: Cambridge University Press, 2010), 59.

16 Citron, *When Opera Meets Film,* 25.

17 The player is led to believe that the game will end with Kefka and the Emperor stopped just before their plan comes to fruition. In a recent interview, Yoshinori Kitase and Hironobu Sakaguchi stated this was the original design of the game, with the World of Ruin added late in development. An English translation of the entire interview is available here: www.onemillionpower.com/25-years-since-the-release-of-final-fantasy-vi-looking-back-at-the-passion/.

18 Both the nonlinear format and the large gap in time (a full year) are rare for the genre.

19 Citron, *When Opera Meets Film,* 26.

20 Without getting into the minutiae of the game's story, this optional flashback sequence is neatly tied into the immediate aftermath of the opera sequence, which connects Edgar and Sabin more directly to Celes, Setzer, and Locke.

21 Players discover via a flashback that the "relic of the past" Locke seeks is something that can bring Rachel back to life—she falls into a coma when Locke fails to save her from an injury.

22 This occurs during the opening scene of Act Three, if Cid dies and leaves Celes alone on the previously mentioned island. Thanks to Jarel Jones for his assistance in transcribing some of these examples. Though instrument names are listed, because the score is digitally produced from sound samples, instrument ranges are often expanded beyond what would be possible – for instance, a flute may play lower than a middle C, etc.

23 Tim Summers, "Opera Scenes in Video Games: Hitmen, Divas, and Wagner's Were-wolves," *Cambridge Opera Journal* 29 (2018), 270.

24 Figure 7.4 is excerpted with permission from a more complete transcription of the opera aria. See Cheng, *Sound Play,* 69–70.

25 Cheng, *Sound Play,* 82.

26 Cheng also notes this similarity of staging between the two scenes.

27 For more on *Final Fantasy IX* and nostalgia, see Jessica Kizzire, "'The Place I'll Return to Someday: Musical Nostalgia in *Final Fantasy IX,*" in *Music in Video Games: Studying Play,* ed. K.J. Donnelly, William Gibbons, and Neil Lerner (New York: Routledge, 2014), 183–198.

PART III
Meaningful Memories

8

LUDOMUSICAL DISSONANCE IN *DIABLO III*

Michiel Kamp

Clearing demons from the Gardens of Hope in *Diablo III* (2012) for what felt like the hundredth time, I heard that familiar part of the musical soundtrack again: two "epic"-sounding *tutti* chords that trail off into *Seufzer* or *pianto*-like sighing motifs.[1] The chords had a portentous quality to them that didn't quite fit the routineness of wading through endless "trash mobs" that my usual gameplay experiences in the game consist of.[2] Much like Espen Aarseth's contention that he sees "through and past" Lara Croft's body rather than stare at her behind while playing *Tomb Raider* (1996), the *Diablo* games invite the player to see through and past the liters of blood that are spilled, focusing their attention instead on the shiny yellow and blue glow of gold and magic items—and on occasion even the satisfying golden beam of a legendary item "drop."[3] And, much like these rewards shine through the otherwise bloody red and brown visuals, the two chords "shone" through the ambient music and diegetic screams of my demonic enemies. But, whereas the visuals serve to highlight *Diablo*'s main gameplay loop—kill demons, gather loot, kill bigger demons, gather better loot, rinse, repeat—the chords did not seem to indicate anything in particular. "Whence their 'shine'?" I asked myself briefly, before continuing the endless slaughter.

The answer came only later, in a manner very similar to William Cheng's account of his experience with the game *Fallout 3* (2008).[4] When I decided to capture the event in the Gardens of Hope with the help of recording software, I realized that the chords must be part of a dynamic element in the soundtrack—a short, non-looping cue sometimes called a "stinger"—that occurs when the player's character crosses a certain bridge.[5] On closer inspection, and with the help of several recordings, a narrative function became clear: the narrow bridge allowed the backdrop of the High Heavens—the setting of *Diablo III*'s fourth act, where demons and angels can be seen fighting out battles on distant lower spires and bridges—to occupy a larger visual area of the screen. In their narrative effect, these chords can be construed as a kind of musical "zooming out," alluding to the broader struggle taking place in the game's story, through their almost monumental instrumentation and the open qualities of the half cadence: C sharp minor to D sharp major, iv-V in the key of G sharp minor (mm. 1–2 in Ex. 8.1).

EX. 8.1   Bridge cue, *Diablo III*

Ludomusical Dissonance in *Diablo III*   **133**

In a sense, this narrative effect can be seen as borrowing from a long musical tradition. Although the exact chord content may differ, the trope of musical "horizon broadening" through two *tutti* chords has become familiar. *The Matrix* (1999), for instance, has a two-chord progression by common-tone relation, D minor to B flat major, when protagonist Neo wakes up in "the real world" and peers over the edge of his gooey bathtub. Like the D sharp major chord in measure 2 of Ex. 8.1, these chords are hammered out by the full orchestra repeating the chords. The chords accompany an over-the-shoulder shot of Neo, revealing the almost incomprehensible vastness of the battery farm spires onto which his fellow humans are chained; the tableau visually resembles the isometric perspective of the bridge in *Diablo III* and the heavenly spires in the distance. Another example of the trope is the "vor Gott ..." cadence in the finale of Beethoven's Ninth (mm. 93–94), which modulates from the key of D major to B flat major by manner of octave As that subsequently become the third of an F major chord. As a culmination of the "Ode to Joy" into the word "*Gott*," it gives the experience of going *beyond* the music that has gone before, an experience of "opening up," or "horizon broadening."[6] One could even imagine a similar over-the-shoulder perspective of the cherub standing before God in Schiller's text, to the shot of Neo's bathtub, and the bridge in *Diablo III*.

Going one interpretative step further, the vastness of the scene that is expressed in all three cases—*Diablo III*, *The Matrix*, and the Ninth—could be seen as depictions of Kant's "mathematical sublime."[7] Magnitude plays an important role for Kant in this concept, particularly the apprehension of a greatness that is beyond measurement (even subjective measurement). The magnitude of the subject matter in the three situations—of the battle between heaven and hell, of the machinic enslavement of humanity, of divine joy—is signified musically in two ways: the sheer size of the *tutti* orchestra playing the chords on the one hand, and the "breaking open" of the harmonic progressions through half-cadences and common tone modulations on the other. Particularly the latter "breaking open" function momentarily does away with the teleological certainty of musical progression, leaving the listener/viewer/player in harmonically "unmeasurable," or at least "unmeasured," territory.

However, even if the reader has followed me in this admittedly rather grandiose interpretation of the chords in *Diablo III*, the point is that this is an interpretation of the game not as a player, but as a viewer who considers it as a narrative audiovisual text, recorded and rewatched through external means—in my case, the screen-capture software Fraps. When playing, the music appeared to be "out of place," or "inappropriate"; it was only upon subsequent study and analysis that its suitability was clarified. In this chapter I want to argue that this experience represented a musical form of "ludonarrative dissonance," a term coined by game developer Clint Hocking in 2007.[8] This "dissonance" generally describes a contradiction between a game's story on the one hand, and its mechanics and gameplay (i.e., the game's rules and the actions that it asks a player to perform) on the

134 Michiel Kamp

other. In the case of *Diablo III*, broadly put, there is then an apparent contradiction between the music's narrative function and the gameplay. I will discuss three aspects related to this idea. In the first large section, I address the relationships among music, narrative, and gameplay by further unpacking Hocking's term; then, I consider this experience from a phenomenological and semiotic perspective in terms of Heidegger's theory of signs. Third, in the second large section I return to the case of *Diablo III* itself, and how moments of ludomusical dissonance like this one might be seen as signifiers or markers of genre expectations. In the case of *Diablo III*, certain musical qualities of the action-RPG subgenre as distinct from other RPG subgenres are signified by these moments.

Ludonarrative dissonance and broken musical signs

In a critique of the game *Bioshock* (2007) on his blog *Click Nothing*, Hocking argues that the game "seems to suffer from a powerful dissonance between what it is about as a game, and what it is about as a story."[9] He contrasts the game's "ludic contract" to its "narrative contract." A ludic contract consists of what is needed to complete the game: the tactics one ought to employ to overcome the game's obstacles most effectively, as well as the choices one ought to make in order to progress through the game most smoothly. The ludic contract is commonly referred to as "gameplay," but is more precisely defined by Simon Egenfeldt-Nielsen, Jonas Heide Smith, and Susana Pajares Tosca as "the game dynamics emerging from the interplay between rules and game geography."[10] A narrative contract is a story goal for the player's character: what motivates the character to perform their actions, to fight enemies, and to aid or oppose others. According to Hocking, *Bioshock*'s two contracts contradict one another. In his interpretation, the game is ultimately about the problems inherent in a society based on Ayn Rand's philosophy of Objectivism. On the one hand, the ludic contract offers the player a choice between acting in Randian rational self-interest and altruism: when defeating some of the game's toughest adversaries, the Big Daddies, the player can either choose to harvest (and thereby kill) or rescue their companions, genetically engineered children called Little Sisters. Harvesting the Little Sisters rewards the player with slightly more resources than rescuing them, creating an ethical conundrum.[11] On the other hand, *Bioshock*'s narrative contract is about helping the character of Atlas, and the player has no choice in the matter. Thus, the ludic contract sets up a moral dilemma that the story does not really allow for "playing out"—for which it has no gameplay possibilities—creating a "dissonance" between what the player is doing and the story that their actions are being contextualized in.

In video games, there is frequently a dissonance between what we are asked to do as players and what the game's story is about. In action-adventure games like the *Uncharted* series (2007–2017), for instance, we are asked to believe that the protagonist Nathan Drake is a good-hearted scoundrel in the vein of Indiana Jones (or perhaps even more so that other Harrison Ford character, Han Solo). Quippy dialogue during gameplay sequences and emotional cut scenes with Drake's various love interests throughout the series portray him as such. Those gameplay sequences, however, feature the player character killing scores of enemies with little remorse or second thought. The game even awards trophies for kill counts with various weapons, although none of these are referenced in the diegetic story world. The games' developers, Naughty Dog, even referenced this contradiction (and Hocking's blog post) by giving the name "Ludonarrative Dissonance" to a trophy awarded for killing 1,000 enemies in *Uncharted 4: A Thief's End* (2016).

These examples point to a common form of ludonarrative dissonance in which the violent nature of gameplay in many game genres conflicts with the heroic protagonists of the stories that they tell. This can be explained with the help of Jesper Juul's idea that video games are "half-real": their rules (or "game mechanics") and their fiction are two separate aesthetic entities.[12] This means that, unlike other media such as novels and feature films, a game's fiction—including both its narrative and story world—can be "incomplete" or "incoherent": for instance, there does not need to be a diegetic explanation for why Mario has multiple "lives" in *Super Mario Bros.* (1985), for why there are blocks moving down a field in *Tetris* (1987), and players do not need to be aware of the names and societal status of the pieces in order to effectively play a game of chess. Herein also lies a counterargument to the idea of ludonarrative dissonance as a unidimensional evaluative concept for critique: players do not necessarily require a fiction that is coherent with the gameplay in a game such as *Uncharted* in order to enjoy the game. In fact, central to Hocking's argument is the notion that this dissonance is so engrained in many game genres—especially ones that feature large amounts of nameless, faceless enemies to kill such as third-person action adventure games, first-person shooters, or action-RPGs like *Diablo III*—that it suggests that ludonarrative dissonance is generic, something that is to be accepted as a feature of those genres and to be looked past (and "through," again echoing Aarseth) in order to enjoy or interpret a game.

Considering music's involvement in this ludonarrative contract sheds light on the functions of the soundtrack in games and the various ways in which players can hear background music. In Isabella van Elferen's ALI (affect-literacy-interaction) model of video game immersion, the ludonarrative contract would be part of game-musical literacy.[13] With literacy, van Elferen is referring to José Zagal's concept of "ludoliteracy."[14] The player's understanding of a particular video game's soundtrack is predicated on a familiarity with various musical conventions: those of video game music (tropes like the high-tempo, repeating short motifs of boss battle music); conventions of musical soundtracks in general (action scoring in film and television music, for instance); and those found throughout the history of Western music (such as the augmented second interval in portrayals of cultural Others—on this, see Dana Plank's contribution to this volume). My own sketch of the connotations of the two chords in *Diablo III* followed a similar outward

136 Michiel Kamp

trajectory through concentric circles: from games, to Hollywood cinema, to Western art music. But part of this musical ludoliteracy also includes expectations of musical functions. If the music in any given game suddenly changes drastically from an upbeat, mid-tempo major tonality to a fast-paced, low-pitched minor tonality or Dorian mode, I can either understand this as a ludic signifier, perhaps an indication of the presence of enemies, or as an indication of a narrative development, such as the onset of a cutscene. I can also understand the interruption to be combining both ludic and narrative musical signifiers. Paraphrasing Hocking's terminology, such a situation, where a change in musical signification can be easily interpreted against a change in the game state, would represent a moment of ludonarrative consonance.

In the case of the Gardens of Hope sequence in *Diablo III*, however, there was clear dissonance between the narrative or cinematic event signified by the music, and the ludic music I as a player expected, the horizon-broadening panorama of the High Heavens articulated by the stinger was not accompanied by any changes in gameplay. It was also this dissonance that made me aware of the bridge cue in a more immediate way than the "unheard" background music that makes up most of the musical soundtrack in the Gardens of Hope (see below).[15] In phenomenological terms, the form that this immediacy took is what Martin Heidegger calls "un-ready-to-hand."[16] The un-ready-to-hand is not just an unfamiliar phenomenon encountered in the (here virtual) world that demands explanation or interpretation, but rather a phenomenon that announces itself as what it *should* be doing but does not. This conception works fine for Heidegger's archetypal example of the hammer as equipment: when we are working effectively with a hammer, its presence withdraws from our attention, it is ready-to-hand;[17] when a hammer breaks, we still recognize it as a hammer but one that is no longer able to operate as such. It has become un-ready-to-hand and draws attention to itself in that manner. But I encountered the bridge cue in *Diablo III* as a sign, and Heidegger argues that a sign is a special kind of equipment that we *do* pay attention to when we use it, when it works effectively.[18] So it is not enough to just say that a "broken sign" draws attention through its un-readiness-to-hand: it has to be a different kind of conspicuousness than a normal, "working" sign. Whereas a working sign announces its referent, a broken sign only announces its "signness." The chords in the bridge cue did not actually portent anything, but they *sounded* portentous.

What makes Heidegger's phenomenology of signs, and un-ready-to-hand or broken signs in particular, such a useful approach to this case is that it reveals the extensive preconditions required for such experiences, preconditions that in the present context can be summed up as ludoliteracy. Heidegger describes a sign as "an item of equipment which explicitly raises a totality of equipment into our circumspection."[19] Consider a traffic sign covered over with black tape. To recognize it as a traffic sign and not, say, a sculpture or a piece of technology requires a certain familiarity with traffic laws, or "traffic literacy." However, to recognize

Ludomusical Dissonance in *Diablo III*   **137**

whether this was an act of vandalism or whether this sign was temporarily put out of order by the authorities due to roadwork requires a more intimate knowledge of the totality of (local) traffic conventions. Similarly, to recognize the bridge cue as a broken sign requires more than a familiarity with video game music conventions and the ludic and narrative functions that music can have. Rather, it is predicated on an intimate grasp of the workings of music in the particular genre that *Diablo III* belongs to. In other words, the experience that forms the basis of this chapter reveals the importance of genre in musical ludoliteracy. In the next section, I will outline exactly what the musical conventions of *Diablo III*'s genre are.

Hearing (sub)genre

According to Karen Collins, genre is an important aspect for gameplay, "in that it helps to set the audience's expectations by providing a framework for understanding the rules of gameplay, thereby … reducing the learning curve of the game."[20] But genre is an important discursive concept in video game culture as well, whether in marketing materials, games journalism, popular (online) discourse, or academic study. The RPG genre is often mentioned in all of these discourses, and the *Diablo* series is usually categorized as such. Mark J.P. Wolf, for instance, includes the first *Diablo* (1996) on a list of RPG titles alongside other games and series such as *Phantasy Star* and *Fallout*.[21] For Wolf, in contrast to the delineation of film genres into, say, westerns and science fiction, game genres ought to be defined not by their iconography, setting, theme, or narrative structure, but rather by the type of gameplay or interactivity they enjoy. In Wolf's taxonomy, RPGs' defining interactive characteristic is that they allow players to "create or take on a character represented by various statistics, which may even include a developed persona," requirements which the *Diablo* series meets only partially, through the prevalence of statistics over character building.[22] But other writers exclude *Diablo* as a traditional RPG, precisely because it does not give the player the ability to develop a persona, or place much focus on a story that involves interaction with an expansive cast of characters. In his *GameSpot* review of the first *Diablo*, for instance, Trent Ward describes it as "a title that combines the elegant simplicity of an action game and the addictive storyline of an adventure game with the personalization and exploration of an old-school RPG."[23] The official *Diablo III* website, too, lists the game's genre as "Action/RPG."[24] In his retrospective of the "action RPG" for *1up* Jeremy Parish describes the uneasy fit of *Diablo* into the RPG genre as follows:

> "It's really more of an adventure game with RPG-like battles," sniffed more than one PC publication reviewer with disdain … even then, the notion of Diablo-as-pure-RPG left some people with a stomach ache. And so the world arrived at a compromise by giving Diablo its own genre: The action RPG.[25]

138 Michiel Kamp

Since the first *Diablo*, the label "action RPG" has been applied to a large variety of games, including titles more traditionally associated with genres like the first-person shooter, such as *BioShock* (2007) and *Destiny* (2014). Most of these include elements of character progression and numerical representation of the kind Wolf describes. For this reason, game designer Jordane Thiboust prefers the term "dungeon crawler" for *Diablo*.[26] He goes as far as to say that at the time of his writing, the term "action RPG" had become mainly a marketing term, being "the current marketing slang for 'it is cool to play it on consoles.'"[27] Thiboust has a point: *The Elder Scrolls V: Skyrim*, for instance, a game that fits the traditional RPG category much more than *Diablo*, has been called an action RPG in even academic literature.[28] Be it action RPG or dungeon crawler, whatever name we give to the RPG subgenre to which *Diablo* belongs—I will use the term "action RPG" in this chapter—it is definitely not its sole occupant. *Warhammer 40,000: Inquisitor – Martyr* (2018), *Grim Dawn* (2016), *Victor Vran* (2015), *Path of Exile* (2013), *Marvel Heroes* (2013), *The Incredible Adventures of Van Helsing* (2013), *Darkspore* (2011), *Torchlight* (2009), *Titan Quest* (2006), and *Dungeon Siege* (2002) all feature gameplay and modes of interaction that the original *Diablo* established. They have in common a top-down, isometric perspective, a single avatar for the player to control; some measure of randomized level design, enemy locations and equipment; and a focus on character progression and loot acquisition. They also follow Wolf's maxim that it is not the theme or iconography that defines subgenre but gameplay: while many of these games have medieval fantasy settings like the classic pen-and-paper RPG *Dungeons & Dragons* that the genre originates in, there are examples of action RPGs in virtually any setting imaginable.[29]

In *Understanding Video Game Music,* Tim Summers addresses the relationship between music and genre in a case study of racing game subgenres.[30] He identifies five subgenres: simulation, semi-simulation, arcade, street racing, and fantastic/ futuristic. His taxonomy hinges on two axes: one of realism, which could also be understood as the "gameplay axis," which indicates the terms of the driving model that is part of the game mechanics, and one of the game's fictional setting. The realism axis decides when and where the music is heard in the game: limited to either the game's menus or the car stereo. The fiction axis decides the musical styles and genres that are represented, such as (predominantly) hip-hop in street racing games to "unusual timbres and musical styles" to emphasize the fantastical settings of games such as *Mario Kart* (1992), *Wipeout* (1995), and *Road Rash* (1991).[31] It may not be entirely accurate to reduce Summers' axes to interaction or gameplay on the one hand, and theme, fiction, or setting on the other (the realism axis also has implications for the way in which those games represent racing and driving culture), but it provides a useful blueprint for a similar taxonomy of music in the RPG in terms of style and structure. Here, too, the styles and genres of the soundtrack are predominantly determined by the fictional setting of the games. When the RPG's traditional home of the fantasy setting is traded in for the post-apocalyptic wastelands of the *Fallout* series, players encounter a soundscape made up of metallic synthesizer drones *cum* pre-1960s oldies.[32] When it is set in the transmedial Marvel superhero universe of *Marvel Heroes*, echoes of the 2000s and 2010s Marvel Studios film scores and their Hollywood idiom can be heard: frantic, syncopated percussion both acoustic and synthesized, string ostinatos, sweeping brass melodies, every now and then supplemented by distorted electric guitar power chords.

In his comparison of Japanese and Western RPG soundtracks, William Gibbons makes a distinction between musical style and musical placement or structure.[33] As argued in the previous paragraph, musical style is determined mostly by a game's fictional setting. Because the fictional setting is largely independent of genre, it is the gameplay axis, rather than the fiction axis that best determines the musical soundtrack's structure—the placement of its cues—in an RPG. For example, even though the aforementioned *Marvel Heroes* is set in a very different kind of world than that of *Diablo*, it has much in common with the *Diablo* series from the standpoint of gameplay (perhaps unsurprising, since its creator David Brevik co-founded Blizzard North, the studio behind *Diablo*). The structure of *Marvel Heroes* is largely based around musical cues tied to the games' different areas. A now-standard feature of the genre, first introduced by the original *Diablo* (1996) is that the layout of areas is randomly generated, based on a limited tile set. These areas are then differentiated based on visual themes, such as caves, dungeons, jungles, or, as in my case study, the High Heavens. This randomization increases replayability, while at the same time decreasing the importance of geographical layouts and features. The structure of the musical score suits this randomization and differentiation by having distinctive looping cues tied to the different areas, conforming to their visual themes through the classic Hollywood scoring technique that Aaron Copland would call "creating a more convincing atmosphere of time and place."[34] In other words, the music adds *couleur locale*, often through exoticist topics like augmented seconds and non-Western (or Western folk-musical) instrumental timbres. The structure of these cues suits the randomization of the areas by having no clear teleological development or cadences. Even though these are ultimately linear, non-dynamic tracks in themselves, this allows them to loop and play for any length of time and over any kind of encounter without drawing undue attention to themselves.

The cue that makes up most of the musical soundtrack in the Gardens of Hope suits both those aspects—randomization and differentiation—by adhering to many of the tenets of ambient music: much like Brian Eno's original forays in *Ambient 1: Music for Airports* (1978), it consists of extremely slow note patterns that lack a discernible exact pulse or rhythm. The notes rarely have a clear onset, and no particular instruments can be clearly discerned in their timbres, although there is somewhat of a contrast between solo lines played by a sharp, shawm-like sound and their accompaniment in breathy, vocal sounds in the soprano register. The pitches revolve around D, G, and sometimes A, with the soloist on rare occasion moving down by half-step from these tones. While the key of G or D is often implied, thirds are rarely heard; a rare F# or B suggests chromatic coloration as opposed to articulating a major tonality. This G/D tonal material sometimes shifts dramatically down by whole step, with darker double bass and horn parts entering on C2, and even outlining ascending and descending C minor scales at a moderate pace, with the most striking example being a clear descending staccato horn motif that repeatedly descends C, Bb, Ab, G. But melodic material is rare, and harmonic shifts are either too gradual or too sporadic to suggest any kind of directionality or progression. It is possible to interpret this ambient cue as evoking the narrative situation in the Gardens of Hope, a battle between heaven and hell where the soprano "vocals" in (more or less) D major represent the angelic choirs in conflict with the dark horns and low strings in C minor as the invading demonic armies— the odd bass drum hit, central to the military musical topic going back centuries, can even be heard every now and then, although never indicating a rhythm or pulse.[35] The "shawm" wavers between diatonicism and chromaticism, between rounder, more angelic woodwind timbres and sharper, demonic string and brass timbres; perhaps it echoes the ongoing struggle, or perhaps, as a solo instrument, it represents the player character's part in it. Finally, these "orchestral," "instrumental" sounds are constantly "invaded" by dark, low noises, monstrous screams and unintelligible ghost-like whispers of the soundtrack's "ambient" layer, calling to mind a disruption of an ongoing order.[36]

Whereas the ambient cue in the Gardens of Hope relates to the environment, the bridge cue can be seen to relate to the narrative. Its musical material is closely related to the game's main theme, titled "And the Heavens Shall Tremble" on the soundtrack album, which also features *sforzando tutti* chords, an anvil accompaniment, and prominent augmented-fourth and minor-second intervals. The bridge cue's semiotic function is therefore to evoke a moment of narrative reflection, shifting the musical focus from indicating the location of the player's avatar in the story world—essentially the ambient cue's function—to the location of the player in the story. And the two cues differ sharply not just in musical signification, but in structure as well. Whereas the ambient cue is what Jonathan Kramer would call "vertical music,"[37] featuring no linearity, directionality, or teleology, the bridge cue is instilled with all of these elements from the standpoints of harmony, melody, and rhythm: the chords form a (half-)cadence, they unequivocally descend, and subsequent measures establish a clear pulse through repetition of the *Seufzer* motifs (including the literal repetition of the intervals from mm. 6–9 in mm. 10–13). Moreover, the bridge cue's harmonic material is sharply distinguished from all of that of the ambient cue: its G sharp minor against the ambient cue's G, D, and sometimes C minor. On the basis of these musical differences, one might be tempted to draw the conclusion that the player needs no awareness of their narrative and ludic functions to recognize the bridge cue as standing out from the ambient cue, as "dissonant." The bridge cue's remote key and contrasting instrumentation suggest that my experience might not have been based in ludoliteracy, but musical literacy, which has been shown to be equally, or perhaps

Ludomusical Dissonance in *Diablo III* **141**

even more widely shared throughout Western culture.[38] But this does not explain away the idea of ludomusical dissonance as something purely musical. The bridge cue is not the only narrative cue in *Diablo III*, nor even in the Gardens of Hope. A player entering the area is greeted with a short, non-looping introductory cue before the ambient cue starts, not unlike the opening passage of *Pac-Man* (1980) or the ragtime-like introduction of the Overworld cue from *Super Mario Bros.*[39] Unique enemies are musically labeled as "bosses" through another set of unique cues, a game-musical trope that also goes back to at least *Super Mario Bros.*[40] Both kinds of cues have similar instrumentation and motivic structure to the bridge cue and "And the Heavens Shall Tremble." What distinguishes the bridge cue from these is that it serves a purely narrative function in the Gardens of Hope and has no "ludic" history. In other words, that the bridge cue appeared as un-ready-to-hand to me as a player was based in the same ludoliteracy that made the other narrative cues—and the ambient cue for that matter—appear as ready-to-hand.

In his discussion of regional traditions in RPGs, Summers distinguishes modern Western RPGs from Japanese RPGs based on the former's tendency to score the environment, and the latter's tendency to score the narrative. Summers provides *Diablo* as an example of a Western RPG, with its "non-teleological, state-based approach,"[41] but this description is actually much more suited to the action RPG specifically. Summers' example of an early WRPG series, *Ultima*, that features a mix of both narrative and environmental cues, actually applies to many modern WRPGs as well, such as the *Mass Effect* and *Elder Scrolls* series. Both modern series feature incidental musical cues that build up and underline specific narrative events on the one hand, and more ambient cues tied to specific areas on the other. Moreover, Gibbons suggests that the combination of location-based cues and event or narrative-based cues has existed since the JRPG *Dragon Quest* (1986).[42] In other words, a mixed approach to scoring is a generic, "unmarked" convention of the RPG, both Western and Japanese, and a purely environmental approach to scoring is a "marked" feature of the action RPG subgenre that was started by the first *Diablo*.[43] It is against this subgeneric convention, in turn, that the bridge cue stands out as marked. The reason the event stands out as a case of ludonarrative dissonance, then, is an expectation of an ambient area cue raised by ludic subgeneric conventions that is subsequently contradicted by a narrative cue. Wolf, in his 2001 argument for genre classification based on interaction, leaves room for some historical developments:

> As narrative games grow more complex and cinematic, iconographic and thematic generic classifications from film will be able to be applied more usefully, but interactivity will always be an important factor in the way the games are experienced.[44]

Diablo III could perhaps be seen as Wolf's prediction coming true in full: it is both an example of growing narrative and cinematic complexity in the subgenre of the action RPG, and an example of the importance of player interactivity in game genre signification. Musical signs like the bridge cue in *Diablo* are likely understood as "broken" by players who possess a ludoliteracy based in ludomusical conventions of the action RPG genre.

As Steven Reale shows later in the volume, games like *Diablo III* may evolve over the years through patches, expansions, and downloadable content, and online games even more so. Blizzard has made a number of drastic changes since the game's launch in 2012, including the introduction of several new game modes such as Adventure Mode and Rifts that downplay the linear story progression in favor of randomized, repeatable, nonlinear challenge areas. The Gardens of Hope still exist as an area in Adventure Mode, and, though its dynamic soundtrack has been altered to do away with the area's introductory cue in favor of the looping ambient cue, the bridge cue remains, although it sometimes appears in a truncated version.[45] It can be said that over the years *Diablo III* has moved away from presenting its narrative and back to the attributes that made the original *Diablo* the progenitor of the action RPG genre, with its focus on loot gathering, character progression instead of story progression, repetition and randomization. But *Diablo III*'s soundtrack still includes snippets of narrative music, like the bridge cue, that remain scattered throughout the game like broken signs. Ludomusical dissonance, then, is a particular kind of ludic experience that arises out of (sub) genre expectations in a historical context of ever-changing scoring practices. As Hocking argued, the uneasy friction between narrative and gameplay is an essential part of ludoliteracy, and music's double allegiance to both these poles means it will remain an important signpost of ludonarrative dissonance.

Notes

1 See www.youtube.com/watch?v=oAFG8hDdAFw, www.youtube.com/watch?v=gkq XfEe9FY0, and www.youtube.com/watch?v=EtCLYOyZMP4 for three separate video examples of my encounter with this cue. The chords occur at 0:24 in the first clip; the two-note motifs occur in the lower brass and strings from 0:36 to the end of the clip. Note that the first four bars of the cue are missing in the third clip; I will return to this in my conclusion. For a discussion of the *pianto* motif, see Richard Taruskin, "Afterword: What Else?," in *Representation in Western Music*, ed. Joshua S. Walden (Cambridge: Cambridge University Press, 2013), 291.
2 "Trash mobs" is a term that is normally employed with regards to MMORPGs (massive multi-player online role-playing games) but has been adopted by *Diablo* players as well. See, for instance, the community-built *Diablo* Wiki: www.diablowiki. net/Trash_mobs.
3 Espen Aarseth, "Genre Trouble," *Electronic Book Review* 3 (2004), www.electronic bookreview.com/thread/firstperson/vigilant.
4 William Cheng, *Sound Play: Video Games and the Musical Imagination* (New York: Oxford University Press, 2014), 47.
5 Tim Summers, *Understanding Video Game Music* (Cambridge: Cambridge University Press, 2016), 23.

6 Mark Evans has described the chords in *The Matrix* as "a 'heavenly' choral piece," suggesting another relationship to the moment in Beethoven's Ninth. See Mark Evans, "Mapping the Matrix: Virtual Spatiality and the Realm of the Perceptual," in *Off the Planet: Music, Sound, and Science Fiction Cinema*, ed. Philip Hayward (New Barnet, UK: John Libbey, 2004), 130.
7 Immanuel Kant, *Critique of Judgment*, trans. J.H. Bernard (Mineola, NY: Dover, 2005). 64–66.
8 Clint Hocking, "Ludonarrative Dissonance in *Bioshock*: The Problem of What the Game Is About," *Click Nothing* (blog), October 7, 2007, http://clicknothing.typepad.com/click_nothing/2007/10/ludonarrative-d.html.
9 Hocking, "Ludonarrative Dissonance in *Bioshock*."
10 Simon Egenfeldt-Nielsen, Jonas Heide Smith, and Susana Pajares Tosca, *Understanding Video Games: The Essential Introduction* (New York: Routledge, 2008). By "geography," the authors refer to the physical features of a game environment that restrict and allow certain actions, such as walls.
11 It has to be said that strategy discussions on multiple websites contradict this assumption that Hocking makes. Rescuing the Little Sisters provides fewer immediate rewards, but further down the line the player is rewarded for their good deeds in the form of gifts that "more than make up for it; in terms of usefulness for defeating later enemies." See, for example, the game's official Wikia: "Little Sister Gift," last modified May 5, 2017, http://bioshock.wikia.com/wiki/Little_Sister_Gift.
12 Jesper Juul, *Half-Real: Video Games Between Real Rules and Fictional Worlds* (Cambridge, MA: MIT Press, 2005); Egenfeldt-Nielsen, Heide Smith, and Pajares Tosca, *Understanding Video Games: The Essential Introduction*.
13 Isabella van Elferen, "Analysing Game Musical Immersion: The ALI Model," in *Ludomusicology: Approaches to Video Game Music*, ed. Michiel Kamp, Tim Summers, and Mark Sweeney (Sheffield, UK: Equinox, 2016).
14 José P. Zagal, *Ludoliteracy: Defining, Understanding, and Supporting Games Education* (Pittsburgh: ETC Press, 2010).
15 Here I am referring to Claudia Gorbman's conception of background music in film: Claudia Gorbman, *Unheard Melodies: Narrative Film Music* (Bloomington: Indiana University Press, 1987).
16 Martin Heidegger, *Being and Time*, trans. John Macquarrie and Edward Robinson (Oxford: Blackwell, 1962).
17 Heidegger, *Being and Time*, 98.
18 Heidegger, *Being and Time*, 107–108.
19 Heidegger, *Being and Time*, 110.
20 Karen Collins, *Game Sound: An Introduction to the History, Theory, and Practice of Video Game Music and Sound Design* (Cambridge, MA: MIT Press, 2008), 123.
21 Mark J.P. Wolf, *The Medium of the Video Game* (Austin: University of Texas Press, 2001).
22 Wolf, *The Medium of the Video Game*, 130.
23 Trent Ward, "Diablo Review," *GameSpot* (blog), January 23, 1997, www.gamespot.com/reviews/diablo-review/1900-2538662/.
24 "Blizzard Entertainment: Diablo III," http://us.blizzard.com/en-us/games/d3/. Accessed March 6, 2018.
25 Jeremy Parish, "What Happened to the Action RPG?" 1Up.com, August 3, 2012, www.1up.com/features/what-happened-action-rpg.html.
26 The term "dungeon crawler" is also used for a different subgenre of the role-playing game that can be traced back to *Wizardry: Proving Grounds of the Mad Overlord* (1981). These turn-based games have a particular first-person view and *Dungeons & Dragons*-based party mechanics very different from *Diablo*'s solo, real-time gameplay. For this reason, I will not take up Thiboust's suggestion in this chapter.

144 Michiel Kamp

27 Jordane Thiboust, "Focusing Creativity: RPG Genres," Gamasutra, January 24, 2013, www.gamasutra.com/view/feature/185353/focusing_creativity_rpg_genres.php.
28 Susan Gallacher, "The Sounds of Skyrim: A Musical Journey Through Gaming," in *The Digital Evolution of Live Music*, ed. Angela Cresswell Jones and Rebecca Jane Bennett (Waltham, MA and Kidlington: Chandos, 2015), 99–106.
29 See Thomas H. Apperley, "Genre and Game Studies: Toward a Critical Approach to Video Game Genres," *Simulation & Gaming* 37(1) (March 1, 2006): 6–23, https://doi.org/10.1177/1046878105282278.; and William Gibbons, "Music, Genre, and Nationality in the Postmillennial Fantasy Role-Playing Game," in *The Routledge Companion to Screen Music and Sound*, ed. Miguel Mera, Ronald Sadoff, and Ben Winters (New York: Routledge, 2017), 412–427.
30 Summers, *Understanding Video Game Music*.
31 Summers, *Understanding Video Game Music*, 89.
32 See Cheng, *Sound Play: Video Games and the Musical Imagination*.
33 Gibbons, "Music, Genre, and Nationality in the Postmillennial Fantasy Role-Playing Game."
34 Aaron Copland, "Tip to Moviegoers: Take off Those Ear-Muffs (1949)," in *Aaron Copland: A Reader: Selected Writings 1923–1972* (New York and London: Routledge, 2004), 104–111.
35 See Raymond Monelle, *The Musical Topic: Hunt, Military and Pastoral* (Bloomington: Indiana University Press, 2006).
36 The *Diablo III* options menu distinguishes between four layers: effects, voice, ambient, and music. The effects are sounds created by player interactions with the environment, and characters such as demons in the environment. Voice consists of voices of player and non-player characters, always diegetic, but sometimes what Kristine Jørgensen calls transdiegetic; see Kristine Jørgensen, "Game Studies—Audio and Gameplay: An Analysis of PvP Battlegrounds in World of Warcraft," *Game Studies* 8(2) (December 2008), www.gamestudies.org/0802/articles/jorgensen. The ambient layer consists of mostly diegetic sounds in the environment that are not necessarily tied to any visible sources or player actions, such as barking dogs and street bustle in cities. In the High Heavens, however, this ambient layer overlaps with the music layer because both incorporate ghostly whispers.
37 Jonathan D. Kramer, *The Time of Music: New Meanings, New Temporalities, New Listening Strategies* (New York and London: Schirmer, 1988).
38 See, for instance, David Huron, *Sweet Anticipation: Music and the Psychology of Expectation* (Cambridge, MA: MIT Press, 2006). See 64ff. on expectations of pitch material and key.
39 See Neil Lerner, "The Origins of Musical Style in Video Games, 1977–1983," in *The Oxford Handbook of Film Music Studies*, ed. David Neumeyer (New York: Oxford University Press, 2013), 332–333.
40 See Zach Whalen, "Play Along—An Approach to Videogame Music," *Game Studies* 4(1) (November 2004), www.gamestudies.org/0401/whalen/.
41 Tim Summers, "Video Game Music: History, Form and Genre" (doctoral dissertation, University of Bristol, 2012).
42 Gibbons, "Music, Genre, and Nationality in the Postmillennial Fantasy Role-Playing Game," 418.
43 For a discussion of markedness in music, see Raymond Monelle, *Linguistics and Semiotics in Music* (Chur, Switzerland: Harwood, 1992). For an example of the role of musical markedness and its relation to genre, see Ronald Rodman, *Tuning In: American Narrative Television Music* (Oxford and New York: Oxford University Press, 2010), 237–239.
44 Wolf, *The Medium of the Video Game*, 115.
45 The recordings that attempted to capture my experiences in *Diablo III* were made in March 2014. When revisiting the Gardens of Hope in January of 2018, the chords were gone. Or, rather, the bridge cue still played, but it omitted the first four bars—and with

them the *tutti* chords—leaving only the less prominent "trailing off" bars (mm. 5–16). Had the makers decided that the chords were indeed too "dissonant" with the gameplay? A short investigation into other players' recordings for "Let's Play" videos on YouTube going back to 2012 revealed that the chords had actually not always been there in every playthrough in the first place. In recordings by TheMediaCows (June 2012; www.youtube.com/watch?v=Fwg7Xa5ZB-Q), Gameworld.gr (August 2012; www.youtube.com/watch?v=3j5guGTjTHU), Omakez. Walkthrough (August 2014; www.youtube.com/watch?v=GeNTKgNkXSg), and Scythe Plays (September 2016; www.youtube.com/watch?v=CGfTgv2MSTE), the four measures are missing. In recordings by tehcrazGaming (May 2012; www.youtube.com/watch?v=l6LEhZxjwyM), John GodGames (September 2013; www.youtube.com/watch?v=qal0IjXQJAU), and dwyrin (May 2014; www.youtube.com/watch?v=78lbn2hNONQ), they can be heard. In fact, in the third of my own three recordings the first four bars of the cue are missing as well. This randomness further complicates my interpretations of the bridge cue in this chapter. If the two opening chords of the cue are the clearest sign of a narrative moment on the bridge, why are they sometimes omitted? Perhaps *Diablo III*'s randomization extends beyond its gameplay design and ambient cues and incorporates these narrative cues as well.

9

A HIDDEN HARMONY

Music Theory Pedagogy and Role-Playing Games

Meghan Naxer

Music is part of an intricate web of interconnected systems contributing to the overall experience of playing a role-playing game. Many of the chapters in this volume focus on the various ways music communicates, engages, and establishes environments with players. This chapter invites you to instead consider both what it means to learn in an RPG as well as the elements that make these games excellent learning environments. How do RPGs teach? What can the field of music theory pedagogy learn from RPGs?

Learning music theory is not unlike beginning a new game. At the outset, students create an identity as a student; then they develop their character, choosing what aspects of music to explore, learning new skills, and overcoming challenges.[1] As with RPGs, learning music theory is both skill-based and cumulative in nature, with early skills creating the foundation for more advanced skills (e.g., learning scales and key signatures before learning about diatonic harmony). Nonetheless, it is unlikely that many music students, especially those beginning study in higher education, would describe their experiences in music theory classrooms as being comparable to playing video games. This chapter suggests that reframing the way we think about teaching music theory in higher education—by imagining we are designing an RPG instead of a course syllabus—could potentially improve the learning experience of our students.

What makes video games and RPGs a good role model for music theory pedagogy? Boettcher, Hahn, and Shaw suggest that "the underlying basis of the higher brain functions that apply to mathematics, music or chess is abstract, spatio-temporal firing-pattern development by groups of neurons over large regions of cortex for some tens of seconds."[2] Thus, their research suggests that games, mathematics, and music have much in common cognitively. As such, video games and learning have become the focus of some research in education and psychology.

Music Theory Pedagogy and RPGs **147**

Applications of research on motivation and learning in video games may prove to be very informative for the ways music theory pedagogy can adapt and change to directly address issues of motivation and engagement in music theory. First, the chapter will outline some of the research in psychology and education on the topics of motivation and engagement, particularly the work of Deci, Ryan, and Rigby. Next, I introduce some of the blossoming studies in video game research that investigate the psychological and philosophical role between games and learning. Finally, I outline some key concepts from this research and how it can be applied in music theory course designs and classrooms.

Deci and Ryan's self-determination theory (SDT) "bring[s] together innate human tendencies, social contexts, and the motivators for human action to illustrate how congruence between one's basic needs and core values spur individual agency that, ultimately, results in overall well-being."[3] Three basic psychological needs form the core of SDT: autonomy, competence, and relatedness. Autonomy promotes intrinsic motivation by providing choices and enhancing a sense of self-initiation, whereas "motivational strategies such as rewards and threats undermine autonomy and thus lead to nonoptimal outcomes such as decreased intrinsic motivation, less creativity, and poorer problem solving."[4] The need for competence is linked to motivation primarily through feedback; relatedness, or meaningful connections with others, provides support and a sense of security for intrinsic motivation.[5]

SDT has been applied in many fields, including an investigation into why video games are motivational. Rigby and Ryan directly applied SDT to video games, creating the Player Experience of Need Satisfaction (PENS), which maps the need fulfillment of SDT (competence, autonomy, and relatedness) directly onto video games. Because RPGs are most associated with fulfilling the need of autonomy, this chapter will focus only on this specific need.[6] The need for autonomy is fulfilled in games by providing meaningful choices and the opportunity to act volitionally. Rigby and Ryan warn that autonomy is not simply a feeling of freedom or having a large array of choices, but the ability to act volitionally, which they describe as "one's actions [being] aligned with one's inner self and values; that you feel *you* are making the decisions and are able to stand behind what you do."[7] Video games fulfill this need by giving players the opportunity to form a virtual identity, the option and choice of activities to pursue, the choice over strategies and tactics, and sometimes an open-world "sandbox" for players to freely explore. Even when there are limited choices available, video games may allow players to act volitionally through narrative gameplay, stories, or character building.

There are three main opportunities to fulfill the need of autonomy in RPGs: character identity, choices, and volitional engagement. When we begin to play an RPG, we often do not directly play as ourselves—we create a character that represents our identity in a game's world. A player-controlled character is one of the defining features of an RPG, according to Hitchens and Drachen, and contributes to autonomy by the player realizing their character's individuality and observing the development and change over time of their character. A player also has control over quantitative aspects of their character (skills and abilities) and qualitative aspects (personality).[8]

How does a player create their character? Along the spectrum of character creation options are two extremes: complete customization and no customization. In a game like *Dragon Age: Inquisition* (Electronic Arts, 2014), players create a detailed character before beginning gameplay: character creation begins by choosing their character's sex, race (Human, Elf, Dwarf, or Qunari), class, difficulty, and physical appearance—ranging from preset options to finely tuned choices for things like hair color and even earlobe size. On the other end of the spectrum are games like *Persona 5* (Atlus, 2016) or many of the *Final Fantasy* games, where players have little control over the backstory, appearance, or personal qualities of their character at the outset of the game, but may be able to shape what kind of character they become through their decisions, actions, and game events.[9]

In addition to defining their characters' skills, background, and appearance, some games also allow players to customize their character's morality. *Fable* (Microsoft Game Studios, 2004) and its sequels, as one example of several, illustrates a game that reflects positive or negative ethical decisions made by the player in the game's world, similar to a simplified character alignment system. Players receive feedback in the game about their morality by their visual appearance (e.g., halos for good characters, horns for evil characters) and in the interactions of non-player characters (NPCs). A system of morality can help shape a character's rationale for making certain narrative and interactive decisions, which will affect a player's volitional engagement, discussed more in depth below.

What do these identities help us achieve? Gee states that virtual identities allow us to fully commit to the endeavor of learning: specifically, "that [players] are willing to see themselves in terms of a new identity, ... to see themselves as the *kind of person* who can learn, use, and value the new semiotic domain."[10] These virtual identities also give the player an easy way to conceptualize their progress and abilities in the game ("My dual-wielding elf is level 32!"), and the freedom to explore the kinds of choices and actions they may not make on a regular basis with their real-world identity.

Allowing players to choose how they explore and interact with the game's world adds to a sense of freedom and autonomy in RPGs. This freedom of choice often manifests in quest design, where players may choose what they want to do from a given list of quest-like options. The number of opportunities varies from game to game. Some RPGs follow a fairly linear narrative, like *Final Fantasy XIII* (Square Enix, 2009) or *Persona 5*, both of which involve progress through a predetermined story that largely remains unaffected by player decisions. Other RPGs feature open-world games that enable and encourage players to freely explore a large environment where they may discover the world at their own pace, such as *Elder Scrolls V: Skyrim* (Bethesda, 2011). Additionally, outdoor settings often

Music Theory Pedagogy and RPGs **149**

enhance this sense of freedom and exploration, resulting in many open-world games featuring lush landscapes and picturesque vistas.

Role-playing games may offer the player decisions beyond choice of activity. Many games offer the potential for numerous, creative solutions to a given challenge or problem. For example, a linear game may not give a player much choice in which boss enemy they will face at the end of a story arc, but may instead give the player many choices in how to pursue defeating that boss, either through character customization, choice of party members, or any other number of strategic choices. Games may give players the option to fight a battle head-on or avoid battles through stealth or optional side-quests, or, during battles, the choice to interact aggressively or passively with the enemy; the latter is a notable feature in *Undertale* (Toby Fox, 2015).

Once the player has established an identity for their character and is faced with numerous choices for them to make, how do they make decisions about what to do next? How do games add meaning and volition to the choices we make? Games often provide a context for choices, both in their narrative and though consequences that alter the state of the game's world. For example, near the conclusion of *Dragon Age: Origins* (Electronic Arts, 2009), the player's character and NPC companions are confronted by one of the main villains of the game, Loghain Mac Tir, who betrayed his former king, branded the protagonist as a traitor with a bounty, and named his own daughter as queen. After defeating Loghain, the player must decide between mercy—sentencing him to serve in the character's party as a Grey Warden—or revenge via execution. The game provides additional context by having NPC companions chime in with their thoughts and opinions. If mercy is chosen (generally identified as the "good" action), a close NPC companion will abandon the party before the final quest. Will the player make a decision that aligns with their character's moral code? Or will they decide, against their better judgment, to satisfy a companion?[11]

These types of choices, framed by the narrative context of the game, allow the player to choose an outcome in a way that provides volitional engagement—a player is able to choose an option based on their beliefs and feel ownership in their decision, whether they are making a decision based on quantitative character elements ("I have to do X or my best mage will leave the party") or qualitative character elements ("My character's personality would never agree to this course of action, so I must choose Y"). However, not all games offer such meaningful choices. Rigby and Ryan acknowledge that "one can also feel autonomy when the only option open to you is one that makes sense to pursue, whether or not options are present."[12] In *Persona 5*, the first main quest in the game involves confronting a teacher at the player character's high school who is physically abusing and sexually harassing their fellow students, leading one NPC to attempt suicide. The game ultimately presents the player with a quest to change the teacher's heart, which will result in him publicly apologizing and turning himself into the authorities. This is a required quest—players do not have an alternative narrative choice in the game; nonetheless, if a player feels that this course of action makes sense and aligns with their own beliefs and code of ethics, they may still perceive a sense of autonomy through that volitional engagement.

Having discussed how RPGs fulfill the need for autonomy through identity, meaningful choices, and volitional engagement, I will explore ways to incorporate these design elements into the music theory classroom. One of the first things a student brings to a classroom is their identity. Based on Hitchens and Drachen's definitions of RPG features, a player will feel a sense of identity through character individuality, capability of the character to develop over time, and ability to control the character's quantitative and qualitative progress.[13] What would this application look like in a music theory course design?

Character development in terms of skills and abilities will mostly likely manifest in a course design through assessment.[14] In order for students to feel ownership in their progress in a course, there need to be clear goals based on skills that can be followed and tracked over time.[15] There are any number of ways to incorporate such a system in a course. Designing a course around skills to master and allowing students to choose how to achieve mastery could be one solution. Nilson advocates specifications grading, which matches learning outcomes directly to the way students are assessed.[16] Instead of assessing specific types of assignments and activities (e.g., midterm exam, final exam, homework assignments, reading responses, etc.), learning objectives and outcomes would be assessed individually, which means that one assignment might receive multiple grades based on the different skills included in the assignment. For example, a first-year music theory course might list scales, key signatures, and intervals as some of the learning objectives of a course. However, one assignment may include exercises that practice all of those skills. In this case, each specific skill would be assessed separately.

Each skill in specifications grading is then graded on a pass/fail basis: "with respect to rigor and motivation, student learning seems to thrive in a pass/fail environment when it is the only environment."[17] This binary feedback is even similar to the type of feedback a player receives while playing a game: a goal or task is either completed or not completed, an enemy is either defeated or not defeated, etc. Additionally, criteria for each objective would have a clear outline or rubric for pass requirements, as these rubrics would only require one level of explanation.

Upon experiencing a failure, players in RPGs are seldom given correct answers, but may be provided with hints, reminders, and encouragement to try again. For example, in *Bastion* (Warner Brothers Interactive Entertainment, 2011), when a character's health falls below a certain threshold, the game reminds the player that pressing "F" will heal your character during combat. If you fail completely, resulting in character death, the game prompts you to press the "ESC" key in order to "carry on"; in this case, there is no "game over" dialogue, and the game resets to give you another opportunity to succeed. This feedback signals to the player that there is an opportunity to improve and provides additional information the player may need to turn the failure into a success. Some games are even more blatant about the importance of failure during the game, such as *Dark Souls* (Namco Bandai Games, 2011) using failure as a requirement in order to complete certain goals.

In order that failure during a game not cause a major setback, the stakes for failing during a game are usually low, with players having multiple opportunities to try again with very few, if any, real-world consequence. By contrast, assignments in classes often come with real-world consequences, where graded assessments may have a significant impact on final grades, the ability to progress to the next in a sequence of courses, to remain in a specific degree program, or continue to receive scholarships. Allowing students to "fail safely" and lower the stakes in a class setting may include adjusting the number of graded assignments, a flipped class environment where students work on application of knowledge on their own or in groups and receive more immediate in-person feedback before a more formal assessment, or allowing students to revise and resubmit previous attempts at assignments. While allowing revisions of assignments may sound like extra grading work, instructors may follow RPG models of feedback: instead of revealing answers, they may ask students to problem solve and detect their own errors, saving time in and out of the classroom. These types of adjustments can be applied to a single assignment or activity, a topic-based unit, or an entire course depending on the needs of the students and teachers.

In order to incorporate specifications grading into an even more RPG-like system, individual skills may be grouped together into larger categories. (This grouping is also helpful if a conversion into a standard letter grade at the end of a course is desired—passing X number of categories results in Y letter grade, for example.) For example, a larger fundamentals category may be created that includes the individual skills of scales, key signatures, and intervals, among other topics. To pass fundamentals, students will need to complete their smaller objectives in scales, key signatures, and intervals. Such a setup begins to resemble a quest system that might be encountered in an RPG, with categories or areas of adventure containing smaller quests and objectives upon arrival, creating a clear way for students to chart and conceptualize their progress over time.

Specifications grading is only one option for assessment that may help encourage more motivation in music theory classes. RPGs often give a player control over their character's personality and individuality, which is something that may not be addressed by a course's assessment design. However, time and space for student reflection and personal development can also be incorporated into a class. Providing students with an opportunity to reflect on their progress and their learning can help them cope with any fears and anxieties about the course, help them identify and develop their personal musical tastes, and begin to build a learner identity of a young music scholar. Using this reflective thinking during written assignments can also help improve a student's ability to communicate about music through writing.

152 Meghan Naxer

Another hallmark design of RPGs that can be incorporated into a course design is the amount of choice students will have. Freedom to explore and choose how to embark on a student's own learning can be implemented in a course design on a small or large scale.[18] Simple ways for students to have meaningful choices in a music theory course may range from asking students to contribute to a repertoire list for the course or offering a list of options for students to choose from for projects. However, for these simple implementations to feel meaningful, small acts of agency should be able to be traced back to the larger goals of the course; one way to accomplish this would be to think of smaller decisions as being like single quests in a larger quest chain.

Many of the meaningful choices presented in RPGs stem from allowing players to access large sections of a map or world and choose their own path forward, where revisiting areas is an (often necessary) option. If a course adopts a quest-like system for assessment as described above, using specifications grading or something similar, giving students access to large sections of the course and freedom to pursue any branch of questlines in any order is one way to replicate those types of choices in RPGs. For example, imagine a first-year music theory course that has two main areas of its map: fundamental skills and Baroque counterpoint. The first half of the course will focus on fundamental skills and students may choose their own path through the following objectives: notation, rhythm, meter, pitch identification, clef reading, scales and scale degrees, key signatures, intervals, triads, and seventh chords. Once a student has passed an objective, they do not need to keep practicing the objective on assignments, but they will need to display this mastery during a midterm "boss" before the next large area of objectives unlocks. While students may not need to keep practicing mastered skills, there is always the opportunity to revisit a skill for additional practice and feedback.

The appendix provides one possible course design like this for a course in music theory, but any such designs would likely require a large consideration of other elements of its design. For instance, in order to allow students this freedom of choice, assignment options for each skill might need to be compiled before the launch of each large "map area." Additionally, lecture-style class meetings may not be relevant for all students in the course if they are pursuing different objectives. Activity-based class meetings or flipped classes might be a better solution for realizing this kind of design choice. For example, asking students working on different objectives to work collaboratively on analyzing a piece of repertoire would require teamwork and sharing of knowledge in order to complete the activity, not unlike a plucky group of party members embarking on a challenging adventure in an RPG.

While choices are available for students to decide how they want to pursue their path through a course, including options that engage students volitionally can also improve student motivation. As discussed earlier, the kinds of decisions that provide volitional engagement often involve story or narrative decisions that impact the game world. For Hitchens and Drachen, part of what defines an RPG is "players affect[ing] the evolution of the game world through the actions of their characters."[19] What kind of decisions and actions can students take to affect their music theory classroom?

On a small scale, activities that are flexible enough for a narrative to emerge based on student choices can help students feel a sense of volitional engagement. For example, analyzing a piece of repertoire can yield multiple viewpoints and interpretations. Challenging students with a difficult piece can lead to debates between differing interpretations. Students can then prepare and argue for their interpretation like a case where the piece of music is on trial. After hearing all sides of the argument, groups can cross-examine each other by asking questions and challenging the other group's viewpoints. Finally, the class as a whole can vote on the verdict and may discuss whether they were swayed by a different group's argument. By introducing narrative elements to an activity, where students may even role-play a specific character (a musical lawyer, in this example), stakes in the activity are raised through volitional engagement without the use of grades or assessment as incentives.[20] As an instructor, responding to situations that arise in class by weaving in a narrative story can emulate the kind of volitional engagement players may feel in RPGs. Hitchens and Drachen even go so far as stating that "it could be argued that the narrative elements in role-playing games are a result of other, defining, elements and that it is a corollary, not a necessary element in itself."[21]

A larger-scope option to reflect student choice in the design of a course is to "hack" the syllabus.[22] By allowing students to edit their syllabus, their choices have an immediate impact on the course. This editing may be one way to incorporate student choices mentioned earlier, like repertoire choices. While RPGs may not allow you to change rulesets or how a game engine functions, implementing student decisions in an official document like a course syllabus can be one way for the environment of the course to react to student changes in a real and tangible way. The course syllabus could even be revisited at regular intervals to allow for continuing changes and edits throughout a semester or school year.

While there are many suggestions presented by this chapter, every class and every group of students is different, just like every group of RPG players. Using RPG elements of design in a music theory course can make it a more motivating and engaging experience for students, but there is no one-size-fits-all approach to design. Ultimately, every teacher will need to decide on what elements work best for their teaching philosophy and for their specific student body.

While RPGs present us with a myriad of tools to help make our classrooms motivating and engaging spaces, it is important to remember that these tools work well in video games not only because of any specific tool's design, but because of the psychological models of motivation behind the design and the larger game system as a whole. Incorporating a few disparate tools into a course without considering the larger picture will be less effective than considering the philosophical changes that need to be made in our own approaches to teaching and learning.

There is a large paradigm shift from identifying as a teacher who disseminates content and values outcomes to an instructional designer who creates a learning environment, values the learning experience, and adapts to reflect the choices and abilities of the participating students. The attitudes, beliefs, and philosophies of teachers in a classroom can have a large impact on the philosophies and beliefs of their students. By understanding how RPGs and video games work psychologically and philosophically, we can begin to experience teaching and learning more like a game designer.

Appendix: Sample Course Designs

For each of the following example course-design elements, I will be assuming a first-semester (15-week) music theory course with separate, but coordinated, aural skills courses. These examples and commentaries are intended as design examples and possibilities, not plug-and-play templates.

Assessment: Branching Questlines

Large learning objectives for the whole course will serve as "map" areas like an RPG, where there will be one or more "main quests." Two units of seven weeks each can be divided into Fundamentals I and Baroque I units with the following objectives:

- *Fundamentals I*: demonstrate mastery of basic diatonic skills in music.
- *Baroque I*: identify norms of Baroque style and form, compose music in a Baroque style, apply fundamental analytical skills in Baroque repertoire, realize figured bass, identify and incorporate appropriate embellishing tones.

These large objectives can be further broken down into branching "questlines" of smaller objectives. These objectives will receive pass (P) or not yet (NY) grades on assignments or activities that are cumulative. Once a student achieves a pass for an objective, they are no longer required to continue working on that objective. However, they may always revisit that skill for more practice (or level grinding).

Fundamentals I: Basic Analytical Tools

- Notation
- Rhythm
- Meter
- Pitch Identification
- Clef Reading
- Scales
- Scale-Degree Names
- Key Signatures

Music Theory Pedagogy and RPGs **155**

- Intervals
- Triads
- Seventh Chords

Baroque I: Species Counterpoint and Four-Voice Chorale Style

- First Species
- Second Species
- Third Species
- Fourth Species
- Four-Voice Voice Leading
- Four-Voice Figured Bass Realization
- Embellishing Tones and Ornamentation

Each of these large units may culminate in a cumulative "final boss" that could be a higher-stakes assessment, a final project, or other activity.

Game Over: Press Start to Try Again

There are numerous ways to give students opportunities to "fail safely" or retry an activity/assignment/mission/quest upon a failure. When combined with the specifications-grading assessment above, students continue to have the opportunity to work on skills until a Pass is achieved, which lowers the stakes of any single attempt at a skill. However, not all classes may be able to implement the grading system above. For individual assignments, especially of written music theory, consider providing feedback more like a video game would: only hints, never answers, with strategy and error detection required of the student. For example, a syllabus might include the following statement: "Practice assignments will not receive a grade upon initial completion; instead, you will receive feedback on which areas need further attention and revision. Practice assignments will receive a grade after their first resubmission. No further resubmissions will be accepted." When I have used this style of feedback and revision in my own classes, I have used a highlighter to mark sections of assignments that need corrections instead of a pen, in order to cut down on the temptation to write more hints than I should. After receiving feedback, students have the opportunity to ask questions, seek assistance, and correct their work in a way that encourages learning from mistakes without also penalizing those initial mistakes. Alternatively, a course could be taught using a flipped class style, which would put more emphasis on receiving immediate verbal feedback in class during activities and in-class assignments.

Hack the Syllabus: Considering Difficulty and Repertoire

When beginning a new game in an RPG, oftentimes there are a variety of choices a player will need to make before embarking on their adventures. Some of those

156 Meghan Naxer

decisions revolve around character creation, while others are important decisions about how you want to play the game in terms of difficulty. For example, *The Witcher 3: Wild Hunt* (CD Projekt, 2015) offers players the following difficulty options:

- Just the Story! (Easy): "Enjoy a smooth ride through the world."
- Story and Sword! (Normal): "You're happy to be challenged."
- Blood and Broken Bones! (Hard): "You're a seasoned, demanding gamer."
- Death March! (Very Hard): "You're truly insane and loving it."

While some games, like *Witcher 3*, allow players to change the difficulty settings at any time, other games lock you into your decision at the beginning of the game. Allowing students to choose some of the settings of a course at the beginning of a semester can simulate the types of decisions a player makes when starting a new game. While students may not have an option for the difficulty of the course as a whole, they can have difficulty options through other means, such as repertoire selections.

The beginning of a course is a good time for instructors and students to communicate about expectations, goals, and setup of a course. While a first-semester music theory course might not be the ideal time to allow students to directly edit all parts of a syllabus, it can be helpful to allow students to input or request musical repertoire they would like to study. With each repertoire selection, an instructor can identify a topic and difficulty level for that work and share a list of requests with the students. Then students are able to choose music to include in a course based on their tastes, interests, and assigned difficulty levels.

In addition to selecting repertoire, students may also have choices about what assignments they may complete in a setup following the earlier specifications grading assessment example or they may have other framing decisions that help guide their learning to a specific final project. If the instructor would like to give students multiple options for a final project, allowing them to make decisions earlier in the class to prepare them for their chosen path can help those decisions be more meaningful for students. For example, the Baroque I unit described above may offer a variety of final project options:

- Write a three- to five-page analysis of a work by Bach or Handel.
- Realize a figured bassline from a Baroque chamber piece.
- Compose an original four-voice chorale warmup for a wind ensemble or SATB choir.
- Compose a fifth-species, two-voice composition.

Instead of asking students to make this decision at the end of a course, ask them to make this decision earlier during a semester and tailor assignments or activities based on their choices. Students composing a four-voice chorale may work more with chorale-style repertoire in class, while students working on fifth-species compositions may study two-voice inventions instead. Students writing an analysis paper may receive more written assignments instead of composition assignments.

While this kind of specification may seem daunting to an instructor, outlining these kinds of design decisions before beginning to teach a class can save time, as well as narrow the decision space based on the capabilities and resources of the instructor. A flipped class environment may also alleviate some extra preparation time by dividing a class into groups based on shared interests and goals and assigning them in-class activities accordingly.

Notes

All websites accessed August 17, 2018.

1 Some students already familiar with studying music theory may be bringing a pre-formed identity into the higher education classroom. While these students may not have a blank slate, they may be like game players who have played an RPG before and understand some of the conventions of the genre that helped form their identity as players before beginning a new game, thus entering with a variety of expectations.
2 Wendy S. Boettcher, Sabrina S. Hahn, and Gordon L. Shaw, "Mathematics and Music: A Search for Insight into Higher Brain Function," *Leonardo Music Journal* 4 (1994), 57.
3 Michael L. Wehmeyer, Todd D. Little, and Julie Sergeant, "Self-Determination," in *The Oxford Handbook of Positive Psychology,* eds. Shane J. Lopez and C.R. Snyder (Oxford: Oxford University Press, 2009), 359.
4 Wehmeyer, Little, and Sergeant, "Self-Determination."
5 David Shernoff adds that "an important insight of self-determination theory is that there are intermediate positions on the continuum between extrinsic motivation, or feeling controlled, and intrinsic motivation, or feeling fully autonomous." See David J. Shernoff, *Optimal Learning Environments to Promote Student Engagement* (New York: Springer, 2013), 56.
6 The needs for competence and relatedness are also relevant to the educational application of SDT and PENS, though often discussed in the context of other types of games. See Edward L. Deci and Richard M. Ryan, "The 'What' and 'Why' of Goal Pursuits: Human Needs and the Self-Determination of Behavior," *Psychological Inquiry* 11(4) (2000), 227–268; and Scott Rigby and Richard M. Ryan, *How Video Games Draw Us in and Hold Us Spellbound* (Santa Barbara, CA: Praeger, 2011).
7 Rigby and Ryan, *How Video Games Draw Us in and Hold Us Spellbound*, 40.
8 Michael Hitchens and Anders Drachen, "The Many Faces of Role-Playing Games," *International Journal of Role-Playing* 1 (2009): 3–21.
9 This distinction between player-controlled character creation and pre-made characters is one of many hallmarks of Western- vs. Japanese-style role-playing games, respectively. See Matt Barton, *Dungeons and Desktops: The History of Computer Role-Playing Games* (Wellesley, MA: A K Peters, 2008).
10 James Paul Gee, *What Video Games Have to Teach Us About Learning and Literacy,* 2nd ed. (New York: Palgrave Macmillan, 2007), 54.
11 The *Dragon Age* series of games raises the stakes of these moral and game-impacting decisions even more by not only reflecting your choices in the current game's world, but also by maintaining those choices in future titles in the series.
12 Rigby and Ryan, *How Video Games Draw Us in and Hold Us Spellbound*, 41.
13 Hitchens and Drachen, "The Many Faces of Role-Playing Games," 12.

158 Meghan Naxer

14 For a more literal way to incorporate role-playing into the classroom through students assuming the role of an actual character or historical figure, see Mark C. Carnes, *Minds on Fire: How Role-Immersion Games Transform College* (Cambridge, MA: Harvard University Press, 2014).

15 This discussion is also linked to the competence need in SDT and Csikszentmihalyi's Flow Theory. See Rigby and Ryan, *How Video Games Draw Us in and Hold Us Spellbound*; and Mihaly Csikszentmihalyi and Isabella Selega Csikszentmihalyi, *Optimal Experience: Psychological Studies of Flow in Consciousness* (Cambridge: Cambridge University Press, 1988).

16 Linda B. Nilson, *Specifications Grading: Restoring Rigor, Motivating Students, and Saving Faculty Time* (Sterling, VA: Stylus, 2015). Specifications grading is related to several other types of assessment methods, including standards-based grading or criterion-referenced grading, which have successfully been implemented in music theory classrooms. See Brian Moseley, "Using Criterion-Referenced Assessment to Encourage Active Analytical Listening," *Engaging Students: Essays in Music Pedagogy* 2 (2014), http://flipcamp.org/engagingstudents2/essays/moseley.html; and Philip Duker, Kris Shaffer, and Daniel Stevens, "Problem-Based Learning in Music: A Guide for Instructors," *Engaging Students: Essays in Music Pedagogy* 2 (2014), http://flipcamp.org/engagingstudents2/essays/dukerShafferStevens.html.

17 Nilson, *Specifications Grading*, 150.

18 On an even larger scale, a more modular design for an entire music theory curriculum would result in students having the freedom to choose their own path of courses based on their interests and areas of specialization. See Megan L. Lavengood, "Modular Music Theory," *Personal Blog*, June 28, 2018, https://meganlavengood.com/2018/06/28/modular-music-theory/.

19 Hitchens and Drachen, "The Many Faces of Role-Playing Games," 16.

20 Introducing narrative elements in the classroom can also support and improve problem solving by providing a cognitive framework. See Michele D. Dickey, "Game Design Narrative for Learning: Appropriating Adventure Game Design Narrative Devices and Techniques for the Design of Interactive Learning Environments," *Educational Technology Research and Development* 54(3) (2006): 245–263.

21 Hitchens and Drachen, "The Many Faces of Role-Playing Games," 15.

22 Jonathan D. Becker, "Hacking the Syllabus," *Personal Blog,* May 13, 2015, www.jonbecker.net/hacking-the-syllabus/; and Daniel J. Cohen and Tom Scheinfeldt, eds., *Hacking the Academy* (Ann Arbor: University of Michigan Press, 2013), www.press.umich.edu/6195993/hacking_the_academy.

10

SOUNDWALKING AND THE AURALITY OF *STARDEW VALLEY*

An Ethnography of Listening to and Interacting with Environmental Game Audio

Kate Galloway

I wait. My baited hook bobs up and down at the surface of the water with a rhythmic pulse. The waves crash against the wooden pier and roll onto the beach. The piercing cries of seagulls ring in my ears as I attempt to concentrate on reeling in my last catch of the day. I place the freshly caught anchovy in my pack next to a sardine, some seaweed, and two pairs of broken glasses I mistakenly caught earlier that afternoon, and start my walk home to Fuzzy Acres Farm. In the morning I'll sell these items and use the proceeds to purchase parsnip seeds. I'm growing weary because my fishing expedition kept me out a little too late, but I still have a few crops left to water before I could turn in for the night. The sun is beginning to slip away below the treeline. Strolling through the town square, I pass Evelyn, one of Pelican Town's elders, as she tends to the gardens in the town center. She noticed that I was coming from the dock and smelled the residue of salt water on my clothes, remarking how she "loves living close to the ocean and listening to the lapping of the waves." It's a soundmark that defines the coastal region of the valley. Every day (and every time I restart my saved gameplay) is a new listening experience as I discover new places, people, and tasks in the valley. I finally arrive home, put away my watering can, and crawl into bed. I select "sleep," to save my progress from another productive and reinvigorating day in the valley, and close my laptop. Just another day on Fuzzy Acres Farm.

(Fieldnotes excerpt, April 10, 2018)

With the growing interest in back-to-nature living, farm-to-table eating, and organic consumerism, farming simulation RPGs such as *Harvest Moon* (1996–), *Farmville* (2009), or *Stardew Valley* (2016) can offer a compelling way to challenge players to confront and reevaluate their own preconceptions that the "digital" and "natural" are mutually exclusive concepts. Video games are an interactive

160 Kate Galloway

space where players may participate in ludic, reparative acts that reestablish the virtual urban farmer's connection to nature and the nonhuman world. Ecologically informed games like *Stardew Valley* challenge the dominant narrative that human-made technology is responsible for nothing more than environmental degradation. These games demand that we listen past this implicit assumption and come to understand how the "digital" and "natural" converge in productive ways to reframe and extend public discourse surrounding the environment. As the ethnographic vignette from my fieldnotes above indicates, these games use a combination of narrative, visuals, gameplay, and—crucially—sound to convey knowledge about an environment and how it operates to players. As farming simulation RPGs continue to gain popularity, scholars have addressed their visual and ludic elements, but the soundscapes of farming RPGs are unaddressed.[1]

In this chapter I focus on the sound culture of the popular indie farming simulator *Stardew Valley*, and how its game audio reconnects players with nature and ecology, using music and environmental sounds that model ecological principles and facilitate ludic interaction with the materiality of nature. While the soundscapes of other forms of green media have received sustained attention, eco-conscious digital games remain overlooked.[2] Sound provides "a fundamentally different knowledge of the world than vision," argues literary sound studies scholar Bruce R. Smith, and "most academic disciplines remain vision-based, not only in the materials they study, but in the theoretical models they deploy to interpret them."[3] We need to listen in many different ways with different sets of ears to fully understand how and why digital worlds and the world around us sound the way they do and what those sounds mean. Pauline Oliveros left us with the lesson that listening is a form of activism, a tool for understanding difference, increasing mindfulness, and facilitating environmental awareness.[4]

The musical score and ambient soundscape of *Stardew Valley* play a vital role in communicating information about the in-game environment, how it operates, and how the player shapes it. My understanding of *Stardew Valley*'s soundscape and its role in both the ecology of the game environment and the communication of the "back to nature" narrative is informed by thick description of gameplay fieldwork and autoethnography. I conducted fieldwork over the course of four months, playing one in-game week per day of fieldwork. Drawing on autoethnographic fieldwork, I examine what I heard in the acoustic ecology of the game, the player and avatar's relationship to these soundscapes, and how my ways of listening to the game world informed my playing and understanding of *Stardew Valley*'s narrative and ludic design.

Stardew Valley, released on February 26, 2016 to critical praise, is an indie farm simulator open-ended RPG published by Chucklefish and designed and developed by ConcernedApe (aka Eric Barone). Barone took four and a half years to design, program, animate, draw, compose, record, and write all the components of the game.[5] *Stardew Valley* is an homage to the *Harvest Moon* series, but it pushes the boundaries of what it means to be a farming RPG. Barone wanted to create a game that retained the mechanics of nurturing the land and making meaningful connections with the community. These are features of *Harvest Moon* that he values as a fan of the series. But he also wanted to give players more flexibility to play their own way and provide a range of goals and activities to ensure gameplay doesn't stagnate. While there are achievements and awards that mark the completion of tasks in a timely manner, Barone opted to not impose a time limit on completing the majority of the farming, social, and crafting activities. This allows players to proceed at their own pace using their own style of gameplay.

To facilitate interactive play during which the player parses out the ecology of Stardew Valley—a combination of social, environmental, and cultural actors—the visual, sonic, and ludic design must simplify rather than precisely replicate the biological and ecological complexities of the actual world. In his discussion of actor-network theory, Benjamin Piekut similarly conceptualizes the interconnections between human and nonhuman actors in musical experimentalisms as an ecology. He writes:

> An ecology is a web of relations, an amalgamation of organic and inorganic, or biological and technological, elements that are interconnecting and mutually affecting. In other words, like experimentalism or anything else, an ecology is an emergent hybrid grouping that connects many different kinds of things.[6]

Game environments are not wholesale substitutes for real-world experiences of the natural world, and farming RPGs don't fully address the environmental limitations of the modern agriculture industry. However, the virtual environments of farming simulator RPGs and walking simulators have opened up alternate spaces for cultivating community participation and mindful nature-play.[7] Game design, as illustrated in *Stardew Valley* and other environmental games such as *Proteus* (2013) and *Viridi* (2015), can be used to create alternate ways of communicating environmental issues and aesthetic experiences beyond those conventionally communicated to the public; to instruct players in natural processes and life cycles; to give them the opportunity to explore how people, plants, animals, and inorganic matter are interconnected and interdependent; and to play through some of the real consequences of responsible agriculture (e.g., if you do not water your crops, they will not grow).

Knowing and Understanding Fuzzy Acres Farm and *Stardew Valley*'s Digital Nature

After selecting a new game, I'm redirected to an avatar personalization mixing console where I select from a series of options to design my avatar's physical features, preferences, and the design of my farm (see Figure 10.1). The player designs their avatar before hearing the background story and knowing the specifics about

162 Kate Galloway

FIGURE 10.1 Crafting my avatar (all gameplay fieldwork stills and any annotations by the author)

the mechanics of their avatar's farm and the citizens of Pelican Town. The player prepares behind the scenes, "much like actors," as Kiri Miller explains, "getting into costume and character backstage before a show."[8] The ability to craft an avatar provides the player with an opportunity to reflect upon the realities of the modern agriculture industry. This could be taken up by the player as an opportunity space for personalized gameplay and any kind of self-representation. As it is, the majority of "[f]arm games, with their default cast of pale, cheerful faces," explains Alenda Y. Chang, "appear intent on ignoring such realities." She continues: "An astonishing number of titles feature fair-skinned, redheaded heroines, who sport nary a freckle or sunburn even after toiling in the hot sun for months on end."[9]

Like most digital games that incorporate identity play, *Stardew Valley* gives the player freedom in shaping the appearance of their avatar. I crafted my avatar from the onscreen options, personalizing it with aspects of my real-world experiences. A young woman, whose pixelated face appears close to me in age, with bright purple hair referencing my former fashion hair color choice from last spring (see Figure 10.1). I name her Darby, my mother's maiden name, which at one point my parents had intended to name me. This process of identity crafting doesn't have a time restriction. I take my time perfecting my avatar while accompanied by a meandering melody of old-time style banjo picking in the track "Stardew Valley Overture," a melody that winds and loops, layered at times with panpipe and harp. This melody continues to play until I confirm that my avatar is complete, and I—as my avatar Darby—wish to proceed in the game.

Soundwalking and Aurality of *Stardew Valley* **163**

In silence, the screen fades to black followed by a prologue that details Darby's "back to nature" origin story and how she came to live in Stardew Valley. Her grandfather lies ill in his bed adjacent to the wood-burning fireplace, tightly holding a sealed envelope intended for her. The non-diegetic sentimental music box melody plinks and repeats as Darby is instructed to take the letter but patiently wait until she senses it's the right time to open it and receive her grandfather's directives (see Figure 10.2). Until then, she must listen closely to his advice: "There

FIGURE 10.2 Opening scenes of *Stardew Valley* gameplay

164 Kate Galloway

will come a day when you feel crushed by the burden of modern life. And your bright spirit will fade before a growing emptiness. When that happens, my girl, you'll be ready for this gift." Grandfather fades away. The narrative skips ahead an indeterminate number of years and to a location inside the glassed-in confining cubicle pen at the Joja Corporation, where employers monitor other employees' every task from behind glass windows. The Joja motto, "Join Us. Thrive," is painted boldly on the wall in view for all employees to see, all of whom are commanded by an endlessly blinking green light labeled "work" beside a red light for "rest" (which we never see illuminate). With a lack of natural light and an incessant soundscape of cycling electrical hum, the blasting air vents recirculating stale air, and computer keyboard clicks, this sterile sensory environment engenders a lethargic workforce disconnected from the natural world and each other.

I find Darby sitting in a bland, gray cubicle struggling through yet another monotonous day at her nine-to-five job. The work she must complete demands no creative thought, and the soundscape lacks vibrancy and variety. Darby is uninspired. She stares at the computer screen in her impersonal cubicle, a half-empty cold coffee sitting at her side, and wonders how much longer she can endure this lifestyle before her personal health and happiness demand a radical change. The computer desk opens with a creak to reveal the letter that rested in wait until Darby was at last "crushed by the burden of modern life." Her grandfather writes:

> *Dear granddaughter,*
>
> *If you're reading this, you must be in dire need of a change. The same thing happened to me, long ago. I'd lost sight of what mattered most in life … real connections with other people and nature. So I dropped everything and moved to the place I truly belong. I've enclosed the deed to that place … my pride and joy: Fuzzy Meadows Farm. It's located in Stardew Valley, on the southern coast. It's the perfect place to start your new life. This was my most precious gift of all, and now it's yours. I know you'll honor the family home, my girl. Good luck.*
>
> *Love, Grandpa*

As Darby reads the letter, the music box melody returns, a sonic memory of grandfather who anticipated her needs. He has gifted her an option to escape the chaos of modern life, the incessant urban soundscape, and the mundane workday of the modern mega-corporation.

The screen reloads, and the soundscape shifts from cyclic electrical hum to a chorus of birds chirping and singing as Darby rides the bus to her destination, Pelican Town, the final stop in the valley. As Darby steps off the bus, she's met by Robin, the local carpenter. Mayor Lewis sent Robin to escort Darby to her farm. Their walk to the farm is accompanied by the upbeat "Settling In" as Robin and Mayor Lewis help me acclimatize, followed by "Spring (It's a Big World Outside)" as Darby starts her first day on the farm. It's a musical cue that returns to introduce each spring as the seasons cycle, signifying rejuvenation and hopeful

Soundwalking and Aurality of *Stardew Valley* **165**

new beginnings.[10] The track is melodically and rhythmically active, capturing the effect of the flora and fauna sprouting and blooming in springtime.

This is the beginning of my explorations with my avatar Darby on her farm, in Pelican Town, and around the surrounding regions of Stardew Valley. As in many games, in *Stardew Valley* an avatar represents the player in the gameworld, while the player manipulates, moves, strategizes for, and makes gameplay decisions on its behalf. It felt like I was working with Darby as I made decisions for her as we collectively tended to the farm and nurtured relationships with the townspeople. In a similar way that William Cheng once challenged why virtual musicians are denied musicality, I question why virtual farmers are denied a green thumb.[11] Over the course of playthrough, the player and their avatar acquire agricultural skills and knowledge that can be mapped (with some adaptation) onto actual-world farming. The decisions I made conditioned how Darby developed her farm and explored Stardew Valley's ecosystem to find her place within it. All the while, I listened to its soundscape and considered my own relationship to my environment on the other side of the screen.

Game environments are more than visual. In my reading and playing of *Stardew Valley*, I'm less concerned with the fidelity of actual world representations of nature and the agriculture industry and I'm instead drawn to the affective affordances among player, place, and soundscape. This isn't a game where player agency is centered on mastery, weaponization, combat, or narratives of overcoming. It's a game that values social and sensory understanding of the world and its actors, one that develops through the avatar and the player's interactions with the things, objects, and nonhumans of the gameworld. You play the role of a farmer, but—like a farmer in the actual world—you are also a puzzle solver, figuring out how nature operates, what it responds to, and whether that response enhances or encumbers gameplay. By putting the appropriate pieces together, the player discovers how the environment they are a part of operates. The player farms along with their avatar, evaluating and sensing the environment and their place in it. According to Lawrence Buell, an ideal environmental text is one that fosters involvement, moral responsibility, and participation in the text's world and the reader's world.[12] It's not the player's goal to master or overcome the environment in *Stardew Valley*, but rather, to be a productive part of it and acknowledge their moral responsibility to contribute to its ecology.

Game environments are obviously not substitutes for actual world experiences of nonhuman nature (though Michiel Kamp and Mark Sweeney question this premise in the following chapter), but they are an accessible option for those unable to access "nature" directly due to physical, geographic, or socioeconomic limitations. Video games—specifically indie games for PC or mobile media platforms that require a low financial investment—provide alternative opportunities for community participation in nature play, whether in the form of a walking simulator, world builder, farming RPG, or another kind of environmental game. These game genres deliberately shift gameplay away from combat toward a mode

166 Kate Galloway

of gameplay where players collaborate and socialize with, and come to depend on, the gameworld actors. Instead of fighting the world around them, avatars nurture and maintain their environment, mindfully clean it up when necessary, and patiently wait for it to grow and restore.

Players care about places they connect with. To provide this sense of connection with—or belonging to—place, it's important that game environments exhibit realistic qualities and actions even when they are not depicting places that are possible to visit and experience in the real world. This is because human beings are "placelings" as cultural geographer Edward S. Casey argues: "we are not only in place but of them."[13] *Stardew Valley* and other environmental games take places seriously in their rendering of environments, but also in their detailed weather conditions and the interactions among human and nonhuman-organic and inorganic actors. The sound design of each actor in the game environment is carefully planned—the audible foreground and background soundscape layers and how the soundscape shifts and cycles from day to night. Writing specifically about the relationship between sound and vision, Tim Ingold proposes that "the eyes and ears should not be understood as separate keyboards for the registration of sensation but as organs of the body as a whole, in whose movement, within an environment, the activity of perception consists."[14] Gameworlds are environments we are meant to listen to.

Soundwalking *Stardew Valley*

Early on in my fieldwork, I observed that my gameplay resembled a soundwalk. I was experiencing a moving sonic environmental and the flexible gameplay of *Stardew Valley* provided an opportunity space for me and my avatar Darby to amass embodied sonic experiences that I would use to know this virtual environment. A substantial amount of each day was spent walking around my farm, Pelican Town, and the playable game space of Stardew Valley, but I walked at a staggered pace, pausing often to listen for extended stretches of time. Anytime I'm in a new place, whether traveling or getting to know a new fieldwork site, I listen to it through soundwalking. Hildegard Westerkamp, an early proponent of the activity, provides a deliberately broad definition of a soundwalk, describing it as "any excursion whose main purpose is listening to the environment. It is exposing our ears to every sound around us no matter where we are."[15]

Andra McCartney further defines soundwalking as a "creative and research practice that involves listening and sometimes recording while moving through a place at a walking pace. It is concerned with the relationship between soundwalkers and their surrounding sonic environment."[16] McCartney highlights in her soundwalking practice an emphasis on "slowness, human movement and a focus on particular places brings attention to the presence of the soundwalkers and their ways of interaction in that place."[17] Avatar movement in *Stardew Valley* is deliberately slow and its slow pace resembles the preferred pace of soundwalk practitioners. Your avatar can't run and bound through the forest and fields with

Soundwalking and Aurality of *Stardew Valley* 167

abandon. This slowness encourages contemplation and careful exploration of place. Soundwalking in *Stardew Valley* does differ in some ways from the soundwalking practices of Westerkamp and McCartney, but there are many points of convergence. In each of these cases, for example, the soundscape—"digital" *and* "natural"—contains a finite number of sonic components. There are only so many sounds in the actual world, and the same is true for a digital gameworld. Westerkamp and McCartney conduct their soundscapes in real time; therefore, like a player starting a new game, they cannot predetermine the sounds they will encounter. In any given environment, an array of spatially and temporally contingent sonic possibilities are present.

On my first day on the farm in *Stardew Valley*, I—as my avatar Darby—didn't do any farming. Darby woke up to the crow of the rooster, and as she opened her eyes the loading screen transitioned from black to inside her farmhouse. Following the opening measures of "Spring (The Valley Comes Alive)," Darby rolled out of bed at six o'clock in the morning and ventured outside to begin her soundwalk. Darby walked and explored, and I intensely listened until midnight when my avatar grew tired (see Figure 10.3).[18] I, the player, could hear this music layered over the ambient soundscape, but I wondered what was audible to Darby and the other non-player characters (NPCs) from their unique listening perspectives. While the diegetic environmental soundscape is a constant part of the game audio, the non-diegetic music isn't present in all of the spaces that Darby walks. It's not present, for instance, when Darby crosses onto the seashore or enters the forest. And, while it plays in the town center and on Darby's farm throughout the day, it is absent at night, and replaced by a vociferous ensemble of crickets.

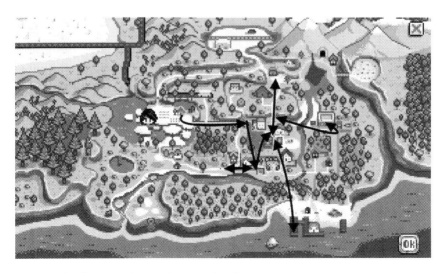

FIGURE 10.3 Annotated gameplay soundwalk map

168 Kate Galloway

As Darby walked, the varied mix of animal sounds, the changing timbre of her footsteps against different terrain, the burbling stream flowing into the ocean, and the shimmer of grasses and trees in the breeze were a source of curiosity and reflection as I listened while moving through the natural and built architecture of the valley. According to Tim Ingold and Jo Lee Vergunst, "social relations," and I would add sonic relations, "are not enacted *in situ* but are paced out along the ground."[19] Our experience of the soundscape is largely acousmatic, but I still found myself redirecting my avatar's body in the direction of the sound source, as I would turn my own body while listening on a soundwalk. The transmission of knowledge about the gameworld environment, like the actual environment, is perceived through our embodied interactions with places and their materiality.[20] Even in a digital game the environment responds to our presence and actions. A tree cracks, bends, and crashes to the ground when Darby chops it down. The choreography of her footsteps changes in pacing, pitch, and organization on different kinds of terrain. When she chases after a seagull on the beach in the game as I did as a child on the beach in Vancouver, it squawks, loudly beats its wings, and flies away.

After the first two in-game hours of walking, I found that I was listening closely to the aural culture of distinct regions. I asked myself: How did Pierre's independent grocery store selling exclusively local seeds and produce sound different when compared to the corporate supermarket Joja Mart? What are the Cindersnap Forest's soundmarks? Where could I hear non-diegetic music and where is the game audio exclusively diegetic environment sounds? I was particularly interested in exploring how these soundworlds transitioned as I moved from one location into another (see Figure 10.4). As Darby entered and exited the built architecture of Pelican Town and walked the paved and unpaved paths linking the countryside and forests to the town, I listened to how the balance of the soundscape shifted as my proximity to different landmarks and water bodies changed. I continued this practice of soundwalking the game's different seasons throughout my gameplay ethnography.

During the late afternoon, I heard the distant chugging of the steam train. The text box "A train is passing through Stardew Valley" pops up in the bottom right-hand corner of my screen. Darby missed the train again. Trains cut through the valley at irregular intervals between 9 a.m. and 6 p.m. Earlier that day Darby stood on the station platform, and I had hoped this would be the day a train passed through. I'd guided her to the station to seek out the sounds of the steam train, and although I was disappointed to miss the train I discovered it was an ideal location to place Darby while I listened to the chorus of birdsong. Here, unlike other gameworld regions, there are audible layers of birdsong with individual voices advancing into the foreground and receding into the background. There are melodies and staccato chirps at different dynamic levels, and varied timbral qualities indicate the presence of multiple species: what Schafer refers to as a "bird symphony" in his analysis of the aurality of life in the modern soundscape.[21]

Soundwalking and Aurality of *Stardew Valley* **169**

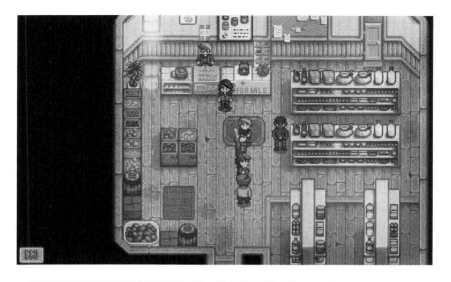

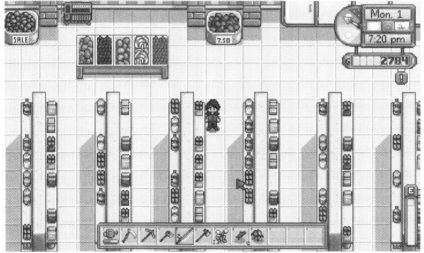

FIGURE 10.4 Sample regions of *Stardew Valley*

As the seasons changed, my progress in the game unlocked new playable game-world regions in Stardew Valley. My soundwalking with Darby reminded me that I was a listener who connects with music and sound while moving through place, and this shaped both my gameplay and my ethnography. Applying the practice of soundwalking to my gameplay revealed the subtle yet significant role of listening in *Stardew Valley*'s gameplay that is not explicitly stated in the directions for the game. While the player's goals include the development of their agricultural

170   Kate Galloway

skills, completing clearly outlined tasks and quests, and socializing with NPCs and animals on the farm and in town, the game mechanics allow for flexibility and interpretation. Although the game directions don't explicitly tell the player to take cues from the sonic environment, the avatar's success in being-in-the-world benefits when the player listens to and analyzes to subtle sonic nuances that contribute to the complexity of their sonic environment.

Listening to *Stardew Valley* and Performing the Farm

> Waking up to the pitter-patter of rain pelting against the farmhouse roof instead of what is typically a rooster crowing, I prepare for my day. The sound of the rain signaled that today I will have more time for other activities because I don't have to water my plants. While walking into town I listened to my feet slop against the damp cobblestones. I observed that the soundscape contained minimal bird calls or other sonic signals of animal life, and fewer townspeople were in the streets. Both the birds and humans were sheltering from the weather, and this response to the weather shaped the soundscape. A few days earlier I walked a similar path and encountered a trio of birds pecking away at the ground. As I approached they chirped loudly. Startled by my presence, they flew away off-screen.
>
> *(Fieldnotes excerpt, May 1, 2018)*

As the player launches *Stardew Valley*, the first sound they hear is vociferous birdsong. Most games open with some kind of sound effect, but in this instance the choice of bird song foregrounds the diegetic soundscape and the back-to-nature narrative. This opening wildlife fanfare shaped how I listened to *Stardew Valley* while playing. It indicated from the outset that the diegetic environmental soundscape is important, and that listening to the sound design would be an appropriate aural strategy during playthrough. In *Stardew Valley* the gameplay, sound design, and narrative welcomes the player into the tight-knit rural community where every person, their actions, and what they contribute to the world around them is central to the health and resilience of the local culture and environment. By using the soundscape, the player comes to understand how *Stardew Valley*—both the game and the place—operates. For the player this means listening to both the diegetic and non-diegetic sounds of the gameworld, because the player has aural access to sonic information (e.g., the non-diegetic music) that is inaudible to their avatar.

Sound is an aural signature of our dynamic and actively sensed surroundings. By attending to embodied experiences of gameplay, as Aubrey Anable has explored in *Playing with Feelings*, we gain a richer understanding of "how games make complex meanings across history, bodies, hardware, and code."[22] As my gameplay experience deepened, it became apparent that Darby was living in (and I was playing in) a world that was alive and dynamic. It responded to her actions

Soundwalking and Aurality of *Stardew Valley* **171**

and presence as Darby and I interacted with its vibrant materials and developed social, emotional, and ecological connections.

The changing of the season brings about different wildlife encountered in the valley, shifts in the characteristics of the valley's flora and fauna, and fluctuations in the resources available for foraging. The soundscape and the music also change with the seasons. Most crops are seasonal, meaning their seeds can grow only during one particular time of year, and when the season changes (which happens every 28 days) the crop will gradually wither and die in your garden (Figure 10.5). Barone extensively researched the fundamentals of farming mechanics to recreate their functions, behaviors, scarcities, and cycles and adapt them to the mechanics and interface of a video game. Over the course of the hours of gameplay it takes to complete one year in the game, the player comes to understand how the ecology of the nonhuman world operates and how our decisions and actions (e.g., farming behaviors) shape the landscape and soundscape of Stardew Valley and the dynamics of this unique ecosystem.[23]

The soundscape and music contribute to the process of understanding one's being-in-the world. If the world is to feel like a living place, the in-game ambient soundscape and music must behave and sound similar to the actual world. It can't predictably loop and repeat. The music was composed using the digital audio workstation Propellerhead Reason, and each track ranges in length from 30 seconds to just over four minutes. Seasonal music is stylistically mimetic of distinctive seasonal characteristics (e.g., hopeful spring, energetic summer, melancholy fall, and lonely winter). Upon first listen, the non-diegetic music might sound like it loops and repeats with interspersed extended non-diegetic "silence"

FIGURE 10.5 Fuzzy Acres Farm over the seasons

172   Kate Galloway

(or soundscape breaks), but it's actually generated at random from a set of tracks assigned to the season, time of day, and region the avatar occupies.[24] Special events, such as the Dance of the Midnight Jellies, the Luau, and other seasonal festivals, character events, and cutscenes, have their own exclusive music. Music is almost continuous when an avatar is inside certain spaces, but music plays less predictably outdoors, and this reduction in music heightens the ambient soundscape. The music and the soundscape of *Stardew Valley* don't loop and repeat in predictable patterns, because this is not how nature operates. The seasons change and cycle through the year, but the seasons do not return in direct repetition: something is always different. This is why the sheer number of sounds heard in *Stardew Valley* is of ludic and narrative significance—from the calls of different bird species, to the train that passes periodically through the countryside, to the crashing of ocean waves against the shoreline, to the cycling hum of the refrigeration system in Joja Mart. The variety of sounds and music creates the possibility for an always-the-same-yet-always-different soundscape. Each sound or track of music, by itself or in combination, communicates to the player something new about *Stardew Valley* and its in-game ecology.

Listening continues to be a strategy taken up by a number of disciplinary perspectives to understand how environments operate and change over time. Composer and ecologist R. Murray Schafer and the World Soundscape Project advocated for the systematic study of soundscapes and how human activity participates in the composition of those soundscapes. Similarly, the writer, scientist, and ecologist Rachel Carson also spent time listening to human-inflicted environmental harm.[25] In 1962, Carson published her influential call to arms *Silent Spring* in response to the environmental effects stemming from the misuse of synthetic chemical pesticides, including Dichlorodiphenyltrichloroethane (DDT), following World War II.[26] As a figure at the forefront of the environmental movement in the United States, Carson was what Linda Lear called a vocal "witness for nature"[27] and what Denise Von Glahn would refer to as a "skillful listener" to the nonhuman world.[28] *Stardew Valley* lays the groundwork for players to play (or learn to play) as skillful listeners. Because, what happens when we no longer sense, or more precisely hear, those voices, echoes, and resonances of the nonhuman world?

Listening skillfully to the environment of Stardew Valley extends to the citizens of Pelican Town. To be accepted into the community, the player with their avatar must listen to, socialize with, and get to know the members of this tight-knit town. Listening in these gameplay moments means reading the on-screen text and, in some instances, responding to the question posed to your avatar by the townsperson by selecting an option from two or three pre-programmed question responses. The response choice results in an increase or decrease in friendship points, or no change at all. Both the visual experience of communication and the aural experience of the game's soundscape require the player to parse aural information that informs their gameplay decisions, and their relationship to Stardew Valley and its inhabitants.

Soundwalking and Aurality of *Stardew Valley* **173**

Early on in my gameplay I tried to woo a partner for Darby. The NPC Alex was quite forward when Darby met him for the first time underneath a tree outside his house. Before introducing himself, he acknowledged the introduction of Darby's presence in the ecosystem of *Stardew Valley*. "Hey, you're the new girl, huh?" Alex wasn't the most articulate. He continued, "I think we're going to get along great. I'm Alex." I was optimistic. Days later, with an outstretched hand, Darby presented her gift that I selected from the item menu, waiting for the textbox and the data beep-boops as each word is typed into the textbox to reveal his response: "Are you serious? This is garbage." He refused her bouquet of seaweed. Like the many failed dishes I cooked in *Harvest Moon* in my childhood, this was a failed gift. I listened to Alex, adjusted Darby's approach, and returned with a sunflower ("This is cool! Thanks."). In the cutscenes that played as Darby and Alex's relationship developed, Darby and I quietly listened to Alex's story, his feelings, and aspirations (see Figure 10.6). It was only by listening to the community members of Pelican Town and the nonhuman actors of Stardew Valley that I understood my avatar's place in this digital world and how she contributes to its ecology.

Throughout my playthrough I was aware of the sounds produced by Darby's activities on the farm and her? (my?) being-in-the-world of Stardew Valley. I listened to the sounds she contributed to the soundscape and the dynamic audio produced by my avatar's actions dominated the soundscape. Chopping wood, crushing stone, scything long wild grasses, and harvesting crops: all of these forms of gameplay labor have associated sounds. If I didn't allow Darby time to rest, the sounds produced by her actions, movement, and body, and those emitted by

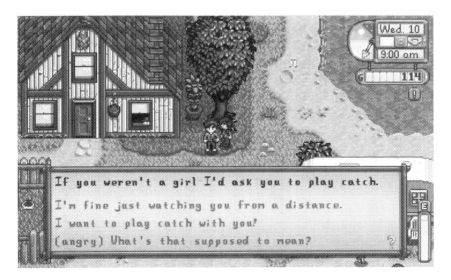

FIGURE 10.6 Alex and Darby

174 Kate Galloway

human-made technologies overwhelmed the sounds produced by the nonhuman living and nonliving things and phenomena of the sonic environment.[29] A soundscape dominated by the incessant clearing of farmland could be heard as unhealthy. As soundscape ecologist Bernie Krause has argued, a loud, lively, and varied soundscape communicates a healthy ecosystem, while a silent soundscape is one that signals decline and disrepair.[30] As Schafer has long questioned: "is the soundscape of the world an indeterminate composition over which we have no control, or are we its composers and performers, responsible for giving it form and beauty?"[31] I learned to farm slowly, but efficiently, taking into account how Darby's daily labor composed the soundscape. If one listens with care to the nonhuman gameworld ecology, *Stardew Valley* reveals to the player how individual actors in the soundscape and in the game—humans, sounds, plants, and animals—are entangled with each other in circumstances that are always shifting.

As I continued to listen to the game's soundscape, I attended to the lack of voice acting throughout the game. There are sounds that accompany each action your avatar makes, yet there are no instances of audible speech aside from the sound effects of strain during agricultural and foraging labor. The only inhabitants of the valley that vocalize are the wild and domesticated animals. The sonic residue of the avatar and NPCs, however, is made audible through interactions with the materiality of *Stardew Valley*'s natural and built environment. Echoes of their activity are heard in the opening of a door, the whoosh from casting off a fishing rod, the patter of our footsteps on different terrain textures, and the sounds produced during avatar-animal interaction.

Listening in Stardew Valley also extends to the different interior and exterior locations across the valley and in Pelican Town. The diversity of *Stardew Valley*'s soundscape is an indicator of ecological health. There are, however, select spaces where the sonic content is a reminder of the aural, physical, and social toxicity of urban life, such as the Joja Corporation in the opening cutscene and Joja Mart in the playable gameworld. As mentioned previously, Bernie Krause argues that a dynamic and diverse soundscape is evidence of a healthy ecosystem, while a silent or monotonous soundscape signals a decline in health. In *Voices of the Wild*, Krause reveals that more than half of his audio data comes from sites "so badly compromised by various forms of human intervention that the habitats are either altogether silent or the soundscapes can no longer be heard in any of their original forms."[32] Joja Mart has a lo-fi soundscape saturated with ambient "keynote sounds" including the hum of neon lights, and a regular beep that pulses and punctuates the loud mechanical drone of multiple electric-powered generators and rows of refrigeration units.[33] Darby's footsteps sound harder and hollow as they strike the industrial tile floors, the sound reflected off of rather than absorbed by the space. Unlike other spaces in Stardew Valley that change with the time of day, weather conditions, and the season, the soundscape of Joja Mart remains the same throughout its hours of operation, all year, and every year.

Darby first visited the Stardrop Saloon on a rainy evening, the rain pelting against the roof of the establishment and echoing into the bar. The Stardrop Saloon, owned and run by Gus, is a central meeting place for villagers, but it has sentimental value for my avatar Darby, as it was the site of her first date with Alex—the place where he confirmed his commitment to their in-game relationship and "made it official." The Stardrop Saloon offers a variety of entertainment options. You can socialize with villagers, purchase a variety of recipes and a daily rotating selection of prepared dishes, play pool and arcade games, use the Joja Cola soda machine, and operate the jukebox (see Figure 10.7). This was the first time my avatar could audibly interact with the music soundtrack of the game. The player uses the jukebox to change the current song playing in the bar, so it gives the player the opportunity to curate the soundscape of the Stardrop Saloon, creating a personalized mix from the selection of tracks that are heard in the different spaces, events, festivals, times of day, and seasons. The jukebox allows players to re-experience sonic memories from across the game in the present by listening back to the soundscape. The jukebox also complicates the relationship between diegetic and non-diegetic music experienced thus far in the game. Up until the first time you use the jukebox in the Stardrop Saloon, it's easy to assume that all instances of music are non-diegetic and that only the player but not your avatar can hear this music. Within the Stardrop Saloon, however, the music heard during different seasons and exclusive events is recalled and played back on the jukebox, a visible sound source that the player and avatar can manipulate to suit their own listening preferences.

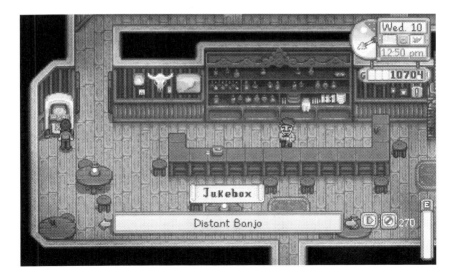

FIGURE 10.7 The Stardrop Saloon

176 Kate Galloway

Conclusion: Just Another Day Listening to the Farm

> I woke up again on a late spring morning to the sound of the rooster crowing somewhere outside my farmhouse. Alex and I had only been married a week, and already he continued to lie there in bed, sleeping in, his sports equipment in disarray and taking up half of our bedroom. The previous evening, he told me that it was OK if I needed some time to myself. I took him up on that offer, watered the vegetables, cleared a new plot of land, and walked through the Cindersnap Forest to Marnie's Ranch. I'd like to think he'd caught on to my mindful listening practices.
>
> *(Fieldnotes excerpt, May 5, 2018)*

Many of the benefits attributed to playing outdoors, going on a hike, or taking an afternoon to sit in a park can also be found in digital media. Games have a growing influence on culture and can be used as tools to inject positive messages and modes of being-in-the-world. In RPGs we play a role and try on a new identity in a digital environment that is equally new to us. In *Stardew Valley* this is a role that reminds humanity that they are not at the center of everything, and the player (and their avatar) is but one individual in an assemblage of actors in this networked ecosystem. This audible focus on the nonhuman world draws the player's attention away from simply the act of looking and refocuses their gameplay to include other sensory observations of the game's environment. *Stardew Valley* calls out to players to listen to their gameworld: we experience and understand our environment using our entire sensorium, so why should a player's experience of a gameworld environment be any different?

Notes

1 See Alenda Y. Chang, "Back to the Virtual Farm: Gleaning the Agriculture-Management Game," *Interdisciplinary Studies in Literature and Environment* 19(2) (2012): 237–252; "Games as Environmental Texts," *Qui Parle: Critical Humanities and Social Sciences* 19(2) (2011): 57–84; and "Playing the Environment: Games as Virtual Ecologies," Conference Proceedings, Digital Arts and Culture, University of California, Irvine, December 2009.

2 Travis D. Stimeling, "Music, Place, and Gulf Coast Tourism since the BP Oil Spill," *Music and Politics* 8(2) (2014). DOI: http://dx.doi.org/10.3998/mp.9460447.0008.202; "Music, Television Advertising, and the Green Positioning of the Global Energy Industry," in *Current Directions in Econusicology: Music, Culture, Nature*, ed. Aaron S. Allen and Kevin Dawe (New York: Routledge, 2015), 188–199.

3 Bruce Smith, "How Sound is Sound History? A Response to Mark Smith," *Journal of the Historical Society* 2(3–4) (2002), 309. See also Michele Hilmes, "Foregrounding Sound: New (And Old) Directions in Sound Studies," *Cinema Journal* 48(1) (2008): 115–117.

4 Pauline Oliveros, "On Sonic Meditation," in *Software for People: Collected Writings 1963–80*, ed. Pauline Oliveros (Baltimore, MD: Smith Publications, 1984), 138–157. Oliveros wrote this essay in 1973 and first published it in *Painted Bride Quarterly* in 1976.

5 In this chapter I use italicized text when I am referring to *Stardew Valley* the game and regular text when I am referring to Stardew Valley the place. *Stardew Valley* was first

released for Microsoft Windows, followed by ports for OS X, Linux, PlayStation 4, Xbox One. In 2017, the game was released for Nintendo Switch, as well as the PlayStation Vita in 2018. A four-player cooperative multiplayer mode was added in 2018. For my autoethnographic fieldwork I played in single-player mode using OS X.

6 Benjamin, Piekut, "Actor-Networks in Music History: Clarifications and Critiques," *Twentieth Century Music* 11(2) (2014), 212.

7 Nik Harron, "Fully Destructible: Exploring a Personal Relationship with Nature Through Video Games," *Alternatives Journal* 40(3) (2014): 16–23; Douglas Heaven, "Inside the Weirdly Calming World of Farming and Truck Simulators," *New Scientist*, November 9, 2016. www.newscientist.com/article/2112187-inside-the-weirdly-calming-world-of-farming-and-truck-simulators/.

8 Kiri Miller, *Playable Bodies: Dance Games and Intimate Media* (Oxford: Oxford University Press, 2017), 66.

9 Chang, "Back to the Virtual Farm," 242.

10 The track titles are taken from the *Stardew Valley OST* (2016).

11 William Cheng, "Afterword—Toadofsky's Music Lessons," in *Music Video Games: Performance, Politics, and Play*, ed. Michael Austin (New York: Bloomsbury Academic, 2016), 300–301.

12 Lawrence Buell, *The Environmental Imagination: Thoreau, Nature Writing, and the Formation of American Culture* (Cambridge, MA: Harvard University Press, 1995), 7–8.

13 Edward Casey, "How to Get from Space to Place in a Fairly Short Stretch of Time: Phenomenological Prolegomena," in *Senses of Place*, ed. Keith Basso and Steven Feld (Santa Fe, NM: School of Advanced Research Press, 1996), 19.

14 Tim Ingold, *The Perception of the Environment* (New York: Routledge, 2000), 268. See also David Howes, *Sensing Culture: Engaging the Senses in Culture and Social Theory* (Ann Arbor: University of Michigan Press, 2003), and *Empire of the Senses: The Sensual Culture Reader* (Oxford: Berg, 2005).

15 Hildegard Westerkamp, "Soundwalking," in *Autumn Leaves, Sound and the Environment in Artistic Practice*, ed. A. Carlyle (Paris: Double Entendre, 2007), 49. See also R. Murray Schafer, *The Tuning of the World* (Toronto: McClelland & Stewart, 1977), 147, 212–213; and Westerkamp, "Soundwalking as Ecological Practice," *International Conference on Acoustic Ecology*, Hirosaki University, Hirosaki, Japan. November 2–4, 2006.

16 Andra McCartney, "Soundwalking: Creating Moving Environmental Sound Narratives," in *The Oxford Handbook to Mobile Media Studies*, vol. 2, ed. Sumanth Gopinath and Jason Stanyek (New York: Oxford University Press, 2014), 212.

17 McCartney, "Soundwalking: Creating Moving Environmental Sound Narratives," 213.

18 Each day the player's avatar wakes up at 6 a.m. and they can stay awake until 2 a.m., but it's advised that they go to sleep at 12 a.m. so that they may fully recharge their energy and health reserves. If your avatar stays awake later than 2 a.m., they pass out, waking up the next morning in their own bed, but finding a bill from the town's local doctor Harvey in the mailbox outlining the specifications of their condition and the amount of money deducted automatically from their account.

19 Tim Ingold and Jo Lee Vergunst, eds., *Ways of Walking: Ethnography and Practice on Foot* (Burlington, VT: Ashgate, 2008), 1.

20 See further Tim Ingold, "Culture and the Perception of the Environment," in *Bush Base, Forest Farm: Culture, Environment, and Development*, ed. Elisabeth Croll and David Parkin (New York: Routledge, 2002), 51–68; "Culture on the Ground: The World Perceived through the Feet," *Journal of Material Culture* 9(3) (2004): 315–340; and *The Perception of the Environment: Essays on Livelihood, Dwelling and Skill* (New York: Routledge, 2002).

21 Schafer, *The Tuning of the World*, 31–33.

22 Aubrey Anable, *Playing with Feelings: Video Games and Affect* (Minneapolis: University of Minnesota Press, 2018), xi.

178 Kate Galloway

23 Sam White, "Valley Forged: How One Man Made the Indie Video Game Sensation Stardew Valley," *GQ*, March 20, 2018. www.gq.com/story/stardew-valley-eric-barone-profile.
24 ConcernedApe, "Dev Updated #16," Stardew Valley Developer Blog, April 20, 2014. https://stardewvalley.net/dev-update-16/.
25 The World Soundscape Project was an interdisciplinary sonic research collective led by R. Murray Schafer, active c. 1969–1975 at Simon Fraser University. The collective worked to raise public awareness concerning the ways human society participates in composing and shaping soundscapes.
26 *Rachel Carson, Silent Spring (Mariner Books, 2002 [1st. pub. Houghton Mifflin, 1962]). See also* Mark Hamilton Lytle, *The Gentle Subversive: Rachel Carson, Silent Spring, and the Rise of the Environmental Movement* (New York: Oxford University Press, 2007).
27 Linda Lear, *Rachel Carson: Witness for Nature* (New York: Henry Holt and Company, 1997).
28 Denise Von Glahn, *Music and the Skillful Listener* (Bloomington: Indiana University Press, 2013).
29 I apply sound ecologist Bernie Krause's research to the study of digital game environments and their soundscape ecology. The technical terms coined and used by Krause to analyze sonic environments include are geophony (naturally occurring non-biological audio coming from a habitat), biophony (sounds created by nonhuman living things), and anthropophony (all sounds produced by humans and human-made industry). See further Krause, "Anatomy of the Soundscape: Evolving Perspectives," *Journal of the Audio Engineering Society* 56(1–2) (2008): 73–80.
30 See further Carson, *Silent Spring*, and Jeff Todd Titon, "The Sound of Climate Change," *Whole Terrain: Reflective Environmental Practice* 22 (2016): 28–32. Environmental historian Peter A. Coates also explored how historical documentation of sound is interpreted to understand environments of the past and changes in society's relationship to these environments. See Peter A. Coates, "The Strange Stillness of the Past: Toward an Environmental History of Sound and Noise," *Environmental History* 10(4) (2005): 636–665.
31 Schafer, *The Tuning of the World*, 4–5.
32 Bernie Krause, *Voices of the Wild: Animal Songs, Human Din, and the Call to Save Natural Soundscapes* (New Haven, CT: Yale University Press, 2015), 29.
33 "Keynote" sound is a term developed by the World Soundscape project to refer to a sound that a listener is not aware they're hearing—not because it's inaudible, but because our body tends to tune out continuous and ever-present sounds in the soundscape. See further Schafer, *The Tuning of the World*, 271–276.

11

MUSICAL LANDSCAPES IN *SKYRIM*

Michiel Kamp and Mark Sweeney

From the towering cliffsides in Ma Yuan's paintings to the birdcalls in Beethoven's sixth symphony, artists have represented scenes of nature to varying degrees of realism, idealism, and taste. Painters and composers such as Edvard Grieg and Caspar David Friedrich attempted to go beyond representation in their works by expressing not only the look or sound of a landscape, but the emotional or aesthetic experience thereof, the sense of being awestruck by the beauty of nature. Many of Friedrich's paintings, including his most famous *Wanderer Above a Sea of Fog* (c. 1818), offer us over-the-shoulder perspectives of solitary wanderers—*Rückenfiguren*—in sublime wilderness scenes. In a sense, these figures are our avatars: we are made to identify with their experiences of nature, their serendipitous encounters with a vista after an arduous climb to a viewpoint.

Video games can offer players very similar experiences. Even though their digital nature might imply an artifice greater than that of older artforms—at least Friedrich's canvases and the wood of the instruments that Grieg composed for have some indexical relation to nature—their interactivity allows us to make precisely the kind of treks that Friedrich's figures make. Our case study in this chapter, the open-world role-playing game *The Elder Scrolls V: Skyrim* (Bethesda, 2011), along with its dynamic score, is one example of a class of video games that put these experiences at the center of their gameplay. We argue that *Skyrim* offers players not just visuals reminiscent of Friedrich's paintings (compare Figure 11.1 and Figure 11.2), but experiences that are in some ways closer to experiences of natural beauty than those afforded by Grieg and Friedrich's works. The game's non-diegetic musical soundtrack, perhaps even more of a stranger to the natural world than *Skyrim* and Friedrich's avatar-wanderers, plays an essential role in evoking these experiences. This is because the temporal quality of the game overall is contingent on both the micro aesthetic of individual ambient musical cues

FIGURE 11.1 Caspar David Friedrich's *Morning Mist in the Mountains* (1808)

FIGURE 11.2 *The Elder Scrolls V: Skyrim* (2011)

and the macro structure of the score (the particular implementation of cues in relation to gameplay). This temporal quality affords experiences of stillness and serendipity in which the player may feel like they have stumbled upon a vista of a natural landscape. In this landscape experience, the game's digital artifice is suspended in favor of seemingly unauthored "happy accidents" similar to aesthetic experiences of natural beauty. While ultimately players of video games are hooked up to technology in the comfort of their own homes, confronted with a virtual world carefully crafted by game and sound designers, visual artists, and composers, we argue that there is something unique about the design of games like *Skyrim* that allows for experiences akin to those of nature, and we outline the central role of music in this design.

We compare two main cases of the use of music in *Skyrim*, composed by Jeremy Soule, and how they relate to experiences of natural and artistic landscapes.[1] While the landscapes in *Skyrim* are closely associated (visually and musically) with a particular socio-cultural group within the game's fictional world—the "Nords"—the implementation of the music also creates a specific sense of time and place or, rather, a state of consciousness in which awareness of these dimensions is somehow heightened. *Skyrim*'s dynamic soundtrack consists of cues for incidental events, generic combat encounters, and generic exploration.[2] Incidental cues are triggered by specific events in quests and serve to highlight some of the unique moments in the game's story. Combat cues are not closely synchronized to player actions and tend to alert the player to danger, but can then immediately fade into the peripheries of the player's attention. By contrast, exploration cues sound not as ludic signals, but intermittently, as players freely explore the game's open world and are under no pressure by time or threats. It is during these moments that the score, by virtue of the musical structure of its cues and their dynamic implementation, affords experiences closer to aesthetic experiences of natural beauty than more "framed" media, such as landscape paintings or even *Skyrim*'s own incidental cues. Our approach to this phenomenon is therefore twofold. On the one hand, we will analyze the musical scores of certain cues on the soundtrack, to argue how their construction relates to Carl Dahlhaus's notions of *Naturklang* and *Klangfläche* to afford a "static" (game-)musical experience, and we look at how these cues are implemented in the game. For this, we provide a more micro musical analysis of the cues, and then turn to Bethesda's game engine editor for *Skyrim*, the Creation Engine, which reveals the macro structure of the dynamic implementation. On the other hand, to provide an interpretation of this experience during gameplay, we take a more auto-ethnographic or phenomenological approach, building on encounters with these musical cues in the game world. Three important concepts—authoredness, framelessness, and serendipity—result from the comparison of encounters with two musical cues: the incidental cue "Unbroken Road" and the exploration cue "Under an Ancient Sun." These encounters can in turn be related to the aesthetics of landscape paintings and compositions and the aesthetics of natural landscapes.

Klangfläche Aesthetics

Skyrim's soundtrack is reminiscent of the music of Nordic composers such as Grieg and Sibelius in multiple ways. First, the Nordic countries that these composers sought to represent through their naturalistic nationalist music serve as a

182 Michiel Kamp and Mark Sweeney

model for the land of Skyrim and its inhabitants, the Nords. Second, and more importantly to our argument, Daniel Grimley's reappraisal of specifically Grieg's musical depiction of Norway highlights that landscape is not merely an imitative representation, but an ideological construct that expresses a particular time and place.[3] Grimley notes that landscape

> presupposes both a process of composition (the creation of frames of refer- ence or forms of spatial organization) and the presence and active participa- tion of a viewer (their sense of perspective). Furthermore … landscape is not merely concerned with spatial perception, but also possesses a temporal dimension.[4]

For these reasons, music is well suited to depict landscape sonically. Grieg described beholding the mountain landscape of western Norway as an "ecstatic or epiphanal experience," which he sought to capture in his composition; Grimley pinpoints that goal, combined with the sense of home and nation evident in his composi- tions, as being markers of high romanticism. Grieg's compositional response to this experience of landscape generates enchantment, distance, and nostalgia through a "suspended temporality" or "radical spatial quality," and a "heightened sense of aural awareness or sensitivity to sound," aspects that may be found in both the structure of the musical pieces and the listening experience thereto.[5] This duality of musical structure and listener experience plays a crucial role in our argument.

Grimley finds these aspects in the music's structure by drawing on Dahlhaus's conception of *Naturklang* and *Klangfläche*—two closely related concepts that are both antithetical to the "teleological process" that Dahlhaus characterized as the hallmark of 19th-century symphonic music. *Naturklang* is a sense of stasis para- doxically reliant on an inner drive generated by ostinatos and a proto-minimalist rhythmic repetition of "cells." Dahlhaus defines *Klangfläche* very similarly, as "the sound-sheet … outwardly static but inwardly in constant motion," but to ensure that the music is not so static that it becomes "dull and lifeless," this constant motion of *Klangfläche* is characterized not only by rhythm, but also by unresolved non-harmonic notes (seconds and fourths).[6] He argues that, for music to depict nature, the teleological impulse of the "imperative of organic development" must be subverted. In other words, through avoiding the normal (at least, as Dahlhaus and others see it) "character of musical form as process," in musical landscapes a particular kind of stasis is permitted, regardless of any amount of internal rhythmic interest. Examples Dahlhaus cites include, most obviously, the development sec- tion of the first movement of Beethoven's Pastoral Symphony, which Dahlhaus characterizes as an "idyll" or "refuge" from Beethoven's own formal principles, the Forest Murmurs from Wagner's *Siegfried*, which Dahlhaus uses as an example of harmonic "open-endedness," and even the tumultuous thunderstorm of the Prelude to Act 1 of *Die Walküre*, which "remains riveted to the spot motivically and harmonically, no matter how gentle or violent its rhythmic motion."[7] By

Musical Landscapes in *Skyrim* 183

thwarting the usual logic of harmonic dissonance and resolution, and layering this with a set of rhythmic patterns that operate on a minimalist or cellular basis, rather than a classically balanced aesthetic, the necessary sense of stasis can be achieved that is the prerequisite to any landscape imagery.

In Grieg's music, Grimley creatively but precisely locates these concepts of landscape in the tensions caused by juxtaposing Norwegian folk music with European diatonic harmony. Many of these elements are also present in the music for *Skyrim*, although there are some significant differences in scale and form. It will be useful to investigate a number of specific features of the music categorized in the Creative Engine under "exploration." That this music is particularly pertinent to the sorts of concepts discussed above is largely self-evident, especially when compared to other categories of music in the game such as the combat cues. However, we also argue that the combination of these features contributes to a sense of *Klangfläche*, affording the experience of a suspended temporality and natural beauty. The cue "From Past to Present" (the opening of which is transcribed in Ex. 11.1), so named on the game's official soundtrack, is a string-based composition that the Creation Engine reveals is used as both "mus_town_day_02" and "mus_explore_day_02," suggesting that it tends to be heard when exploring in the daytime, and in towns or while exploring the open landscape.[8]

The music continually hangs on imperfect cadence points. Ex. 11.1 is a case in point: the tonal center is ambiguous from the start and shifts through modal inflections of D (aeolian, dorian, ionian), and phrases often conclude open-endedly. In fact, some entire cues come to an end on open-ended harmonies, and even those that feel tonally closed often employ fade-outs, whether composed or electronically imposed. The form is frequently ABA, and the A sections tend to "blossom" in the middle through a buildup of volume and texture. The cues are composed this way, perhaps because the listener tends to experience the music for a short time before moving off or being interrupted by some other action, and indeed cues are frequently not heard in their entirety. Following the cadence point in measure 7, the music in this cue returns to the minor mode with supplementary melodies in the woodwind, and then continues in much the same vein with frequent mode switches. The consistent use of these features does not drive the music forward but leaves it open.

Aside from added reverb, there are other important "effects" that help to create the sensation of wide-open spaces. The melody for the track "Journey's End" is in fact the same as "From Past to Present" (transcribed in Ex. 11.2 as a three-part

EX. 11.1 "From Past to Present," mm. 1–7

184 Michiel Kamp and Mark Sweeney

EX. 11.2 "Journey's End," excerpt

contrapuntal texture). The sound is thickened through the use of enharmonic cluster chords (not notated). For example, the first comes in the second measure with the entry of the second voice and consists of the notes E♭, F and G, as well as the A♭ in the part below. The slow pacing, meandering rhythm and enharmonic suspensions create an ethereal feel with the gentle dissonances of the chord clusters moving in parallel motion. Even in the jaunty "The City Gates" ("mus_town_day_01" in the data structure), these cluster harmonies are pervasive.

As Grimley suggests, "Landscape can be constructed through purely musical means, such as particular harmonic progressions and the prolongation of diatonically dissonant sonorities (*Klangfläche*) to create the impression of temporal suspension, a musical effect which suggests depth and perspective, or it can be evoked through the innovative use of conventional musical signifiers such as herding calls and echo effects to suggest space and distance."[9] In *Skyrim*, too, static *Klangfläche* are embellished by these sporadic herding calls in horns and woodwinds. Ex. 11.3 demonstrates the pastoral combination of horn melody and string accompaniment found in "Awake" ("mus_special_cartintro_01"), although this incidental cue is brief, as it is used at the very start of the game. The violins hold long, high-tessitura lines like those that embellish the theme of "From Past to Present," which create a sense of vertical space.

Horn calls such as this are pervasive across the soundtrack because they fulfill two functions: the horn is often used as a heroic and warrior-like cultural trope, yet it also has a pastoral association, and the many leaping fourths and fifths traditional to horn calls are effective in helping to create a certain sense of time and space. "Far Horizons" (transcribed in Ex. 11.4 and Ex. 11.5), indexed in-game as "mus_explore_day08," starts with another horn solo (with string countermelody), closely related to "Awake."

In summary, the musical elements that make up these exploration cues are:

- String-based instrumentation with themes presented in octaves (cellos and violins).
- Extreme string tessitura and use of horn calls/melodies with open intervals creating sense of vast space.

- Harmonically open-ended phrases and cues, but with an ultimately static sense of a home pitch center.
- Mixture of diatonic harmony and "folk"/modal procedures (parallel motion, mode switches indicative).
- Wash of rhythmic harmonic "accompaniment" using static harmonies.
- Themes built up through repetition of smaller motifs; accompaniments also based on ostinatos. Repetition creates timeless quality; themes don't drive the music forward.
- Few "main themes" and many subtle variations ensure balance is struck between repetitiveness and familiarity.
- Reverb and long-held chord clusters.
- Blossoming "A" sections with contrasting "B" sections in ABA structures.

Nearly all of these elements, but particularly those related to *Klangfläche*, come together in "Under an Ancient Sun" ("mus_explore_day_01"). The cue consists of almost nothing but slowly revolving string clusters played in an extreme tessitura over the course of around three and a half minutes. As such, traditional musical transcription is less helpful, and so we offer a spectrogram of the passage in Figure 11.3. High, airy G and B♭ octaves are exchanged between string sections (Y and X in Figure 11.3; the vertical lines in the spectrogram indicate changes in the bass notes) in a kind of static shimmering, like that of light reflecting on water. The high strings are supported by horn (Z in Figure 11.3) and double bass drones

EX. 11.3 "Awake," horn melody

EX. 11.4 "Far Horizons," excerpt 1

EX. 11.5 "Far Horizons," excerpt 2

that shift even more gradually from an emphasis on G to Eb, C and F, before returning to G. There is a sense of an Eb pitch center that is slowly revealed but at the same time destabilized both by the F and C in the bass register, as well as a drone on the mediant G instead of the tonic Eb. The only significant elements missing are horn calls (the horn is present but just to join the string clusters) and other more melodic elements found in the other cues, making "Under an Ancient Sun" an even more extreme example of *Klangfläche* composition. Like the "A" sections of many of the other exploration cues, "Under an Ancient Sun" does "blossom out," although here this occurs mostly texturally, with lower registers joining the higher strings and the bass becoming more active. This all happens so gradually that the extreme stasis in this cue is not interrupted.

Framelessness, Authoredness, and Serendipity

The aesthetics of *Skyrim*'s cues support experiences akin to those of natural landscapes, but, when analyzed independently of their gameplay setting, they can be heard much like the autonomous pieces of music that inspired them. The music of Grieg, as experienced in a concert hall, remains a *representation* of the experience of a natural landscape, expertly employing techniques like *Klangfläche* and the other devices mentioned in the previous section. In a similar manner, Joseph

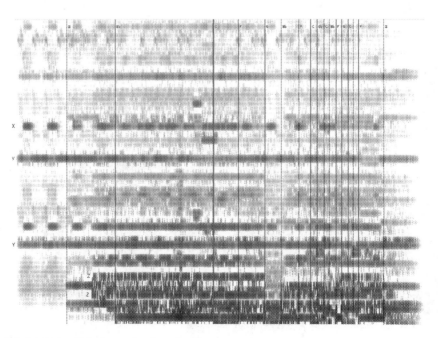

FIGURE 11.3 "Under an Ancient Sun," spectrogram

Musical Landscapes in *Skyrim* **187**

Koerner argues that Friedrich's paintings represent not so much natural landscapes as the experiences of those landscapes, by obscuring shapes and horizons and giving a sense of boundlessness, of views that extend beyond the frame of the painting.[10] But the paintings remain framed in a museum and their experiences authored, just as Grieg's music remains authored and framed in performance, temporally, by applause and silence. What makes the musical experiences in *Skyrim* different from Grieg and Friedrich's representations is not the aesthetic structure of the cues, but their placement in the game. At the heart of this distinction is the difference between the aesthetic experience of nature, including natural vistas or landscapes, and that of art. Philosopher Ronald Hepburn says:

> Where we confront what we know to be a human artefact—say a painting— we have no special shock of surprise at the mere discovery that there are patterns here which delight perception; we know that they have been put there, though certainly we may be astonished at their particular aesthetic excellences. With a natural object, however, such surprise can figure importantly in our overall response, a surprise that is probably the greater the more remote the object from our everyday environment.[11]

There is an important insight here that highlights the importance of "finding" an aesthetic panorama, of serendipity. It raises the question to what extent our knowledge of intention—of how much the scene has been "authored"—can diminish the surprise. Video games offer unique cases for this idea of authoredness and serendipity. Of course, as artefacts, video game elements, be they gameplay design, visual imagery, or musical soundtrack, are ultimately implemented by a game's developers. However, the freedom to traverse game worlds over dozens or even hundreds of hours—especially freely explorable, three-dimensional, avatar-driven worlds like Skyrim—complicates that authoredness. Unlike a film, in which the musical soundtrack is carefully synchronized with events on screen, *Skyrim's* dynamic score allows for surprising moments in which player actions, visual landscapes, and musical events suddenly appear perfectly complementary. The structure of the musical cues can ultimately only create potentials for the game to afford these moments; it cannot dictate when and where they might occur—and this audiovisual indeterminacy is crucial. Consider the following autobiographic account of a serendipitous musical landscape by one of this chapter's authors—we will refer to it as the "hilltop experience"—which highlights both the structure of the cue encountered, as well as its implementation:

> Walking through the snowy plains of northern Skyrim, reaching a hilltop and surveying the countryside to get my bearings, I am suddenly struck by the beauty of the distant mountaintops against the tumultuous grey sky (1'10" in the video).[12] The sense of openness and space is accentuated by the "Under an Ancient Sun" cue in the soundtrack, which consists

188 Michiel Kamp and Mark Sweeney

of instrument groups playing single notes that alternate so gradually that any sense of time or musical progress is absent. Sustained notes—high-pitched strings and disembodied, wordless soprano voices—seem to "hang" in the air, even above the wind sounds that remain anchored to the flurries of snow closer to the ground. I know that the music was playing before I got to the hilltop, and continues playing for a while afterwards (even as I encounter a group of enemies and it is drowned out by the sounds of swords clashing and men shouting), but it is in the moment I encounter the vista at the top of the hill that the music acquires this significance. It is as if the music was made for the moment.

In this moment, the music has gone from something that was there in the background to quite a clearly distinguishable and definable set of things: sustained notes that ever so gradually changed, had a location in musical space (being quite high in pitch) and stood in a certain relationship to other elements in the diegetic environment. In other words, these elements of the music became more object-like, not in the sense that I could walk around and manipulate them, but in the sense that I could "think around" them and relate and compare them with other things in the environment, such as the distant mountains, the gushing wind and the grey sky. While there is movement in the scene, and movement in the music (to a small extent), the moment seems suspended in time: I am not worried about having to move on, or about what comes after this particular experience—I am squarely in the moment, unconcerned with time.[13]

This attempt at a close examination of an experience playing *Skyrim* clearly shows how the moment was afforded by the *Klangfläche* of "Under an Ancient Sun," but it also raises a number of questions. Before we return to how this particular nature scene relates to Hepburn's aesthetics—authoredness and serendipity—it would be useful to more closely examine some of the concepts that surfaced in the earlier description. The two that we want to focus on are musical objects and musical moments. Particularly in the case of music, the concepts are interrelated: only in a particular kind of moment can a musical event or process (e.g., a melody, a trill, a phrase, a crescendo, an entire piece) become object-like to the extent that one can reflect on it and relate it to other objects in that moment. Time and objects have been central themes of phenomenology, occupying everyone from Edmund Husserl as he established the field to Shaun Gallagher and Dan Zahavi's contemporary investigations.[14] For this reason, a phenomenological approach to these concepts can bear fruit.

In Thomas Clifton's phenomenology of musical time, musical objects are the same as any kind of object in that they are determined by continuity. When we walk around a solid object it presents different perspectives to us, but we do not question whether they are of the same object because of a fundamental continuity in the phenomenon. Similarly, when we listen to a tone, its continuity causes us

Musical Landscapes in *Skyrim* **189**

not to hear it as something different now than a fraction of a second ago, but as a single "object."[15] Continuity is also what allows us to hear a melody as a melody, rather than a meaningless succession of notes. But there are two fundamental differences between the way in which we hear sounds extended in time and the way we see objects extended in space. The first is that a sound always has a duration. Owing to the energy it takes to produce a sound, we conceptualize even very long sounds, or potentially infinite ones, as entities that will ultimately cease to be. We think of spatial objects, however, as persistent. The second has to do with the kind of agency we have in perception: we can look around an object at will, whereas we have only limited spatial control over a sound, such as muffling it or distancing ourselves from it. (Even when we are producing a tone on an instrument, we can only manipulate it so that it transforms into a different object.)

But objects can acquire sound-like qualities. We cannot look around the trees in a landscape painting, and the landscape that we see outside the window on a train journey "ceases to be" as it passes us by. Furthermore, a sound can become object-like when we "think around" it spatially, or in other words reflect on it while it is present to us.[16] What distinguished the hilltop experience in *Skyrim* from other musical experiences was the way in which both the sound-like qualities of the musical sounds, and the object-like qualities of objects in the scene, were suspended. In the durationless moment afforded by the music's *Klangfläche* structure, we are free to reflect on these qualities separately, and to consider their relationships to each other, enabling us to "think around" the sounds and vistas; to see the spatial elements of sound and hear the landscape. The musical elements— the shimmering string octaves on G and Bb—become part of the landscape, on equal terms with elements seen and felt in what Nicholas Cook might term a moment of "quasi-synaesthesia," wherein attributes of music and image mutually complement and map onto each other,[17] or what Michel Chion might call synchresis, "the spontaneous and irresistible weld produced between a particular auditory phenomenon and visual phenomenon when they occur at the same time.[18]

The hilltop experience can be compared to what Amy Herzog calls a "musical moment" in Hollywood musicals, when "music, typically a popular song, inverts the image-sound hierarchy to occupy a dominant position."[19] During such moments, "the temporal logic of the film shifts, lingering in a suspended present rather than advancing the action directly"; "movements within the frame are not oriented toward action but toward visualizing the trajectory of the song"; "space … is completely reconfigured into a fantastical realm that abandons linear rationality"; and there is a "dissolution of the space-time continuum that orders the reality of our everyday existence."[20] The notion of "lingering in a suspended present" is a particularly important similarity between musical moments and the hilltop experience. The player might describe their personal "narrative" as "I climbed the hilltop to survey the countryside," but on the hilltop this narrative is paused as the player lingers on the mountaintops and dwells on the music. Like the characters who break out into song in a musical, the player is temporarily suspended in

190 Michiel Kamp and Mark Sweeney

music. The typical linear and clear verse–chorus setup of Hollywood songs make them more perceptibly dominant than the *Klangfläche*-landscape combination, but that does not mean that the latter is mere background music. The *real* difference between Herzog's musical moment and the hilltop experience is very close to Hepburn's distinction between beauty in art and nature. Whereas a film frames the musical moment, authored by the director and crew, the moment in *Skyrim* frames my experience of the landscape, and I can only conclude in hindsight that I serendipitously framed it myself.

Hepburn notes three main distinctions between the appreciation of beauty in nature and in art:

1. With beauty in nature there is a sense of involvement, whereas in art there is a distancing. Moreover, encountering beauty in nature somehow makes us experience our*selves* in an "unusual and vivid way … and this difference is not merely noted, but dwelt upon aesthetically."[21]
2. Art is *framed*, in that we can usually see a distinct demarcation from the environment. We can see both the boundaries and what lies beyond the boundaries: the silence before a concert, the white walls of the museum and the applause and frames that separate them. Scenes of nature, however, seem to be pervasive.
3. There is a difference in grasping an art object and a scene of nature as a perceptual whole: in the case of the artwork, it is the delight we find when we see how some aspect of the artwork has been put into place for a purpose; namely, achieving the artistic whole. In the case of beauty in nature, we marvel at the fact that nature in general can seem beautiful to us at all; that there is natural beauty and that the present scene is an instance of it.

The sense of involvement in encountering natural landscapes can be found in the hilltop experience, as well: it is the player's interaction with the game world that makes possible the experience of a musical landscape. The framelessness of the musical moment is related to this sense of involvement: although we did speak of the experience as demarcated or "framed" from the rest of the gameplay experience, this framing is experienced as an act on the part of the player, not the makers of the game. Although in some way this makes us the authors, this is a conclusion at which we only arrive in hindsight, not during the experience itself. This in turn relates to the unauthoredness and the serendipity of the experience, Hepburn's third distinction. We marvel at the fact that an experience like this can occur in the musical game world of *Skyrim* at all; not just at the aspects or elements like the music that have been put into place by the game's developers.

Natural Landscapes and Landscape Paintings

It might be objected that *Skyrim*'s "nature" still is authored to its digital core, that we do not so much experience ourselves as we do our in-game avatars in an "unusual or vivid way," and that we ultimately admire the developers' arrangement of musical and visual assets. But it is the manner in which we don't experience these as being arranged that makes possible the serendipitous moments described in the previous section. By way of comparison, consider the incidental use of the cue "Unbroken Road" in the game, which is experienced much more like a landscape painting by Friedrich or a tone poem by Grieg than as a natural landscape. The track (Ex. 11.6) is in a simple ternary ABA form, with each "A" section culminating in a sweeping rendition of the slow version of the *Elder Scrolls* theme heard in the horn part of Ex. 11.3 above. In the data structure it is entitled "mus_explore_day_06," and in the Creation Engine we see that, unlike most of the other "explore" tracks, it is only used in one unique instance: MUSSpecial-ElderScrollSequence. (By way of contrast, "Under an Ancient Sun," Music Track MUSExploreDay01 is used in MUSExploreSnow, MUSExploreMarsh, MUSExploreCoast, MUSExploreMountain, MUSExploreTundra, MUSExploreReach, MUSExploreForestPine, and MUSExploreFall.) This instance concerns a particular moment in the game that is important to the main questline.

The horn melody that commences the track is a fragment from the tail end of the main theme that appears in the strings at measure 25 (cf. measures 1–8 with 32–37). The stepwise rising third is the principal motivic component of the track, and it originates from the start of the main *Skyrim/Elder Scrolls* theme. The music builds gradually in both volume and texture, culminating in the presentation of the main theme that is doubled in the violins and cellos encompassing three octaves. The sweeping character of the melody is greatly enhanced by its contrasting but supportive accompaniment in the rest of the strings—a pulsating but static wash of a single harmony. The music dies down in a similar fashion, repeating the final phrase of the melody. The "B" section is marked by the solo flute entrance. Although the horn continues to echo the closing phrase from the previous section, and the wash of harmony remains largely unchanged, the character is decidedly different. The instrumental solos benefit from added clarity, since the texture of the accompaniment is less rich. Eventually the passage dies away and the music proceeds to the final "A" section. In the buildup section before the main theme returns for the second time, a choir joins the violin part at the moment parallel to measure 9 below, though there is no public record of what the lyrics are. This additional punctuation adds to the building tension and supplements the sweeping aesthetic with a sense of the player's role in an epic saga.

The cue's rhythmic string ostinatos in the "A" sections exhibit *Naturklang*, blossoming with the main theme but not driving forward. The woodwinds over the static *Klangfläche* wash of string harmony in the "B" section can be compared to other static pieces, such as the birdcalls in Beethoven's sixth symphony and the "Forest Murmurs" sequence from Wagner's *Siegfried*. The other stylistic features identified in the musical excerpts above are also combined in "Unbroken Road" to create an archetypal example of *Naturklang* or *Klangfläche*. The use of reverb (throughout the soundtrack) enhances the generally slow pacing of the explore music and gives the impression that the music is being heard in a vast landscape.

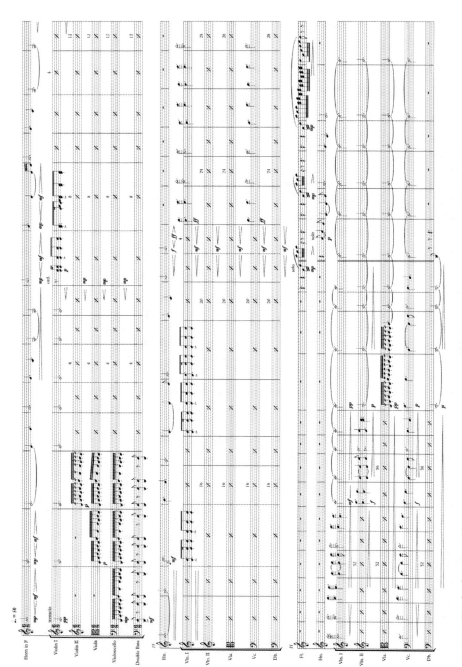

EX. 11.6 "Unbroken Road," excerpt

Musical Landscapes in *Skyrim* **193**

The tumultuous string ostinatos provide rhythmic interest but remain static. Great washes of slow harmonic rhythm with unresolved non-harmonic notes (seconds) support long sweeping themes for strings and, frequently, the horn. This sense of movement within stasis sets up a particular subject position from which the landscape is surveyed. In addition to this, a particular temporal experience is created. The principal musical process is that of repetition, which by its very nature does not progress, develop, or change. Even the larger scale structure is a form of repetition, the "B" section providing some contrast but with a strong sense of continuation. Dahlhaus's concepts provide a useful way of describing the particular aesthetic sense of time and space created by the music, and this aesthetic is well suited to the phenomenological experience of exploring the virtual world.

However, even though "Unbroken Road" exhibits some of the same static elements of *Klangfläche* composition found in "Under a Dying Sun," it differs in the manner in which it is encountered. The cue appears about two-thirds of the way through the game's main questline. Players have found the game's titular Elder Scroll, which must be read atop Skyrim's tallest mountain to allow players to see back in time. In this gameplay sequence, captured in a video, the game offers very clear instructions of where to go and what to do, via compass markers at the top of the screen and journal entries (1'55" in the video).[22] In fact, the only searching done by the player—perhaps the equivalent of the hilltop climb—involved looking for the scroll in the game's inventory screen. When activated in the right spot, the Scroll immediately triggers a semi-interactive flashback scene, accompanied by the "Unbroken Road" cue (3'04" in the video). Although the player has control over where to look in this scene, they are unable to move or interact in any other way, and their view is literally framed by bluish arcane markings representing the magic of the scroll. As a semi-interactive cutscene, the sequence as a whole is clearly framed by the game's developers in terms of gameplay, visuals, and narrative. Even though there is no close synchronization between music and images, this is the cue's only occurrence in the game.[23] Players "visit" the cue like a painting in a gallery, rather than stumble upon it like a natural landscape. The sequence is framed like Herzog's musical moments in film: the narrative sequence of events is interrupted, and musical stasis is provided, but, as these elements are clearly authored and put in place by the game's developers, none of Hepburn's criteria for the experience of natural beauty are fulfilled.

It might be objected that, even though the cue "Unbroken Road" exhibits elements of musical landscapes, the visuals in the flashback sequence do not emphasize the landscape, and this is therefore an unfair comparison with the "Under an Ancient Sun" landscape described earlier. Although the sequence takes place on a mountaintop, the player's eyes are drawn to the actions of the figures—the Nord heroes fighting the dragon Alduin—in the foreground rather than the landscape of Skyrim in the background. The music is neither directly underscoring a vista or the battle, but does allude to the continued presence of Skyrim's landscape and reinforces the sense of place throughout the vision, despite that not being the primary visual focus. Furthermore, framed and authored landscapes certainly occur in video games. Most famously, there are the "synchronization" sequences in the *Assassin's Creed* series, wherein the player is asked to climb towers and other high viewpoints in order to survey the landscape and unlock new missions and side quests. Although slightly different for each entry in the series, these sequences are usually accompanied by a musical stinger of sorts, a short musical motif that scores the vista as the camera swings around the player's avatar. Another example is from the *Tomb Raider* remake (2013), whose title card is framed similarly to the climb to the hilltop in *Skyrim*: climbing out of a dark cave, its protagonist Lara Croft can oversee the island she has been stranded on for the first time from a cliffside. Here, again, a specifically designed short cue plays to accompany the vista. While the similarities to the hilltop sequence in *Skyrim* should be apparent, the difference is that it is not the player's memory of their climbs that frames the panorama, but the games' "authors"—their designers and composers. Like Herzog's musical moment, in these authored sequences the games linger in a suspended present. But this is not the *player*'s present; it is a depiction of their avatars' present, represented through a combination of gameplay, music, and graphics. The player does not stumble upon the viewpoints in *Assassin's Creed*, the cliffside vista in *Tomb Raider*, or the flashback sequence in *Skyrim*, their avatars do. Of course, this does not necessarily stop one from having an aesthetic experience when confronted with the beauty of the landscapes in these sequence, but they would be more akin to that of a Friedrich painting framed on a museum wall. Ultimately, the flashback sequence that "Unbroken Road" accompanies is one in which players do not experience "themselves"—paraphrasing Hepburn—but their avatars having this encounter.

The exploration cues on *Skyrim*'s musical soundtrack concern landscape. Their manner of composition shows similarities to the *Klangfläche* structures that Nordic composers such as Grieg and Sibelius employ in their tone paintings of their countries' landscapes. The cues tend towards musical stasis as epitomized in "Under an Ancient Sun," but also present in the more common cyclical forms of tracks like "Unbroken Road." These examples highlight the fact that there are two distinct ways of experiencing a landscape. On the one hand, we can visit a museum to look at landscape paintings framed on a wall, or similarly we can visit a concert hall to hear a piece framed by classical concert practice—experiences ostensibly authored by composers and performers. On the other hand, we can stumble upon a beautiful vista while trekking through nature, climbing a hilltop, and discovering a natural landscape laid out before us. In this experience, we feel ourselves as having "framed" and "authored" the landscape experience, not deliberately, but serendipitously. In a way, we frame these landscapes in our mind's eye, often reflecting on "how perfect the form is," "as if" (it should have been) authored. The manner of implementation of the exploration cues in *Skyrim* makes possible similar serendipitous moments. Even though the game's creators have created every part of its digital world and its soundtrack, the structure of the open world and the semi-indeterminacy of the non-diegetic soundtrack afford musical, or rather audiovisual, moments like these. When Ronald Hepburn says that in an experience of nature we ourselves are involved more so than in experiences of art, this distinction finds a parallel in the manner in which certain moments in *Skyrim* allow us to experience *ourselves*, rather than our avatars. In a sense, this avatar/self distinction is emblematic of the RPG genre, and exemplified by the nameless guise of the Dovahkiin (or Dragonborn) protagonist that players take on.

We do not wish to deny the aesthetic qualities of more scripted moments in games such as the flashback sequence in *Skyrim*, but we hope to have shown that these are experiences of a different sort. If there is any truth to the nostalgic idea that the digitalized and mediatized world we live in has pushed us ever further away from nature, our suggestion that a video game of all things can offer experiences similar not merely to other artistic depictions of landscape but to the experiences of natural beauty itself might seem hyperbolic—particularly when we suggest that a non-diegetic musical soundtrack is essential to this experience. However, the temporal experience of how we explore and re-explore *Skyrim* for a few hours at a time actually parallels the temporal patterning of exploring the countryside on a hike at the weekend in "real life" before returning home. In this sense, playing an RPG is markedly different to the paintings and concert pieces we find in galleries and concert halls. While these spaces can be revisited, the experiences they contain are whole and unified, but an open-world RPG like *Skyrim* is rarely played and "completed" in a single sitting. On the macro level, the placement of cues such as "Under an Ancient Sun" is tailored to this manner of playing the game. As a consequence, the way in which cues can appear to players— sneaking in unnoticed to coincide serendipitously with the landscape—can afford literally arresting moments. Here, on the micro level, *Klangfläche* and related features of *Skyrim*'s cues offer the temporal experience of a perpetually extended present that opens up the game's vistas to the player. In these moments, the sense of a frame and an author that guides the player's hand are temporally suspended, in favor of a musical moment of natural beauty more at home in a countryside trek than in a gallery. *Skyrim*'s music, then, matches its nature.

Notes

1 The composer is also in the process of completing his first symphony in the same idiom as his *Skyrim* soundtrack, *The Northerner*. See www.kickstarter.com/projects/499808045/from-the-composer-of-skyrim-soule-symphony-no-1 (accessed June 6, 2018).
2 With the use of the word "dynamic," we are referring to Collins's concept of dynamic game music, see Karen Collins, *Game Sound: An Introduction to the History, Theory, and Practice of Video Game Music and Sound Design* (Cambridge, MA: MIT Press, 2008), 125–127.
3 Daniel Grimley, *Grieg: Music, Landscape and Norwegian Identity* (Woodbridge, UK: Boydell Press, 2006), 223.
4 Grimley, *Grieg*, 56.
5 Grimley, *Grieg*, 79–80.

6 Carl Dahlhaus, *Nineteenth-Century Music*, trans. J. Bradford Robinson (Berkeley, Los Angeles, and London: University of California Press, 1989), 307.
7 Dahlhaus, *Nineteenth-Century Music*, 307.
8 All transcriptions by the authors.
9 Grimley, *Grieg*, 109.
10 J.L. Koerner, *Caspar David Friedrich and the Subject of Landscape*, 2nd ed. (London: Reaktion Books, 2009), 12.
11 Ronald W. Hepburn, "Contemporary Aesthetics and the Neglect of Natural Beauty," in *British Analytical Philosophy*, ed. Bernard Williams and Alan Montefiore (London: Routledge and Kegan Paul, 1966), 302.
12 See www.youtube.com/watch?v=ZV7Ou3BoviU (accessed October 13, 2018).
13 Michiel Kamp, "Four Ways of Hearing Video Game Music" (Ph.D. dissertation, University of Cambridge, 2015), 108. This account is quoted in full to preserve as much of the original experience as possible. Similar experiences have been noted by William Cheng about another Bethesda game, *Fallout 3* (2008). See William Cheng, *Sound Play: Video Games and the Musical Imagination* (New York: Oxford University Press, 2014), 52–53.
14 Edmund Husserl, *On the Phenomenology of the Consciousness of Internal Time (1893–1917)*, trans. John Barnett Brough (Dordrecht, Boston, and London: Kluwer, 1991). Shaun Gallagher and Dan Zahavi, *The Phenomenology of Mind: An Introduction to Philosophy of Mind and Cognitive Science* (London and New York: Routledge, 2008).
15 Thomas Clifton, *Music as Heard: A Study in Applied Phenomenology* (New Haven, CT and London: Yale University Press, 1983), 97–98.
16 See also Jonathan Kramer's discussion of "vertical music"—music that invites hearing akin to looking at a piece of sculpture. Jonathan D. Kramer, *The Time of Music: New Meanings, New Temporalities, New Listening Strategies* (New York and London: Schirmer Books, 1988).
17 See Nicholas Cook, *Analysing Musical Multimedia* (Oxford and New York: Oxford University Press, 1998), 28.
18 Michel Chion, *Audio-Vision: Sound on Screen*, trans. Claudia Gorbman (New York: Columbia University Press, 1994), 63. Chion's examples of synchresis involve a "tighter" synchronization than the hilltop experience in *Skyrim*, which does not involve individual sounds coinciding with visual motions.
19 Amy Herzog, *Dreams of Difference, Songs of the Same: The Musical Moment in Film* (Minneapolis: University of Minnesota Press, 2010), 6.
20 Herzog, *Dreams of Difference*, 6–7.
21 Hepburn, "Contemporary Aesthetics and the Neglect of Natural Beauty," 289.
22 See www.youtube.com/watch?v=41wfzONqTwI (accessed October 13, 2018).
23 Several comments on a YouTube upload of the track suggest that players are aware of the unique appearance of this cue in the game. See www.youtube.com/watch?v=EK3q3Jb3TCQ (accessed October 13, 2018).

12

BARRIERS TO LISTENING IN *WORLD OF WARCRAFT*

Steven Reale

It is a well-rehearsed cornerstone of postmodern literary theory that texts are inherently unstable. "All literary works," Terry Eagleton reminded us in 1983, "are 'rewritten,' if only unconsciously, by the societies which read them; indeed there is no reading of a work which is not also a 're-writing.'"[1] Of course, Eagleton is not claiming that literal words on literal pages are changing in some substantial way, but rather highlighting the fact that today's cultural values and the meanings that we assign to utterances are quite different from those in, say, Elizabethan England. I may never be able to access quite the same constellation of meaning from Shakespeare's Sonnet 18 as might the poet's contemporary, my colleague in the English department, or you, dear reader, but I can at least be reasonably confident that the words that appear in my anthology of poetry do so in the same order and with the same punctuation and line breaks as they do in yours. Even if the poem is an unstable text, its notations are fixed in place. Indeed, our ability to engage in scholarly discourse at all generally relies on our agreement that we are studying the same object.

In general terms, we can make the same observation about a musical work as we can a poem—from a certain perspective, texts are texts irrespective of their medium. Yet scholars have noted that a thornier complication emerges in trying to even locate the musical text, or to determine what even constitutes a musical work.[2] Few writers would claim that the musical score independent of performance fully encapsulates the work. Nattiez, for example, notes that the semiology of Western art music requires an extra interpretive step between its poiesis and realization—that being the role of the performer.[3] Nicholas Cook takes up this thread in his recent volume that reimagines music scholarship from the standpoint of performance studies, specifically destabilizing the role of the score in its contribution to musical discourse and advocating for a closer alignment of music with the related medium of theater.[4] In a radical case, Carolyn Abbate and Roger Parker began their volume *A History of Opera* by announcing in its preface that they decided "at a very early stage … that this history would contain no musical examples," because they "wanted to write a book without reference to musical scores."[5] In the case of music, then, the work cannot be taken to be either stable or fixed, even if there exists some *Urtext* that fixes some of its parameters—and Stanley Boorman has even cautioned us against implicitly trusting that an *Urtext* serves as an unimpeachable document of textual authenticity.[6] Nonetheless, only the fussiest of musical ontologists would reject as dysfunctionally imprecise a statement like "I have tickets to see the symphony perform Beethoven's *Eroica* this evening." As with poetry, Beethoven scholars must be able to agree on the stability of at least *some* aspects of their object of study in order to engage in any discourse on it.

The genre of the massively multiplayer online role-playing game (MMORPG), by contrast, represents texts in systemic flux. *World of Warcraft* (Blizzard, 2004–) is perhaps the best-known title in the genre, having at its peak boasted 12 million concurrent subscribers. The game was such a cultural phenomenon that it was featured both in a Toyota advertisement as well as in an episode of the television series *South Park* (1997–). Since the game's original release, Blizzard has added seven expansions, each of which substantially changes not only the geography of the game—presenting around a half-dozen new zones and several handfuls of new dungeons to explore—but also many rules governing gameplay. The game requires a persistent internet connection, and all players, regardless of whether they have purchased the expansions, are subject to these gameplay changes. This is significant: I can be confident that if I replay the original *Legend of Zelda* (Nintendo, 1986) in 2019, the game will be exactly as it was decades ago, just as I am that if I reread Sonnet 18 in 2024, it will feature the same words in the same order with the same punctuation and line breaks as it does now. Today's *World of Warcraft*, however, is a substantially different game than it was is 2004. In fact, owing to the August 2018 release of its seventh expansion, *Battle for Azeroth*, *World of Warcraft* was a substantially different game as I made the final edits to this chapter than when I completed its first draft; was different still as this chapter went through copyediting, due to the March 2019 release of the version 8.1.5 content patch; and with the expected release of version 8.2 in summer 2019, will almost certainly be different still by the time you read these words. Much writing on video game music has focused on its indeterminacy: in a manner very different from film scores, whose soundtracks play out the same way from viewing to viewing, a characteristic feature of video game music is that its soundtracks may never be heard twice in exactly the same way.[7] The score to *World of Warcraft* is, then, even less stable than what might be called the "possibility spaces" established by dynamic video game scoring techniques: a game subject to periodic renewal and revision, music that once frequently accompanied a player's journey through the land of Azeroth might never be heard in-game again.

This chapter focuses on barriers that prevent players from listening. Its first part lays out a theoretical framework for how such barriers operate, with interspersed,

Barriers to Listening in *World of Warcraft* **199**

autobiographical examples of my own experiences of them as a *World of Warcraft* player. I categorize these barriers as either *synchronic* or *diachronic*, where the former exist at specific moments during the game's lifespan, and the latter emerge when patches and expansions alter the game. The second part of the chapter takes a meta-diachronic approach, showing that even the diachronic analysis of the first section begins from a synchronic standpoint, and describes how the very nature of diachronic barriers to listening to *World of Warcraft* are in flux. The chapter then concludes by drawing comparisons to *World of Warcraft*'s diachronic barriers to those that appear in media beyond the MMORPG. Though perhaps unexpected, it may be that diachronic barriers to experiencing works of art are far more common than we may first assume and, by extension, that the MMORPG represents a far more normative mode of storytelling than we may imagine.

I played World of Warcraft *predominantly during the "Burning Crusade" era, roughly 2007–2008, in which players spent the bulk of their time on another planet known then as Outland. Those days, I found myself spending a lot of time in the Terrokar Forest zone. I imagine that I was in the minority of players for doing so: after all, it lacks the beautiful vistas of nearby Nagrand, and there were few important resources to gather. Instead, it was designed as a low-level area in which players would spend a brief amount of time before outleveling it and moving on. With the exception of a hub of dungeons in the southern expanse, there was not much reason for a player to return and even less to linger. But I kept returning and I kept lingering, because I found myself obsessed with a fragment of the zone's musical accompaniment: a dreamy organ elegy that reminded me of some of my favorite pieces by Messiaen:* Le Banquet Céleste *(1928), for example, or the first movement of* L'Ascension *(1933–1934) (See Ex. 12.1).*

Part of the enjoyment of playing an MMORPG arises from the unstructured freedom in how players may spend their time. Some might race to the maximum level

EX. 12.1   Excerpt from "Terrokar Forest" scoring. *World of Warcraft: The Burning Crusade* (Blizzard, 2007). All transcriptions by the author with minor simplifications

200 Steven Reale

and begin progressing through the game's most difficult dungeons—encounters that might require the coordinated efforts of several handfuls of players to complete; others might roam the world of Azeroth amassing a collection of exotic in-game pets; still others might spend their time in competitive Player-vs.-Player (PvP) combat in the game's arenas and battle-grounds. During these quiet visits to Terrokar Forest, I was choosing to spend my in-game time—time that I was paying for at the rate of $15 per month!—just listening to the game's non-diegetic score. The game's incentive structure was pushing me towards higher-level, more rewarding zones; that structure itself was a barrier to my ability to continue listening to some music that had captivated me.

Synchronic and Diachronic Barriers

The nature of the MMORPG is such that virtually no player will be able to experience all of the available game content: a barrier, then, is anything that prevents a player from experiencing content. Although this chapter is specifically focused on the game's music, the concept could be extended to any parameter of the game experience. These barriers can be represented on a two-dimensional framework with a temporality axis on the one hand and a permeability axis on the other. The temporality axis indicates whether a barrier is synchronic or diachronic, where, broadly speaking, synchronic barriers exist within the structure of a game at a particular moment of gameplay, while diachronic barriers emerge over time as patches and expansions alter that structure.[8] The permeability axis indicates whether a barrier is fine or coarse. Fine barriers represent hard-coded limitations, whereas coarse barriers represent incentivization structures that discourage players from experiencing content that is otherwise available.

A synchronic barrier is any game mechanic present during a moment of play-through that restricts, hinders, or disincentivizes a player from experiencing game content that is theoretically accessible during that playthrough. The permeability of a synchronic barrier, then, is a function of a player's degree of agency in choosing whether to cross it. On the one hand, a fine synchronic barrier exists when a player wishes to experience content but is prevented from doing so; while, on the other, a coarse synchronic barrier exists when some content is freely accessible to the player, but he or she does not wish to experience it. In practice, a barrier will fall somewhere between these two extremes, and in the various scenarios outlined in Table 12.1, there is likely *some* degree of player choice—to purchase a new computer system, for example, or to dedicate time to improving their skills as a player.[9]

Synchronic barriers are not unique to the MMORPG genre or to *World of Warcraft* in particular; they are features of virtually all video games. Given advances in technology, a computer built in 2009 will likely not be able to run a game released in 2019, nor is it reasonable to expect that a PlayStation 3 will be able to run a game released for the PlayStation 4. The *Dark Souls* franchise of games (Namco Bandai Games, 2011–2018) is famous for its punishing level of difficulty

Barriers to Listening in *World of Warcraft*   **201**

TABLE 12.1 A spectrum of hypothetical synchronic barriers from the perspective of a player who owns a game for which a recent paid expansion features a particular encounter

Finer	Player's computer does not meet system requirements of most recent expansion
	Player has not purchased most recent expansion
	Player is not skilled enough to experience encounter
	Player has not yet had enough time to experience encounter
	Player is not skilled enough to complete a prerequisite encounter
	Player has not yet had enough time to complete a prerequisite encounter
Coarser	Player deems encounter unrewarding and chooses to engage in some other activity

that demands countless hours of skill refinement from its players to succeed—many players, including this author (and his co-editor!), abandon the titles without finishing. Many other games, such as *The Legend of Zelda: Breath of the Wild* (Nintendo, 2017), are packed with optional side-content (cooking, treasure hunting, city building, etc.) that the player can skip without missing the essential gameplay experience. Of these examples, *Dark Souls* represents a finer barrier, while *Breath of the Wild* represents a coarser one.

In 2008, I was a member of a modest guild focused on Player-vs.-Environment (PvE) encounters. On the one hand, this meant that I spent almost no time participating in PvP content; on the other hand, it also meant that I was not embedded in a group that was able to advance through the entire progression of endgame dungeons. While I chose to spend a lot of time listening to the music in Terrokar Forest, I also chose to spend little to no time listening to any of the martial strains that sound in the game's PvP battleground zones; my lack of interest in this aspect of the game became a coarse synchronic barrier to hearing this scoring. Similarly, my guild's limitations in skill and available time prevented us from progressing past the first couple of raiding tiers. There was thus a fine synchronic barrier that prevented me from hearing the music that accompanied the battle against the demon Kil'jaeden, the final enemy of the Burning Crusade *era.*

In contrast with synchronic barriers, which are common in many video games, diachronic barriers are a quintessential feature of MMORPGs like *World of Warcraft*. The nature of the game's revenue model requires that the studio develop and release content on an ongoing basis to encourage players to continue paying a monthly subscription fee. Since the game's 2004 release, each of the expansion packs have added new regions for players to explore—but, especially in one high-profile case, expansions may also remove previously existing content. With the release of the game's third expansion, *Cataclysm* (2010), the designers reshaped the world of Azeroth in accordance with the expansion's premise that a dimensional rift wreaked geological disaster upon the land. One resulting change was the

202 Steven Reale

radical transformation of the zone Thousand Needles. In the game's initial release, the zone existed as a desert of spires resembling the dramatic landscapes of southern Utah; after the cataclysm, the zone flooded, and what had been the ground upon which countless players quested for countless hours is now an ocean floor well beneath the surface (see Figure 12.1).

As I mentioned above, this is a remarkable situation, because even players who choose not to purchase an expansion are subject to an ever-changing synchronic game state. Even if they wanted to, players cannot revisit the old Thousand Needles zone (at least, not through official channels). Thus, the release of *Cataclysm* creates a fine diachronic barrier to experiencing the Thousand Needles in its original form.

One of my earliest memories from playing World of Warcraft *was the experience of entering Orgrimmar, the capital city of the orc race, with whom I had chosen to ally. Up to that point, my low-level questing had taken place in remote, sparsely populated areas. The day that I ventured to the city for the first time, recall I glimpsing the city's imposing stone barbican from afar, and when I finally approached and crossed its threshold I was greeted with a musical cue featuring low brass and a martial drumbeat (see Ex. 12.2). When I entered the city and saw a vast number of other players going about their business, I began to grasp just how unimaginably large the number of my fellow adventurers was, and it gave me goosebumps. Even after countless visits to Orgrimmar, this cue became intimately associated with that first experience of entering the city. I was surprised, then, to enter Orgrimmar after the cataclysm, and to learn that the entrance cue had been rescored: the new music still features the warlike drums and horn, but, whereas the older cue had been clearly in B flat minor, the new version is replete with tritones and chromatic inflections that obscure a clear tonal center (see Ex. 12.3). While the reimagined theme is effective at capturing the Horde's bellicose nature, and the original music can still be triggered at other locations within the city, I found myself missing the punctuation of my arrival into Orgrimmar with the familiar entry music; a fine diachronic barrier has been erected, and I no longer have access to that experience.*

If a fine diachronic barrier emerges when Blizzard removes content from the game, then coarse diachronic barriers arise when new content is released that eliminates the incentive to experience older content that may still be nonetheless present. A primary reason this might happen is because each expansion features two broad categories of content: *leveling content*, which players move through to gain levels, and *endgame content*, designed for players who have attained the maximum level for that particular release. A player may spend a week or two leveling and the next year or two at max level; since the vast majority of the gameplay experience will thus be at the level cap, the game designers need to develop a considerable amount of endgame content to incentive players to continue subscribing.

Table 12.2 lists all of the endgame zones as they appeared at the end of the original *World of Warcraft* content cycle and all of the high-level zones as they

FIGURE 12.1 The Thousand Needles zone: before (above) and after (below) *Cataclysm*

EX. 12.2 Entrance to Orgrimmar cue, *World of Warcraft* original release

EX. 12.3 Entrance to Orgrimmar cue, post-*Cataclysm*

appeared at the end of *The Burning Crusade*. There are two noteworthy aspects: first, three of the eight new high-level zones (nearly 38 percent) were designed with the endgame experience in mind, a sensibly large percentage if your players could attain maximum level in several weeks, but you want them to continue p(l)aying for the entire 23 months that the *Burning Crusade* cycle lasted. Second, the first new high-level zone, Hellfire Peninsula, was designed to be experienced by characters as low as level 58. This meant that players new to the game during the *Burning Crusade* era would likely spend minimal time in the five endgame levels of the game's original release. Additionally, when *The Burning Crusade* was released, Blizzard adjusted the rate at which characters level, allowing them to move from level 1 to 60 considerably faster than they could before. The upshot of all of this is that players new to *World of Warcraft* would have few if any ludic reasons to experience, say, the Silithus zone, and thus to hear the dissonant, insect-inspired ambient accompaniment therein. The release of *The Burning Crusade* rendered this important endgame zone obsolete, and its geographical remoteness created a strong disincentive to journey out to it. As it was still available in-game, however, determined

TABLE 12.2 High-level zones in *World of Warcraft* and *The Burning Crusade*

Level Range	Zone Name	Zones as they appeared at the end of:
53–60	Eastern Plaguelands	*World of Warcraft*
53–60	Winterspring	*World of Warcraft*
55–60	Deadwind Pass	*World of Warcraft*
55–60	Silithus	*World of Warcraft*
58–63	Hellfire Peninsula	*The Burning Crusade*
60–64	Zangarmarsh	*The Burning Crusade*
62–65	Terokkar Forest	*The Burning Crusade*
64–67	Nagrand	*The Burning Crusade*
65–68	Blade's Edge Mountains	*The Burning Crusade*
67–70	Netherstorm	*The Burning Crusade*
67–70	Shadowmoon Valley	*The Burning Crusade*
70	Isle of Quel'Danas	*The Burning Crusade*

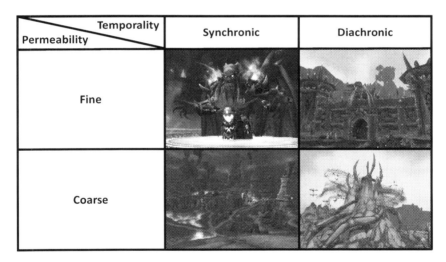

FIGURE 12.2 The entire barrier complex. From left to right, top to bottom: the demon Kil'jaeden; the gates of Orgrimmar; the Eye of the Storm battleground; and the wasteland of Silithus

players could still experience it if they wished. Thus, the release of *The Burning Crusade* created a coarse diachronic barrier to listening to the Silithus music. The entire preceding discussion is summarized in Figure 12.2. The fine diachronic barrier is represented by Kil'jaeden; the coarse diachronic barrier by the Eye of the Storm battleground; the fine synchronic barrier by the gates of Orgrimmar; and the coarse synchronic barrier by the infested wastelands of Silithus.[10]

Complications and Barrier Flux

During the final stages of revising this document, I flew my character outside the gates of Orgrimmar and spotted some tents that were not usually there. As I approached them, some music played that I had not heard in over a decade (see Ex. 12.4). In fact, I had completely forgotten that this polka existed, and yet, the moment it began playing, accompanied by the sounds of drunken goblin chatter, it was as though I were transported back in time. Brewfest, the in-game version of Oktoberfest, had arrived! Every September, a set of beer-related quests and events become available and then a week or so later disappear. Clearly, this represents a fine diachronic barrier to listening, but I was stunned to learn as I researched the polka and prepared my transcription that this tune only plays outside of Orgrimmar. The Alliance has a completely different polka that plays at their *Brewfest celebration. I had never heard that* music *before, nor knew that it even existed. In addition to the fine diachronic barrier that restricts players from hearing this music in-game save for one week per year, I learned that there is also a coarse synchronic barrier that prevented me, because of my allegiance to the Horde, from hearing or knowing of the Alliance's Brewfest music. The lesson here is that identifying barriers to listening is often more complex than categorizing them into a single quadrant of the diagram in Figure 12.2.*

The barriers of Figure 12.2 all exist within the frame of the game, but it is important to note that even its diachronic barriers have been explored from stable synchronic moments—those being predominantly the state of the game at the end of *The Burning Crusade* and the beginning of *Cataclysm*. The nature of diachronic analysis, though, means that insights gleaned at one synchronic moment may

EX. 12.4 Excerpt from the Brewfest polka, hordeside

be false at others. Indeed, to my considerable amusement, after choosing in the initial stages of this research to adopt the Silithus zone as my archetypal coarse, diachronic barrier, not only did Blizzard release a set of endgame quests for *Legion* that took place in the zone, but the very first quest of *Battle for Azeroth* requires the player to journey there. In addition, like Thousand Needles in *Cataclysm*, the zone was fundamentally changed: after completing the final raid of *Legion*, players view a cinematic in which the demonic titan Sargeras plunges his massive sword into the zone; healing the resulting wound becomes one of the central conceits of *Battle for Azeroth* (see Figure 12.3). *Unlike* Thousand Needles post-cataclysm, there is a way of revisiting the older version of the zone: a non-player character will allow the player to "travel back in time" to see Silithus as it was before Sargeras's strike. Thus, in addition to diachronically falsifying my statement about the obsolescence of Silithus, this example serves as evidence of a philosophical change on Blizzard's part to seek ways of eliminating, rather than erecting, barriers to content. This is a sensible move, for it would be a shame for Blizzard to design so much content and to subsequently prevent players from experiencing it. The remainder of this chapter, then, will detach the study of barriers to listening from a singular, synchronic, in-game moment. It will consider not only the ways in which barriers change diachronically, but also ways that barriers may be circumvented from outside the game's diegesis, and ultimately how the nature of the barriers themselves are subject to diachronic changes to the designers' gameplay philosophies for *World of Warcraft*.

FIGURE 12.3 The blade of Sargeras's sword and the wound of Azeroth now occupy the location of the insect mound in Figure 12.2

208   Steven Reale

There had been a longstanding problem with the game's endgame dungeons (called *raids*), in that they require the cooperation and skills of potentially dozens of players to complete perhaps dozens of prerequisite encounters to even enter them. The musical scoring for these events would then seem to be locked away, accessible only to an elite minority of players. This was never exactly so, but it is much less true today than it was a decade ago. To begin with, since the game arose during a period of widespread internet access, that very same internet access became a means by which players could research important information about the game outside of the frame of its gameplay. Indeed, websites such as Wowhead (wowhead.com) are an important tool for players studying game mechanics, featuring a wealth of detailed data concerning optimal ways of assigning stats or selecting gear; suggestions for efficiently leveling both the character and its secondary skills (e.g., how to quickly and inexpensively increase skill in cooking, or how to find specific recipes that feature a strong synergy with other aspects of the gamer's play-style); and, importantly, strategies for defeating endgame enemies. Although it may seem like "cheating" to consult a guide on defeating a monster rather than to learn its weaknesses through gameplay trial and error, in practice it is considered poor form to arrive at a high-level raid without having studied its encounters in advance.[11] Raiding takes time and organization, and it is wildly inefficient, on the one hand, for a raid leader to have to explain how an encounter should work while everybody is assembled in-game; or, on the other, for an ill-informed neophyte to make an error that ultimately causes the group to fail the encounter and have to restart it from the beginning. Thus, out-of-game research is not just encouraged by the community, in many ways it is essential, and since video footage of the encounters is available on Wowhead and YouTube, anybody may experience *World of Warcraft* content in at least a secondhand way. Moreover, since gameplay footage can be found from as early as the game's initial release, external sources become a way for interested parties to "peer over" boundaries both synchronic and diachronic. Furthermore, watching top raiding guilds complete these difficult encounters can be a form of entertainment in and of itself. On September 19, 2018, the guild Method was the first in the world to defeat the final boss at the highest difficulty setting of the then-current raid, Uldir, and reportedly over 160,000 viewers watched the feat on a TwitchTV livestream.[12]

Still, there is a fundamental difference between viewing content on YouTube and experiencing it in game, so Blizzard began to soften fine synchronic barriers over the course of individual content cycles. For example, the Kil'jaeden fight may have been extraordinarily difficult upon its initial release during *The Burning Crusade*, but Blizzard eventually retuned the encounter, decreasing its difficulty so that more players would have the opportunity to experience it (a diachronic softening of a fine synchronic barrier). This was among the first of many such moves toward increasing player accessibility to the endgame raid dungeons. The most difficult *World of Warcraft* raids were designed for 40 players to complete.

Noting the logistic difficulty of organizing such a large group of people, Blizzard eliminated 40-player dungeons from their design language and instead designed two tracks of raids for the *Burning Crusade*: one set of dungeons for groups of 10 players, and another for groups of 25 players. In *Wrath of the Lich King*, Blizzard designed each raid dungeon so that it could accommodate groups of either 10 or 25 players, with the 10-player raids being less difficult to complete. As a result, greater numbers of players could experience end-game content that had previously been inaccessible. In the current iteration of the game, Blizzard now offers four tiers of difficulty, ranging from a version that can be completed by unorganized groups of players, known as *pick-up groups* (*PUGs*), to the world-class "mythic" setting, mentioned above; and, rather than being tuned for specific player counts, most of these tiers scale to accommodate various group sizes. Blizzard's strategy, then, is to soften even the finest synchronic barriers of the game, creating opportunities for virtually any motivated player to cross them.

As we have seen, a diachronic study of barriers itself implies that the very nature of the barriers themselves are subject to change over the course of the game's lifespan. Boundaries that were once synchronous may become diachronous, and vice versa. For example, players who choose to align themselves with the game's Horde faction will almost certainly hear an entry cue for Orgrimmar, but a player who chooses to align with the Alliance faction might never set foot in it at all and thus never hear its entry cue. The opposite is also true: a truly dedicated Horde player may never visit the Alliance capital Stormwind City and thus may never hear its musical accompaniment. In these cases, a player's choice—which faction they will play—establishes a coarse synchronic barrier to hearing music that is heard frequently by players of the opposing faction. Significantly, then, what was once a coarse synchronic barrier to hearing the original Orgrimmar entry cue *becomes* a fine diachronic barrier in *Cataclysm*.

At the end of *The Burning Crusade*, the Kil'jaeden encounter, even after retuning, still required a certain degree of organization and ability to complete. Upon the release of later expansions, however, as players elevated their characters far beyond the level cap intended for this encounter, it became considerably easier—so much so that, though originally designed for a 25-player group, it could be completed by a single player.[13] At the same time, any rewards for defeating Kil'jaeden have by now been long rendered obsolete. As was (up until recently) the case for the Silithus zone, the only reason to visit Kil'jaeden now would be to engage in a kind of "endgame tourism," to experience artifacts of previous iterations of the game, in much the same way that Dana Plank has shown earlier in this volume that modern tourists might find themselves fascinated with ancient Egypt. Thus, what was previously a fine synchronic barrier over time may become a coarse diachronic barrier.

But even changes like these are not necessarily stable. The most difficult dungeon that existed before the release of *The Burning Crusade,* Naxxramas,

210 Steven Reale

represented an extremely fine synchronic barrier. This encounter, requiring the coordination of 40 players, was considered to be one of Blizzard's finest pieces of game design up to that point, and yet, due to its difficulty and the long, complex sequence of prerequisite encounters, only a small fraction of players got to experience it. When the company designed the third expansion, *Wrath of the Lich King,* they reused the dungeon as an introductory raid experience, showcasing with it their new design philosophy of presenting raid dungeons in both 10-player and 25-player versions, and allowing most of its player base a chance to experience what has been described as "the absolute pinnacle of old *WoW* raiding."[14] In so doing, they removed the original, 40-player dungeon from the game, rendering it permanently inaccessible. Thus, charting the barriers to listening to the eerie music of Naxxramas, citadel of the undead, reveals a complicated path through this chapter's two-dimensional framework. The fine synchronic barrier to Naxxramas gave way to a coarse diachronic barrier upon the release of *The Burning Crusade*, when players' elevated stats lessened the difficulty of the dungeon.[15] Upon release of *Wrath of the Lich King*, however, a fine diachronic barrier to the original 40-player experience was erected (as it was removed from the game); and a new fine synchronic barrier was established for the new version of the dungeon, though one considerably softer than in its original iteration. Finally, as new expansions were released and the level cap continued to rise, the barrier once again became coarse and diachronic.

A third way that these barriers change over time might be termed "diachronic reinstatement," where Blizzard either restores access to content that had been removed or reincentivizes experiencing content that had previously been rendered obsolete. In the latter case, during the game's fifth expansion cycle, Blizzard created a "timewalking" mode, in which players could explore lower-level dungeons with their characters' stats being artificially scaled down to restore the intended level of challenge (e.g., a level 100 character might have their abilities decreased to those of a level 70 character). At the same time, loot earned during these encounters would be scaled *up* so as to be appropriate for the character's actual level. This system thus encourages players to explore older content, lowering some coarse diachronic barriers that may have developed over time.

One aspect of diachronic reinstatement is particularly pertinent for the present discussion. During the game's fifth expansion, *Warlords of Draenor* (2014), one of the central conceits was that each player would build and customize a unique garrison to serve as their base of operations. Though all Horde garrisons are located in one place and all Alliance garrisons in another, the game employed what Blizzard called "phasing," so that when players enter the garrison zone they would only see and interact with their own instance of it. The garrison system represented Blizzard's response to fans who had long been asking for player housing, and it allowed each player to customize their home base to their liking. One significant way players could customize their garrison was by building a jukebox that would allow them to play music from rolls they could collect out in the world, considerably lowering some boundaries to listening, but not all. The music from Terrokar Forest does not appear on a music roll; if I want to hear it in-game, I still need to travel to Outland to do so.

Finally, on November 3, 2017, Blizzard made a stunning announcement: for many years, fans had been clamoring for the opportunity to revisit and replay *World of Warcraft* as it existed before the release of *The Burning Crusade*. During a now notorious 2013 Blizzcon event, a fan asked the development team if they would ever consider releasing a legacy server, and J. Allen Brack, *World of Warcraft* Production Director, replied: "No. And you don't want that either. You think you do, but you don't."[16] Many people did, however, as evidenced by the numerous unofficial legacy servers that arose to fill that demand. The largest, Nostalrius, boasted 800,000 accounts (150,000 of which were active) in a press release written after they acquiesced to a cease-and-desist order request from Blizzard.[17] Ultimately, though, in part due to subsequent conversations with the lead developers for Nostalrius, Blizzard decided to develop official legacy servers.[18] When these servers are released, players will once again have official access to game content that has been unavailable for many years. The fine diachronic barriers to the original *World of Warcraft* experience will be lifted: Hordeside players entering Orgrimmar will once again be greeted by the old cue; and players at the level cap will once again have a good incentive to listen to Silithus's haunting ambience, to experience the zone as it existed more than a decade ago.

Conclusion

I recently wanted to revisit the original Star Wars *trilogy, so a friend loaned me his DVD box set. As the trilogy came to an end, I was looking forward to hearing a song that I had loved as a child—the Ewok celebration that closed* Return of the Jedi. *I was surprised to discover the ending was substantially revised in a way that incorporated and resolved the storylines of Episodes 1–3, and that the entire sequence featured a brand-new musical accompaniment. As lovely as the sequence was, I was mildly disappointed; a fine diachronic barrier to listening had appeared in a beloved work.*

While synchronic barriers to listening (and to experiencing other content) are not uncommon in video games, MMORPGs bring a second kind of barrier to the forefront. This barrier emerges—sometimes intentionally, other times as a byproduct—when new content is released that supersedes, obsoletes, or replaces older content. Diachronic barriers might even be described as a defining feature of the genre. Nonetheless, as my experience viewing *Star Wars* will attest, they are not limited to the MMORPG. One straightforward way this occurs is when content creators release revised editions of works that abridge or otherwise remove material that existed in previous editions. Those of us responsible for authoring,

212 Steven Reale

reviewing, or selecting textbooks for the college classroom are well aware of these kinds of changes. A particularly noteworthy example of this kind of diachronic barrier occurred with the game *The Legend of Zelda: Ocarina of Time* (Nintendo, 1998): in the initial release, the soundtrack to the game's fire temple featured some samples of Islamic chanting that were replaced with synthesized sounds in subsequent production runs and in later rereleases.[19] Without "peering over the wall," either by using unofficial emulation software or watching online videos, or else locating what are now rare and valuable first-release cartridges, players who did not acquire the original version of the game may no longer be able to hear the music as originally released. In another example, which is by now becoming a predictable experience, during the final stages of editing this book Nintendo released a new edition of the original *Legend of Zelda*, making some substantial quality-of-life changes to the original release and thereby diachronically falsifying a claim I made in this chapter's third paragraph.[20]

Outside video games, diachronic barriers are becoming more and more common in the world of board games and card games. It has long been a common feature of collectible card games such as *Magic: The Gathering* (*MtG*) that publishers will release expansion sets that introduce more powerful cards than what had existed previously, with the effect of encouraging players to purchase more packages of cards to increase their competitive advantage. While this does not necessarily *prevent* players from using outdated cards, they will struggle when playing against those who are using a current deck—so the release of new cards creates something of a coarse diachronic barrier to using older ones. In some cases, such as with the *MtG* card "Black Lotus," the designers become aware that a released card is overly powerful and creates an imbalance to play. While they (of course) cannot repossess these cards from the players, they can ban their use in official competitive play, creating a fine diachronic barrier to their use.

The lifespan of the cooperative board game *Pandemic* (Z-Man Games, 2007) demonstrates two additional examples of diachronic barriers. First, a second edition of the game, featuring updated artwork and components, was released in 2013. All expansions for the game released after that point adopted the new design standards and thus were incompatible with the version of the game at initial release. The publisher did make available a set of updated components for the original version, and it is only through purchasing them that owners of the first printing could cross the diachronic barrier to playing the game's later expansions. In 2015, Z-Man released a new version of the game entitled *Pandemic Legacy: Season 1*. The title begins with the basic framework of the original game, but during each of its 12 scenarios the game changes in fundamental ways: players are directed to open compartments revealing new rules and new components; or to apply stickers to the game board, so that incidents from one playthrough have consequences that permanently affect the subsequent scenarios. Other times, players will be instructed to destroy certain game components, further reinforcing the permanence of in-game events. By the end of the 12th scenario, the board game and its components will have been fundamentally transformed, and without purchasing a new set players cannot return to a previous game state. The diachronic boundaries are fine—and firm!—indeed.

Ultimately, diachronic barriers are considerably more common than we might first imagine. Carol Poster has shown, adapting the insights of Walter Ong, that the experience of playing *World of Warcraft*, and being an audience to its storytelling, aligns it more closely with ancient traditions of oral storytelling than with what is ultimately a recent and anomalous consumption pattern of media:

> The twenty-first century Homer ... is bound between covers with a fixed shape and sequence, and read silently and privately as part of a literary experience Plato describes as rigidly unresponsive ... Homer as experienced in antiquity, on the other hand, like MMORPGs, was social rather than solitary and interactive rather than monological. No two performances of Homeric epic were identical. Just as when gamers replay episodes or entire games, the course of events and length of time required depends on the ways the players interact with the game universe, so audience reactions and performance situations cause oral performers to vary their performances of what they consider the "same" story.[21]

Though not limited to the MMORPG experience, diachronic barriers nonetheless *do* constitute a primary essence of that experience, and this allows MMORPGs like *World of Warcraft* to serve as a catalyst for reminding us of the manner in which works of art may—and often do—change over time. We can be reminded that texts may be unstable not only in the high-theoretical sense in which we understand that they are re-composed every time an audience experiences, or even re-experiences them, but also in an everyday sense. It is possible—even in the age of internet archiving—that we may never be able to access a remembered work in the form it once took. We may grieve such a loss, but maybe we can take comfort in knowing that we do not suffer in isolation: humankind could never really keep a story in a firm grasp.

Notes

1 Terry Eagleton, *Literary Theory: An Introduction* (Minneapolis: University of Minnesota Press, 1983), 12.
2 Lydia Goehr outlines some of the debates in the philosophy of music concerning the nature of the work in *The Imaginary Museum of Musical Works*, rev. ed. (New York: Oxford University Press, 2007).
3 Jean-Jacques Nattiez, *Music and Discourse: Towards a Semiology of Music*, trans. Carolyn Abbate (Princeton, NJ: Princeton University Press, 1990), 73.

4 Nicholas Cook, *Beyond the Score: Music as Performance* (New York: Oxford University Press, 2013).
5 Carolyn Abbate and Roger Parker, *A History of Opera* (New York: W.W. Norton, 2012), xv.
6 Stanley Boorman, "The Musical Text," in *Rethinking Music*, ed. Nicholas Cook and Mark Everist (New York: Oxford University Press, 1999), 403–423.
7 See Steven Reale, "Transcribing Musical Worlds; or, Is *L.A. Noire* a Music Game?" in *Music in Video Games: Studying Play*, ed. Kevin J. Donnelly, Neil Lerner, and William Gibbons (New York: Routledge, 2014), 77–103.
8 The terms of this axis—synchronic vs. diachronic—are borrowed from Ferdinand de Saussure, and are particularly apt for a study of games, as he uses the analogy of a chess match to exemplify these forces as they apply to language. Ferdinand de Saussure, *Course in General Linguistics*, ed. Charles Bally and Albert Sechehaye (New York: Philosophical Library, 1950), 88–89.
9 Naturally, the ability to make such choices is itself a function of certain kinds of socio-economic privilege.
10 Below, this chapter considers ways that Blizzard's design philosophy has evolved in order to reduce or eliminate barriers to experiencing content: as an example of one such change, the sixth expansion, *Legion* (2016), zones now scale along with the player's level. This means that there is now less of a distinction between leveling zones and endgame zones, and players will now continually be incentivized to return to all of the main zones of a content release.
11 Of course, *someone* must have figured out these strategies in the first place: the general pattern is that the top guilds in the world will be the first to experience newly released encounters. These guilds will undertake the encounters without foreknowledge and through some trial and error will determine a workable strategy. This information is then disseminated through forums and video footage that other players may study in preparation for their own encounters. Much of this data gathering and dissemination occurs while forthcoming content is undergoing public beta testing, so that by the time an encounter reaches the live servers, it is already widely documented by the player base.
12 See Wowhead, "The Viewer Impact of Streaming the World First Mythic Uldir Race" (accessed April 18, 2019), www.wowhead.com/news=287311/the-viewer-impact-of-streaming-the-world-first-mythic-uldir-race.
13 The footage of the solo encounter by YouTube user HeelvsBabyFace at www.youtube.com/watch?v=42xAe-JXg7U not only provides a great example of this, but his commentary touches upon many of the issues of diachrony discussed here (site accessed April 18, 2019). Today, where the level maximum is 40 levels higher than it was when the encounter was released, it is so trivial that, after I took the screen capture for Figure 12.2, I was able to defeat the demon in about seven attacks, while taking no damage myself.
14 See Matthew Rossi, "Wrath of the Lich King Retrospective: Naxxramas," Engadget.com (June 3, 2010; April 18, 2019), www.engadget.com/2010/06/03/wrath-of-the-lich-king-retrospective-naxxramas/.
15 But by no means was Naxxramas easy for a level-capped player during *The Burning Crusade*. See discussion thread: www.wowhead.com/forums&topic=8478/how-many-for-naxx-70 (accessed April 18, 2019).
16 See transcription of the event: http://wowwiki.wikia.com/wiki/BlizzCon_2013/WoW_Q_%26_A_About_Almost_Everything_panel (accessed April 18, 2019).
17 Nostalrius, "Nearly One Million Gaming Accounts Lost in Legacy Servers," https://en.nostalrius.org/pr1.pdf (2016; accessed April 18, 2019).
18 Chris Bratt, "World of Warcraft Classic: We ask Blizzard Our Biggest Questions," Eurogamer.com (April 11, 2017; accessed April 18, 2019), www.eurogamer.net/articles/2017-11-04-wow-classic-blizzard-answers-some-of-the-big-questions.

19 A longstanding rumor that the change was made due to outcry by the Muslim community seems to have been debunked. See Gametrailers, "Pop Fiction: Season 1: Episode 9: The Fire Temple Chants [Update 2]" (accessed April 18, 2019), https://youtube/U34MFcJdGCo.

20 Andrew Webster, "The Nintendo Switch Just Got a Much Easier Version of the Original NES Zelda," TheVerge.com (October 10, 2018; accessed April 18, 2019), www.theverge.com/2018/10/10/17959040/nintendo-switch-online-legend-of-zelda-nes-special-edition.

21 Carol Poster, "Walter Ong's *World of Warcraft*: Orality-Literacy Theory and Player Experience," *First Person Scholar* (October 12, 2016; accessed April 18, 2019), www.firstpersonscholar.com/walter-ongs-world-of-warcraft/.

NOTES ON CONTRIBUTORS

Kevin R. Burke is an Associate Professor of Music and Director of Music Programs at the Florida Institute of Technology. His emerging research and teaching interests involve classic video game music, particularly the compositional trends and culture developing around the sound chips for 8- and 16-bit systems. He has presented this research at meetings of the North American Conference on Video Game Music and the Ludomusicology Conference. Kevin remains active in the study of music pedagogy, recently serving as the Secretary-Treasurer for the American Musicological Society's Pedagogy Study Group, and his work with instructional technology and the "Reacting to the Past" (RTTP) platform appear in *Hybrid Pedagogy*, *Engaging Students*, *Journal of Music History Pedagogy*, and the forthcoming *Norton Guide to Teaching Music History*.

Karen M. Cook is Assistant Professor of Music History at The Hartt School at the University of Hartford. Her primary research is on theoretical approaches to rhythmic notation in the late medieval period, with her current work focusing on lesser-known or fragmentary treatises. She also maintains strong interests in medievalism and in ludomusicology, with several publications focusing on the creative repurposing or reimagining of medieval music in video game soundtracks. Recent work appears, or is forthcoming, in *Studies in Medievalism XXVII: Authenticity, Medievalism, Music*; *The Oxford Handbook of Medievalism in Music*; *Musica Disciplina*; *Plainsong & Medieval Music*; and *Oxford Bibliographies in Music*. She is a recipient of the inaugural ACLS Professional Development Grant, which she will use toward her work on her forthcoming monograph on the development of rhythmic notation in the 14th and early 15th centuries.

Kate Galloway is Lecturer at Rensselaer Polytechnic Institute. She specializes in North American music that responds to and problematizes environmental

Notes on Contributors **217**

issues and relationships, sonic cartography, musical Indigenous modernities, sound studies, science and technology studies (STS), new media studies, and the digital humanities. Her monograph *Remix, Reuse, Recycle: Music, Media Technologies, and Remediating the Environment* (under contract with Oxford University Press) examines how and why contemporary artists remix and recycle sounds, musics, and texts encoded with environmental knowledge.

William Gibbons is Associate Professor of Musicology and Associate Dean of the College of Fine Arts at Texas Christian University. His research focuses broadly on issues of musical canons, national and cultural identity, and music in media. In addition to a number of book chapters and journal articles on these topics, Gibbons is the author of *Building the Operatic Museum: Eighteenth Century Opera in fin-de-siècle Paris* (Rochester, 2013) and *Unlimited Replays: Video Games and Classical Music* (Oxford, 2018), as well as co-editor of *Music in Video Games: Studying Play* (Routledge, 2014).

Julianne Grasso is a PhD candidate in Music History and Theory at the University of Chicago. She holds a BA in Music with a certificate in Neuroscience from Princeton University. Her current project, "Video Game Music, Meaning, and the Possibilities of Play," analyzes how gameplay and musical subjectivity interact in virtual worlds. Her wider interests include music cognition, fandom studies, and broader issues of sound in multimedia.

Michiel Kamp is Assistant Professor of Musicology at Utrecht University, where he teaches on music and audiovisual media. He is co-founder of the UK-based Ludomusicology Research Group, which has organized yearly conferences on video game music in the UK and abroad since 2011, and co-edited a volume of the same name (Equinox, 2016). Michiel has previously contributed to a special issue of *Philosophy & Technology* on video game music and ecological psychology.

Meghan Naxer has a Ph.D. from the University of Oregon, and is an instructional design specialist at Oregon State University. Prior to joining OSU, Dr. Naxer was an Assistant Professor of Music Theory at Kent State University. She has presented research on music theory pedagogy, late 19th-century form, and rhythm and meter at regional, national, and international conferences, including "Engaging Students: An Unconference on Music Pedagogy," the Mythopoeic Society Mythcon, and the European Music Analysis Conference. Her work also can be seen in *Engaging Students: Essays in Music Pedagogy*. Dr. Naxer is on Twitter @mnaxer.

Dana Plank holds a Ph.D in Historical Musicology from The Ohio State University, with a dissertation on representations of disability in early video game soundscapes. Her publications on game music include articles in *The Soundtrack* and a chapter in *Music Video Games: Performance, Politics, and Play* (2016), while contributions to *BACH: Journal of the Riemenschneider Bach Institute* and the *Cambridge*

218 Notes on Contributors

Companion to Video Game Music are forthcoming. Aside from video game music, her diverse research interests include the sacred music of Carlo Gesualdo, minimalist and post-minimalist opera, Egyptology, disability studies, and music and identity. In addition to her scholarship, Plank remains active as a violinist and chamber musician.

Steven Reale is Associate Professor of Music Theory at Youngstown State University, and has become an acknowledged leader in the field of video game music, a topic on which his scholarly publications and presentations have attained an international impact. He is a co-founder of the North American Conference on Video Game Music and was the lead organizer of the first conference, held at YSU in 2014. He received the UK Ludomusicology Research Group's inaugural Award for Excellence in Game Audio Research for his 2015 Society for Music Theory presentation on transformational geographies in *The Legend of Zelda: Ocarina of Time*. In 2016, his two-part video series on the music from the *Portal* franchise of video games was published by *SMT-V*, the peer-reviewed video journal of the Society for Music Theory.

Tim Summers is Lecturer in Music at Royal Holloway, University of London. His research concerns music in popular culture, with a particular focus on video game music. He is the author of *Understanding Video Game Music* and he has written articles on game music for journals including *Cambridge Opera Journal* and *Twentieth-Century Music*. He co-founded the Ludomusicology Research Group, which holds conferences on game audio. He has broadcast on game music for the BBC and is finishing his second book while editing *The Cambridge Companion to Video Game Music*.

Mark Sweeney is the Executive Director and co-founder of the Society for the Study of Sound & Music in Games. After completing a BA in Music at Oxford University, he received an AHRC award in support of an MSt (Distinction) in musicology, with a dissertation on non-linear video game music, which was expanded into a DPhil thesis on aesthetic theory and video game music. He has taught faculty classes and college tutorials across the University and was a Stipendiary Lecturer in Music at St Catherine's College, Oxford. He has also supervised dissertations on video game music at the universities of Oxford and Cambridge. As a co-founder of the Ludomusicology Research Group, Mark is co-editor of the Intellect series "Studies in Game Sound and Music," has co-edited journal special issues and a book anthology, and has also contributed conference papers, book chapters, and articles on a range of topics.

Ryan Thompson is a Professor of Practice in the College of Communications Arts and Sciences at Michigan State University, where he teaches video game audio and online broadcasting. He received his Ph.D. in Musicology from the

University of Minnesota in 2017. His research tends to focus on game audio's potential to guide and influence the actions of a player. Future projects will likely involve his growing interest in esports as a subject of academic study. Ryan has spoken multiple times at the North American Conference on Video Game Music, and has also presented at the Game Developers Conference and GameSoundCon. He has been featured in interviews with Game Informer and Minnesota Public Radio, and has served as an expert source quoted on *Polygon*, *Kotaku*, and in Boss Fight Books. Ryan streams regularly with colleagues in game audio at twitch.tv/bardicknowledge, and can be reached on Twitter as @BardicKnowledge.

INDEX OF VIDEO GAMES

The Adventures of Willy Beamish 11
Akalabeth: World of Doom 2
Ar Tonelico 14
Assassin's Creed (series) 194

Baldur's Gate (series) 20n32, 30
The Bard's Tale (series) 21; *The Bard's Tale* (2004 game) 4, 21–34
Bastion 32n7, 150–151
Bayou Billy 68
Bioshock 134, 138
Black Knight 33n27
Bloodborne 3–4

Castlevania 74n17
Chrono Trigger 102, 108
Cleopatra no Ma Takara 4, 76–79, 83–96
Contra (series) 74n18, 75n28

Darkest Dungeon 30
Darkspore 138
Dark Souls see Souls (series)
Destiny 138
Diablo (series): *Diablo* (1996) 3, 137–138, 139; *III* 5, 131–145
Donkey Kong 24
Dragon Age (series): *Origins*, 32n7, 149–150; *II* 32n7; *Inquisition* 20n30, 148

Dragon Quest (series) 35–36, 46–48, 57; *Dragon Quest* (1986) 2, 44, 53n28; *III* 78, 79, **80**, 83, **84**, **88**, 91–93; *XI* 2
Dragon Warrior (series) *see Dragon Quest* (series)
Dragon's Dogma 26
Dungeon Siege 138

EarthBound see Mother (series)
The Elder Scrolls (series), 141; *Skyrim* 2, 5, 19n30, 138, 148, 179–195

Fable 148
Fallout (series) 137, 138–139; *3* 131
Farmville 159
Final Fantasy (series) 35, 44, 46–48, 57, 78, 108, 109, 113, 117, 127, 148; *I* 76, 78; *II* 92, 128n4; *III* 118; *IV* 5, 9, 30, 97–116, 117; *V* 92, 96n43, 118; *VI* 5, 12, 102, 117–128; *VII* 128n6; *VII* 128n6; *IX* 128n27; *X* 14, 17, 24, 128n6; *X-2* 19n30, 128n6; *XII* 128n6; *XIII* 74n16, 148; *Tactics* 32n7 *see also Theatrhythm: Final Fantasy*

Gauntlet 11
Grandia II 13–14, 16–17
Grim Dawn 138
Guitar Hero 31

Index of Video Games **221**

Harvest Moon (series) 159, 160–161, 173

The Incredible Adventures of Van Helsing 138

Journey to Silius 75n27

Lagrange Point 4, 57–75
Laser Invasion 64
The Legend of Zelda (series) 50; *Breath of the Wild* 201; *The Legend of Zelda* (1986) 50, 198, 212; *Ocarina of Time* 52n12, 212
Loom 12, 52n12
Lunar: Silver Star Story Complete 9–11, 13–18

Marvel Heroes 138, 139
Mario Kart 138
Mass Effect (series) 141
Max Payne 2 24
Mōryō Senki MADARA 64
Mother (series) 4, 35–53

Ni no Kuni: Wrath of the White Witch 20n32

Pac-Man 141
Path of Exile 138
Persona 5 148, 149
Phantasy Star (series) 62, 137
Prince of Persia: The Sands of Time 32n7
Proteus 161

Rakuen 3
Rhapsody: A Musical Adventure 20n33
Road Rash 138
Rocket Knight Adventures 74n18
Rollergames 64

Sacred (series) 26
Senki Madara 2 74n18

Shadow of the Colossus 33n19
Shovel Knight 30
The Sims Medieval 30
Sinistar 11
Sonic the Hedgehog 11
Souls (series) 4, 26, 200–201; *Dark Souls* 151, 200–201
Skyrim see *The Elder Scrolls: Skyrim*
Stardew Valley 3, 5, 159–176
StarTropics see *Zoda's Revenge: StarTropics II*
Super Mario Bros. 24, 50, 135, 141
Super Mario RPG 108

Tales (series) 17
Teenage Mutant Ninja Turtles 68
Tetris 135
Theatrhythm: Final Fantasy 113
Titan Quest 138
Tomb Raider (2013) 194
Torchlight 138
Twin Bee 3 64

Ultima (series) 2, 44, 141
Uncharted (series) 134–135
Undertale 2, 149

Victor Vran 138
Viridi 161

Warhammer 40,000: Inquisitor—Martyr 138
Wing Commander II: Vengeance of the Kilrathi 12
Wipeout 138
The Witcher 3 33n18, 33n22, 155
Wizard and the Princess 24
Wizardry (series) 2, 32n7, 143n26
World of Warcraft 2, 5, 197–213

Zoda's Revenge: StarTropics II 96n37

GENERAL INDEX

Aaresth, Espen 131
Abbate, Carolyn 198
action RPG 2–3, 21–23, 32n6, 134–135, 137–138, 141, 142
Adorno, Theodor 120
Almén, Byron 100
Anable, Aubrey 170
avatars: player identification with, 148, 160–161

bard 9, 12, 22, 26, 29–32, 37, **38**
Barone, Eric 160–161
Barthes, Roland 114n6
Beethoven, Ludwig van 133, 143n6, 179, 182, 191, 198
Blizzard (video game publisher) 139, 142, 198, 202, 204, 207–211, 214n10
Boettcher, Wendy S. 146
Boorman, Stanley 198
Buell, Lawrence 165
Brack, J. Allen 211

Carlson, Rachel 172
Casey, Edward S. 166
CD-ROM: audio capabilities of 11–13, 18n9
Chang, Alenda Y. 162
Cheng, William 6n2, 13, 18n5, 19n16, 47, 124, 128n7, 128n12, 131, 165
Chion, Michel 9–10, 12–13, 102, 189
Clifton, Thomas 188

Citron, Marcia 121–122
Collins, Karen 20n31, 101, 137, 195n2
ConcernedApe *see* Barone, Eric
Cook, James 33n18
Cook, Nicholas 189, 197
Copland, Aaron 139
Csikszentmihalyi, Mihaly 111, 115n29, 115n32, 158n15 *see also* flow (state)

Dahlhaus, Carl 181–182, 193 *see also* *Naturklang* and *Klangfläche*
Deci, Edward L. 147 *see also* self-determination theory (SDT)
Dobashi, Akio 63
Donnelly, Kevin 51
Drachen, Anders 147, 150, 152–153
Dungeons & Dragons (tabletop game) 2, 12, 20n32, 29, 138, 143n26

Eagleton, Terry 197
early film: connection to games 10–18
Eco, Umberto 114n6
Egenfeldt-Nielsen, Simon 134
Egypt, cultural fascination with 79–82
Eisler, Hanns 121
van Elferen, Isabella 135
Enix *see* Square Enix
Eno, Brian 139
exoticism 78–80, 82–83, 86–88, 90–91, 93–94

General Index **223**

Famicom *see* NES, *see also* Famicom Disk System
Famicom Disk System 64, 73n2, 75n28, 76, 95n2
flow (state) 111, 115n29, 115n32, 158n15 *see also* Csikszentmihalyi, Mihaly
FM Synthesis 57, 60–61, **62**, 63, 66–67, 70, 72–73, 74n15
Fraps (screen capture software) 133
Frequency Modulation *see* FM Synthesis
Friedrich, Caspar David 179, 187, 191
Fujio, Atsushi 63–64, 72

Gee, James Paul 148
Genette, Gerard 114n3
Gibbons, William 26, 32n19, 44, 47–48, 139, 141
genre 1–4, 6, 22–31, 44, 91, 96n39, 134–142
The Godfather (films) 121
Grieg, Edvard 179, 181–182, 183, 186–187, 191, 194
Grimley, Daniel 182, 183, 184

Hahn, Sabrina S. 146
Hasty, Christopher 101
Hata, Aki 63, **64**
Heide Smith, Jonas 134
Heidegger, Martin 134, 136
Hepburn, Ronald 187, 188, 190, 193–195
Herzog, Amy 16–17, 189–190
Hitchens, Michael 147, 150, 152–153
Hocking, Clint 133–134, 136, 142 *see also* ludonarrative dissonance
Hubbert, Julie 12, 18n3
Husserl, Edmund 114n11, 188 *see also* phenomenology

Ingold, Tim 166, 168
Itoi, Shigesato 35–36, 40–41, 42, 48–50
Iwadare, Noriyuki 15

Japanese role-playing game *see* JRPG
The Jazz Singer 10, 16
JRPG 3–5, 9–10, 13–15, 17–18, 20n31, 26, 35, 44–45, 47–48, 51, 52n5, 76, 78, 86, 90–93, 96n39, 98, 118–119, 121–122, 139, 141
Jørgensen, Kristine, 144n36
Juul, Jesper 103–104, 111–113, 135

Kant, Immanuel 133 *see also* sublime, mathematical
Kinne, Jesse 115n16
Kizzire, Jessica 47
Klangfläche 181–186, 188–191, 193–195
Koerner, Joseph 186–187
Konami 57, 59, 62–64, 66, 68–70, 73
A Knight's Tale 33n27
Krause, Bernie 174, 178n29
Kramer, Jonathan 101, 140, 196n16

Langer, Susanne 103
leitmotif 26, 117, 120–121
Leonard, Kendra 27
Lewin, David 114n11
Little, Todd D 157n3.
loop (music) 44, 47, 50
Lord of the Rings (films) 2, 121
ludoliteracy, 135–137, 140, 142
ludonarrative dissonance 98, 133–142

Magic: the Gathering 212
Margulis, Elizabeth 106, 111
Mateas, Michael 115n17
The Matrix 133, 143n6
McCartney, Andra 166–167
Medina-Gray, Elizabeth 111
Messiaen, Olivier 199
MIDI 11
Miller, Kiri 116n34, 162
minimalism 49
MMORPG 5, 142n2, 198–201, 211, 213

narrative 97–116, 134
Nattiez, Jean-Jacques 197
Naturklang 181, 182, 191
NES 3–4, 45, 52n5, 57, 59–60, 62, 64–68, **69**, 70, 72–73, 74n10, 74n20, 76, 82–83, 95n2, 96n37 *see also* Famicom, Famicom Disk System
Nintendo (company) 11, 36, 48, 60 *see also* NES, SNES
Nintendo Entertainment System *see* NES
Nintendo Family Computer *see* Famicom
nostalgia 3–4
Nyman, Michael 49

objectivism 134 *see also* Rand, Ayn
Oliveros, Pauline 160
Ong, Walter 213
opera: in *Final Fantasy VI* 117–128

224 General Index

Pajares Tosca, Susana 134
Pandemic 212–213
Parker, Roger 198
Parish, Jeremy 137
parody 22–31, 32n4
pedagogy 5, 50–51, 146–157
phenomenology 101, 114n11, 136,
    188–189 *see also* Husserl, Edmund
Piekut, Benjamin 161
Plank, Dana 114n12
PlayStation (console series) 9, 13–14,
    20n33, 21, 32n3, 200
Poster, Carol 213
The Princess Bride 27

Rand, Ayn 134 *see also* objectivism
Reale, Steven 142
Robin Hood: Men in Tights 27
rhythm games 116n34
Rigby, Scott 147, 149 *see also* self-
    determination theory (SDT)
Ryan, Richard M. 147, 149 *see also* self-
    determination theory (SDT)

Saint-Saëns, Camille 115n20
Sakaguchi, Hironobu 113n1
Saussure, Ferdinand de 214n8
Saturday Night Fever 28
Schafer, R. Murray 168, 172, 174, 178n33
Sega CD 11
Sega Genesis 11, 14, 74n18
self-determination theory (SDT) 147 *see*
    also Deci, Edward L., Ryan, Richard M.,
    and Rigby, Scott
Sergeant, Julie
Shakespeare, William 197
Shaw, Gordon L. 146
Shore, Howard 2, 26
Shultz, Peter 116n34
Sibelius, Jean 181, 194
sign 136–137, 142
silent film *see* early film
Smith, Bruce R. 160
Smith, Jonas Heide 134
SNES 3–4, 11, 52n5, 74n18, 96n43, 98,
    102, 113n1, 117
Sony PlayStation *see* PlayStation
Soule, Jeremy 181 *see also The Elder Scrolls:*
    Skyrim
soundtrack 5, 15, 26–28, 31, 33n19; albums
    39, 48–49, 50
soundwalking 166–170

specifications grading 150–151, 152, 155
Star Wars (films) 2, 121, 211
Steam (gaming platform) 32n3
sublime: natural 179; mathematical 133 *see*
    also Kant, Immanuel
Summers, Tim 35–53, 124, 138, 141
Super Famicom *see* SNES
Super Nintendo Entertainment system *see*
    SNES
Square (software company) *see* Square Enix
Square Enix 93, 98, 102, 108, 113
Sugiyama, Koichi 78, 79, **80**, 83, **84**, **88**, **89**
    see also Dragon Quest (series)
Suzuki, Katsuhiko 63–64
Suzuki, Keiichi 36
synchresis 189; kinesonic 102

Takahashi, Noriyuki 63
Takemitsu, Toru 108
Tanaka, Hirokazu "Hip" 36
Thiboust, Jordane 138
Tolkien, J.R.R. 29, 35
Tosca, Susana Pajares 134

Uematsu, Nobuo 4–5, 13, 76, **77**, 79, 83,
    85–**87**, 88, **89**–**94**, 90, **93**–**94**, 98, 102,
    108, 121

Vergunst, Jo Lee 168

Wagner, Richard 2, 121, 182, 191 *see also*
    leitmotif
Ward, Trent 137
Wardrip-Fruin, Noah 58
Westerkamp, Hildegard 166–167 *see also*
    soundwalking
Western RPG 3, 13, 17, 20n32, 26, 44, 60,
    139, 141
Williams, John 2, 26, 121
Winters, Ben 41–42
Wittgenstein, Ludwig 3
Wolf, Mark J.P. 137, 141

Xbox 21

Zagal, José P. 115n17, 135 *see also*
    ludoliteracy
Zbikowski, Lawrence 108, 115n25

Printed in the United States
By Bookmasters